Winnipeg

A PRAIRIE PORTRAIT

Photo by Mike Grandmaison.

Winnipeg

A PRAIRIE PORTRAIT

Written by Martin Cash

Corporate Profiles by
Wendy Stephenson and Judy Waytiuk

Featuring the Photography of
Mike Grandmaison and George Siamandas

Winnipeg, A Prairie Portrait

PRODUCED IN COOPERATION WITH THE WINNIPEG CHAMBER OF COMMERCE
167 LOMBARD AVENUE, SUITE 500
WINNIPEG, MANITOBA, CANADA R3B 3E5
204-944-8484/FAX: 204-944-8492

BY MARTIN CASH
CORPORATE PROFILES BY WENDY STEPHENSON AND JUDY WAYTIUK
FEATURING THE PHOTOGRAPHY OF MIKE GRANDMAISON AND GEORGE SIAMANDAS

Community Communications, Inc.
Publishers: Ronald P. Beers and James E. Turner
Publisher's Sales Associates: David McKinney, Susan Kokolsky, and Stan Blady
Executive Editor: James E. Turner
Managing Editor: Bonnie Ashley Harris
Profile Editor: Kari Collin
Design Director: Camille Leonard
Designer: Rebecca Hockman Carlisle
Photo Editors: Rebecca H. Carlisle, Kari Collin and Bonnie Ashley Harris
Contract Manager: Katrina Williams
Editorial Assistant: Robin Davies
Sales Assistant: Annette Lozier
Proofreaders: Fran Norris and Wynona B. Hall
Accounting Services: Sara Ann Turner
Printing Production: Frank Rosenberg/GSAmerica

CCI

Community Communications, Inc.
Montgomery, Alabama
James E. Turner, Chairman of the Board
Ronald P. Beers, President
Daniel S. Chambliss, Vice President

Photo by Mike Grandmaison.

TABLE OF CONTENTS   Part I

Chapter 1
MEETING OF THE HUNT & THE PLOUGH - PAGE 15

■ Situated at the confluence of the Red and Assiniboine Rivers, Winnipeg has always been a natural meeting place. It was a combination of the fur trade and the buffalo hunt that brought agriculture to the Winnipeg basin. Agriculture brought trade and that sped the arrival of the railroad. Now the Prairie Metropolis is a city of entrepreneurs with a truly diverse economy and an enviable quality of life.

Chapter 2
CITY DYNAMIC, WINNIPEG MEANS BUSINESS - PAGE 31

■ Winnipeg is a city of 600,000 plus, it has a remarkable mix of peoples and industries, the cleanest of air and water, one of the sunniest climates in North America and a quality of life second to none. It is a city that means business.

Chapter 3
WINNIPEG, A CITY OF TRADERS - PAGE 47

■ The city started as a fur trading centre, then became a supply centre for that industry. As the frontier spread west, Winnipeg became a distribution and supply centre for the rest of western Canada. All the while it was developing a brisk trade relationship with its neighbors in the U.S. and establishing a lock on the commercial end of the grain business. Located in the geographic centre of the continent, it is not surprising that the future prosperity of the city will come from its ability to trade.

Chapter 4
THE CITY THAT MANAGES & FINANCES THE NATION'S BREADBASKET - PAGE 59

■ The 110-year-old Winnipeg Commodity Exchange, the only commodity exchange in the country, helped insure that Winnipeg would be the commercial headquarters for the Prairie grain industry. It also spawned an important financial services industry that supports and services existing businesses and generates new opportunities.

Chapter 5
PLANES, TRAINS & SEMIS - PAGE 69

■ Winnipeg is the largest distribution centre between Vancouver and Toronto. Its location as the geographic centre of the continent makes it a key centre for both Canadian National Railway and Canadian Pacific Railway. Winnipeg is the headquarters for eight of the largest national trucking firms. And plans are underway to establish a circum-polar 747 air cargo route from Asia to Winnipeg with a multi-modal distribution centre based at the Winnipeg International Airport.

Chapter 6
EDUCATION, A PURSUIT OF EXCELLENCE - PAGE 81

■ Winnipeg has a spot at the head of the class with its array of educational facilities and opportunities, boasting of three universities including the francophone St. Boniface College, community colleges and a well-developed elementary and secondary school system that features enhanced, alternative, and french immersion choices.

Chapter 7
HEALTH CARE & TECHNOLOGY, FROM FIBRE OPTICS TO BIODIAGNOSTICS - PAGE 91

■ World class medical facilities and cutting-edge bio-medical research define the area's medical science environment and Winnipeg is home to the recently completed $150 million Health Canada/ Agriculture and Agri-Food Canada Federal Laboratories, better known as the Virology Lab.

Chapter 8
THE WHOLE CITY'S A STAGE - PAGE 101

■ Winnipeg boasts more arts and culture per capita than just about any other city in North America with the internationally renowned Royal Winnipeg Ballet—the oldest ballet in Canada, the Winnipeg Symphony Orchestra, and Manitoba Theatre Centre, the oldest and most influential regional theatre in the country. And then there are the museums and the festivals to entertain all during the summer and the winter.

Chapter 9
WINNIPEG AT PLAY, ONE GREAT CITY - PAGE 115

■ Whether it's rooting for the Blue Bombers, the Manitoba Moose, the Goldeyes or any one of the university teams, spectator sports thrive in Winnipeg. But there's also plenty of hands-on excitement for everyone—from skating on the pond in the winter to canoeing down the Assiniboine River, playing golf or heading to one of the lakes in the summer. Winnipeg is one great city!

Chapter 10
WINNIPEG & ITS PEOPLE - PAGE 131

■ Winnipeg is in the midst of celebrating its 125th anniversary with its number one treasure and resource being its people. Winnipeg, an ethnically diverse city that is very proud of its multicultural heritage, will continue to celebrate next year when the city will host the 1999 Pan American Games.

Photos by Mike Grandmaison.

PART II, WINNIPEG'S ENTERPRISES - Page 145

TABLE OF CONTENTS *Part II*

Photos by George Siamandas.

FOREWORD

*W*innipeg, *A Prairie Portrait*, is a 125th anniversary project of The Winnipeg Chamber of Commerce. The fact that The Chamber of Commerce was formed six months before the city itself was incorporated speaks volumes for the important role played by business in the development of our city.

In a time when society is increasingly mobile, it is notable that almost all of the past Presidents/Chairmen of the Board of The Chamber remain in Winnipeg. "I wouldn't live anywhere else!" exclaimed a recent Chair. From the chapters that follow, you'll understand why.

Located at the geographic centre of North America, Winnipeg is the eighth largest city in Canada with an ethnically diverse population of 650,000. A diversified economic base, a skilled workforce, and competitive operating costs make Winnipeg an attractive option for business starts and expansions. Winnipeg offers a quality of life that combines small town values with big city opportunities, making it an ideal place to raise a family. The beauty and progress of our City is evident from the pictures; the economic base and its roots are conveyed by the words; the community spirit of the people is best experienced first-hand to truly appreciate what makes Winnipeg unique.

To those who call Winnipeg home, we are confident that *Winnipeg, A Prairie Portrait* will instill a renewed sense of pride in the things about our City that we sometimes take for granted. To our visitors, we hope that this book gives you a glimpse into what makes Winnipeg such a great City to work, live and play in.

The Chamber extends its appreciation to the corporations featured in this publication. Their generous support of this project is yet another tangible demonstration of the business community's dedication to Winnipeg's future.

Shelley Morris
President
Winnipeg Chamber of Commerce

◄ ▲ Photos by George Siamandas.

PREFACE

Winnipeg, A Prairie Portrait

started working on this book project at exactly the same time as the people of Winnipeg set to work on protecting the city from the flood of the century.

It was an extraordinary time for the city and the people of the Red River valley. Town after town in the valley was evacuated and an ominous period of hurry-up-and-wait took hold of the city as the crest of the flood water approached Winnipeg at an excruciatingly slow pace. The entire city held its breath not knowing whether the expensive and ingenious Winnipeg Floodway would really work and divert the Red River's flood waters around the city like it was designed to do.

It did work.

Most of the credit for the effectiveness of the city's flood defenses must go to the engineers who designed the Floodway back in the 1960s and the municipal and provincial hydraulic engineers and flood forecasters. Damage in Winnipeg was kept to a bare minimum, although the valley was full of heart-breaking stories that spring and summer.

▲ *Photo by George Siamandas.*

But is seemed like a brilliant victory for all of the city even though most of us did little more than spend a few afternoons and evenings on sandbag lines.

It will forever serve as an historic touchstone. "Remember how everyone worked together back in the spring of '97?"

For me, it provided an excellent context for which to be reminded of the strength and courage around which this city is built. Every city would have you believe it is populated with a breed of people a cut above the rest. In the spring of '97 I became convinced it was true of Winnipeggers.

Having grown up in the suburbs of Toronto I know how the face-lessness of the big city works. Having lived through an event like the Red River flood of 1997, I now know just what it means for a community to pull together.

In researching this book I was also reminded that Winnipeg has a fabulous history and I am thankful to have had the occasion to study it with more than a passing regard.

I wish to acknowledge the assistance provided by the Winnipeg Free Press, my employer for the past nine years, for extensive use of its archives and resource materials. I could not have had the access to the kind of timely information I needed without the co-operation of the Free Press.

I also wish to thank all those who dropped what they were doing to answer questions and dig up information for me, something that we journalists request of others with some regularity yet rarely do we adequately express our appreciation for such generosity.

When asked by friends and acquaintances just how the book was going I regularly replied that at least the photos will be great—and they are.

My wife Susan and children Madeline and Emma could not have been more supportive and encouraging to me while the book was being produced. I dedicate it to them.

Martin Cash

◀ *Leo Mol Sculpture Garden, Assiniboine Park. Photo by Mike Grandmaison.*

I

Winnipeg, A Prairie Portrait

▲ *Photo by George Siamandas.*

◄ *Photo by Mike Grandmaison.*

Photo by Mike Grandmaison.

Meeting of The Hunt & The Plough

▲ Courtesy of the Provincial Archives of Manitoba.

◄ Photo by Mike Grandmaison.

Portage and Main may be one of the most famous intersections in Canada now, but when Henry McKenney decided to build a general store at the site of the now-famous corner in 1862, it seemed an unlikely thing to do.

The commercial centre of the growing community was clustered around the Hudson's Bay Company fur trading post called Upper Fort Garry, to the south of McKenney's new store. A couple of kilometers further north was Point Douglas, where the first agricultural settlement and homesteading had taken place.

But the town—known alternately at the time as either Fort Garry, Red River, Assiniboia or just the Forks—was growing and changing and McKenney knew it. The fur trade and buffalo hunt, now already on the wane, had helped establish trade with organized brigades of Red River carts travelling between Winnipeg and St. Paul, Minnesota and York boats and canoes plying the lakes and rivers all the way up to Hudson Bay.

McKenney picked his location because it was the natural intersection of the north-south traffic of the fur-traders along the Red River and the trail in from the west along the Assiniboine River.

That McKenney would even contemplate diversifying his former hotel business into a general store/hotel was testimony to the high opinion in which Winnipeggers have always held their city.

Five years later in 1873, when it was little more than a collection of shacks with a population of less than 3,700, the community became a city by an act of the newly established provincial government. The post office didn't even start referring to the community as Winnipeg—Cree for "murky water"—until 1876.

Winnipeg began as a centre for the fur trade and the buffalo hunt and evolved into a frontier agricultural town when the fur trade was over and the buffalo herds had dwindled. Enterprising Winnipeggers became suppliers for the growing number of settlements further west. When the railroad arrived in the late 1880s Winnipeg became a boomtown and the "Chicago of the North."

Winnipeg remains a transportation, distribution and agri-food centre to this day. But now it has a manufacturing sector that is the most diversified in the country, a growing cluster of high-technology research enterprises and more cultural activity than just about any other city its size in North America.

The confluence of the Red and Assiniboine rivers has been a meeting place dating back 6,000 years for the nomadic Cree hunters and other First Nations of the region. In his quest to find the fabled western sea the great French explorer, Pierre Gaultier de La Verendrye, established the first European settlement there in 1738, called Fort Rouge, "at the great fork of the Red River."

At the time, the French explorers out of Montreal were developing the fur trade along the Great Lakes and westward,

▲ An exact wooden replica of the British ship, the Nonsuch, housed at the Manitoba Museum of Man and Nature. Photo by Mike Grandmaison.

▲ *Historical painting of Upper Fort Garry in the 1850's. Courtesy of the Provincial Archives of Manitoba.*

while the British were engaged in the same pursuit from their base on the frozen shores of Hudson Bay.

In 1668 the British ship, the *Nonsuch* (an exact wooden replica of which is housed at the Manitoba Museum of Man and Nature in Winnipeg) was sent to Hudson Bay and the fur trade effectively was founded. Enterprising British sailors secured a boat-load of beaver pelts in trade with the natives of the region. In 1670 they convinced the British king, Charles II, to grant the new enterprise, the Company of Adventurers Trading in the Hudson Bay, exclusive trading rights in all of the river basins that flow into the bay. Thus was founded the Hudson's Bay Co., the oldest company in the English-speaking world. Its history and

the history of Winnipeg remain to this day deeply connected.

The British suffered the bitter winters on the bay and in time negotiated the treacherous rapids of the Nelson and Hayes Rivers south into what is now central Manitoba. Meanwhile, the coureuer de bois who were working for the North West Company, founded in 1784 by Scottish merchants in Montreal, were trading with the natives on the rivers of the Winnipeg basin in southern Manitoba and effectively stealing the business from the HBC's posts at York Factory on Hudson Bay.

A classic competitive rivalry had been established between the French and mixed blood Metis hunters and traders of the North West Company, and the British

agents of the Hudson's Bay Co. in the early 1800s.

The North West Company built Fort Gibraltar at the forks of the Red and Assiniboine rivers in 1810 at about the same spot that La Verendrye had built Fort Rouge. With the Metis maintaining a supply system for the posts along the Assiniboine and Saskatchewan Rivers, as well as providing the furs from the buffalo hunt, the NWC felt it was making inroads against the HBC.

So when Thomas Douglas, the fifth Earl of Selkirk, convinced the HBC to deed him lands to establish an agricultural community near the forks of the Red and Assiniboine rivers, it was seen as an overt threat to the wilderness infrastructure that had been set up by the NWC.

▲ Red River Cart Monument, Assiniboine Park. Photo by Mike Grandmaison.

▲ A view of Winnipeg south from Point Douglas, circa 1900, of the Red River looking north. Photo courtesy of the Provincial Archives of Manitoba.

The first Selkirk settlers, led by Miles Macdonell, were a group of 36 Scottish and Irish labourers who settled at Point Douglas, a couple of kilometres downstream (north) along the Red River from Fort Gibraltar, where some of those early houses and commercial buildings still stand. About 120 more Irish and Hebridean settlers followed that year and then, in 1814, 83 Scots from Kildonan arrived.

Through the first couple of years the settlers were harassed by armed Metis huntsmen who feared the settlers' presence would mean the loss of their land. In 1815 the Metis drove the settlers off their meagre riverlots. But when they were allowed to return late in the summer, their crops had yielded a harvest of 400 bushels of wheat, 200 of barley and 500 of oats—with seed for the next year and enough for bread and meal.

It was the first "bumper" crop for the region that would eventually become one of the great breadbaskets of the world. Winnipeg has become the Canadian agricultural industry's commercial, transportation and administrative centre, and, as such, one of the great cities of the country.

After the arrival of a new governor, Robert Semple, "a sincere and earnest but impulsive and indecisive gentleman," the settlers captured Fort Gibraltar from the NWC in 1815 and tore it down, leaving their own Fort Douglas as the main post along the Red threatening the Metis and the North West Company's traffic.

In the most unfortunate event of the period, a group of Metis led by Cuthbert Grant was on its way to meet up with Nor'Westers from the east. Attempting to skirt the Point Douglas settlement, they were spotted and encountered by an armed group of 25 settlers on foot led by Semple. Shooting broke out and the Metis, skilled mounted marksmen as they were, massacred 19 of the 25 settlers including Semple. The so-called Seven Oaks Massacre of June 16, 1816 remains one of the darkest moments in the region's history. It also marked the beginning of

▲ *A 1916 view of the northeast corner of Portage and Main. Photo courtesy of the Provincial Archives of Manitoba.*

▲ *The famous intersection of Portage and Main. Photo by George Siamandas.*

the end for the NWC. In response to the massacre, Selkirk mounted a force from Toronto, re-captured Fort Douglas in 1817 and, in 1821, the Hudson's Bay Company merged with The North West Company.

Although it was an important centre for the fur trade in 1821, the Red River colony was still more casual than permanent. There were fewer than 500 inhabitants, although the first mission church in St. Boniface had already been erected by 1818. The Metis sons of French and Scottish farmers and Cree, Saulteaux or Assiniboine mothers were the largest and most distinct element of the community.

The fur trade continued to be the main source of commerce in the community until the mid-1860s. Up until the

Manitoba Act made the region a province in the Dominion of Canada in 1870, the increased commercial connection with the U.S. led some to believe, even advocate for, union with the Americans.

Selkirk's estate provided the sole authority in the land until 1834, when it fell under the Hudson's Bay Company's jurisdiction again. The company built two forts—Upper and Lower Fort Garry (the latter still standing as a National Historic Site just north of the city). Upper Fort Garry would become the centre of activity in the settlement area until it was torn down in 1882 to make room for development on south Main Street. All that remains at the site of the fort is its gate tucked in behind the stately Hotel Fort

Garry in downtown Winnipeg.

But the company's continuing monopoly in the region was becoming increasingly untenable and, in the late 1850s, the British House of Commons decided that the HBC could retain its monopoly in the far north, but should leave open the possibility of Canada acquiring the Red and Saskatchewan River valleys.

While the Canadian government negotiated with the HBC, the residents of the Red River community were left out of the picture. A garrison of troops accompanied a research party to determine whether the HBC should keep its monopoly, but when they had to leave the settlement in 1861, they were not replaced and the HBC refused to fund another force.

▲ *The railway yards in 1956 before the $20 million rail yard reclamation project—begun in 1988—called the Forks. Photo courtesy of the Provincial Archives of Manitoba.*

▲ *The confluence of the Red and Assiniboine Rivers circa 1960. Photo courtesy of the Provincial Archives of Manitoba.*

▲ Lower Fort Garry National Historic Site. Photo by Mike Grandmaison.

The armed Metis became the de facto law of the land. It should be said, however, that the Metis were closely aligned with the clergy who were instrumental in developing the underpinnings of the social fabric of the community. For example, the Grey Nuns, who arrived in St. Boniface in 1844, founded St. Boniface General Hospital.

With the influx of traders and speculators and farmers from Ontario and from the U.S., who were there to take advantage of opportunities as they might present themselves when the HBC yielded control, concern intensified among the original settlers that they might be pushed off their now well-settled riverlots by the Americans or the aggressive Canadians from Ontario.

Of the process of transfer from HBC ownership to public ownership, it has been said, "One of the greatest transfers of territory and sovereignty in history was conducted as

a mere transaction in real estate." The HBC eventually received 300,000 pounds, one-twentieth of the fertile areas to be opened for settlement and title to all the land where it currently had posts in exchange for ceding the territory to Canada.

However, to the Metis and the original North West farmers it was not just a question of land title, but who would control the new government—the natives of the North West or the swarm of newcomers from Ontario.

A Canadian Party led by the boisterous Dr. Charles Schultz was "more noisy than numerous." Their misguided assumption that the Metis sympathized with a pro-American party fueled suspicions that later erupted into the so-called Red River Rebellion.

One of the most promising Metis, Louis Riel, became their leader and set about organizing a united protest against the Canadian government for refusing to

listen to the concerns of the long time residents. Since the Metis was the only armed presence in the community, they controlled the outcome of events and easily seized Upper Fort Garry on November 2, 1869.

During these tense times, Riel generally comported himself with restraint; however, his erratic nature that would become part of his legacy was still in evidence. A member of an Ontario work crew, Thomas Scott, who had been imprisoned by Riel's armed Metis supporters, so angered his guards that they demanded he be court-martialed and shot. Riel, not wishing to break with his men, agreed. That was in March, 1870. It proved to be a tragic mistake.

Before that point Ottawa believed Riel to be sincere in his attempts to usher the region into Confederation, but the execution of Scott precipitated the mounting of a military expeditionary force from Toronto lead by Colonel Garnet Wolseley.

▲ *St. Boniface Cathedral. Photo by Mike Grandmaison.*

In the meantime, the Manitoba Act was declared in 1870, making Manitoba the fifth province of Canada. But Wolseley and his troops, after their 96-day trek from Toronto, were spoiling for a fight when they finally arrived at Point Douglas on August 24, 1870. Riel was warned and fled the preceding day, allowing Wolseley to take Fort Garry without a shot being fired.

Riel went into exile in the U.S. but, in 1884, he was asked to assist in another Metis uprising, now known as the North West Rebellion, in Batoche, Saskatchewan. He was captured after two months of fighting, charged with treason, convicted and was hanged on November 16, 1885 in Regina.

His remains lie in the cemetery in front of the St. Boniface Basilica and his presence is very much alive in the city and province he helped found.

During the 1870s as settlements in the region grew the commercial-minded former fur traders of Winnipeg became outfitters and hardware merchants. Immigrants like the German Mennonites from Russia started farming the southern region of the province around the Pembina River and fishermen from Iceland settled on the southern end of Lake Winnipeg, at Gimli, 85 kilometres north of Winnipeg.

The dream of a strong Prairie commercial centre held by the enterprising business leaders of the day led to the audacious movement to incorporate as a city in 1873 when there were fewer than 3,700 residents. Winnipeg was already getting a reputation as a rough and ready, hard-drinking town and when the inexperienced provincial legislature was less than supportive of the original papers of incorporation for the city, its speaker, a medical doctor, was lured from his home late one evening on the pretext of seeing a patient. Instead he was tarred and feathered by individuals who remained unknown.

By 1880, with the population of the city around 8,000 there were no less than 59 financial institutions in Winnipeg. The Canadian Pacific Railway was on its way

▲ Prominent Winnipeg leader and businessman, Andrew G. B. Bannatyne, was the first president of the Winnipeg Chamber of Commerce. Photo courtesy of the Provincial Archives of Manitoba.

▲ In 1956 Stephen Juba was the first member of Winnipeg's ethnic communities to be mayor. He then proceeded to win eight succeeding elections, serving the city as mayor, and unofficial ambassador for the Ukranian community until 1977. Photo courtesy of the Department of Archives & Special Collections, The University of Manitoba.

▲ *The $67 million Winnipeg Floodway, completed in 1968, saved Winnipeg from certain flood damage in the recent great flood of 1997. Photo by Mike Grandmaison.*

and real estate speculators were having a ball in Winnipeg with prices reaching levels that weren't matched again for almost 100 years.

Though the boom was short-lived the city's business and political leaders remained focused on economic and population growth. Their first major challenge was ensuring that the trans-continental railroad would indeed pass through Winnipeg. Original surveys done by Canadian Pacific Railroad (CPR) called for the line to cross the Red downstream from Winnipeg, through the town of Selkirk.

Winnipeg's proactive civic and business leaders eventually made a deal with the CPR that ensured it would be a railroad hub as it still is today.

For almost three decades following the

arrival of the trans-continental railway into Winnipeg in the late 1880s, the city enjoyed a period of growth and prosperity that is unequalled in the history of Canadian urban development.

The city reached the height of its power and influence in those years. In 1911 Winnipeg handled 88 million bushels of wheat, surpassing Chicago, Minneapolis and New York. By 1913 it was the third largest city in the country with a population of about 150,000 with flour mills, metals shops, breweries, bustling financial services, wholesale, retail and of course grain handling and processing industries.

The outbreak of World War I, some poor harvests, sagging grain prices and the completion of the Panama Canal in

1915 providing another way to ship goods from one coast to the other knocked the city down a peg or two.

The Winnipeg General Strike in May and June of 1919 ranks as one of the most significant events in labour history in Canada. More than 35,000 people joined the strike. Bloodshed and two deaths were the result of rioting near the end of the strike and the scars were a long time in healing.

In 1956 Stephen Juba became the first member of Winnipeg's diverse ethnic communities to be mayor. He then proceeded to win eight succeeding elections serving the city as mayor, and unofficial ambassador for the Ukrainian community, until 1977.

The city went on a building binge in the '50s, '60s and '70s. A new football stadium, hockey arena, city hall, concert hall,

and theatre were all built in those decades. The $67 million Winnipeg Floodway, that saved Winnipeg from certain flood damage in 1997 and several other years prior to that, was finished in 1968.

The '80s saw a handful of new downtown office buildings built and a continued emphasis on preserving some of the distinctive turn-of-the-century architecture. A major re-development of Portage Avenue, called Portage Place, took place in the mid-'80s, and, in 1987, the city, province and federal government created the 56 acre, $20 million rail yard reclamation project called The Forks.

After the ordeal of the flood of 1997, Winnipeg really has something to celebrate as it turns 125 years old in 1998. The following year, in 1999, the city will host the XIIIth Pan American Games inviting all of North and South America to meet at the Forks. ■

◀ *The Forks at dawn. Photo by Mike Grandmaison.*

2

City Dynamic, Winnipeg Means Business

▲ Photo by Mike Grandmaison.

◄ Now the land at the confluence of the Red and Assiniboine Rivers is alive with public events, shopping, restaurants and entertainment. It functions once again as the meeting place it had been for thousands of years. Photo by George Siamandas.

31

Every community has its shared experiences that help illustrate some underlying reality. For Winnipeggers, one of those experiences occurs when visitors arrive from out of town, particularly from places like Toronto or Vancouver where the real estate markets tend toward the stratosphere. These visitors see the stately elm-lined streets and the Victorian and Edwardian homes of the older riverside neighborhoods along the Red and Assiniboine Rivers in Winnipeg. They see the spacious contemporary homes in any one of several well-designed suburbs and they discover, to their astonishment, that they too could afford to own one of those houses—if they lived in Winnipeg.

Of course, the sheer price of a home is

▲ Broadway's canopy of elm trees. Photo by Mike Grandmaison.

not what makes a city great. But it's a manifestation of the fact that Winnipeg has become one of the most affordable cities in North America. The city provides an enviable quality of life. It is a vibrant, multi-cultural community with a commitment to the future in big, sweeping public-private sector partnerships and its economy in the late '90s is as robust as it has been in some time.

The great outdoors is literally... just outdoors, about an hour's drive to some of the best hunting, fishing and cottage country imaginable. It has some of the cleanest air of any city in North America and according to Environment Canada, the sunniest climate of any city in Canada particularly through Winnipeg's "dry cold" winters.

The Boyd Company, an American research firm, recently ranked Winnipeg as the second least expensive city among 45 manufacturing centres in North America in which to do business. Office space is about half of what it costs in Toronto, hydro rates are the lowest in the country and wages across the board are below national averages.

Twice during the first half of the 1990s Winnipeg was selected as one of the five best cities in the country to do business in by the *Globe and Mail*, Canada's national newspaper.

But just like in its frontier days, Winnipeg is still a little off the beaten track. That too is part of the city's charm.

Maclean's magazine columnist, Allan Fotheringham, once wrote, "As a nationality-surfer who cruises in between the frenetic wanna-be Americanism of Toronto and the hey-man-laid-back Starbucks lifestyle of Vancouver, Winnipeg is an oasis of calm."

There is still something slightly exotic about the big Prairie city whose Canadian Football League Blue Bomber's seem to be perennial contenders; where a disproportionate number of national leaders in business, law and arts and cultural affairs seem to emanate from; and where pitching-in and helping your neighbour is an activity that isn't just reserved for floods like the one in 1997.

▲ Winnipeg provides an enviable quality of life. Photo by Mike Grandmaison.

After the flood of 1997, tossing sandbags became another one of those Winnipeg things to do like drinking cappucino at an outdoor cafe on Corydon Avenue in Little Italy, eating perogies at Alycia's in the North End, taking a stroll at the Forks, soaking up the sun on Grand Beach, and whooping it up at the "Grand Rendezvous on the Boulevard" that kicks off the Festival du Voyageur on a frosty Friday night in February.

At the opening of an auto parts manufacturing plant in one of Winnipeg's industrial parks in the spring of 1997 the president of the multi-billion dollar company, Siegfried Buschmann, looked around at the 300 employees and said quietly to a visitor, "These people are great workers."

The comment was more than just the standard pride a CEO may have in his workforce. The company, Phillips & Temro, supplies 80 per cent of the North American market for block heaters, among other things, and is owned by the $4.6 billion Detroit-based Budd Group, which in turn is owned by the $28 billion per year German-based multi-national Thyssen AG. Buschmann was making a very specific point. Even though the company builds plants all over the world, it chose to do so in Winnipeg and it was because of the people.

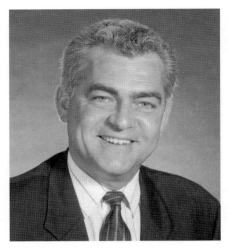

▲ *Klaus Thiessen, president and chief executive officer of* Winnipeg 2000, *the city's economic development agency. Photo courtesy of* Winnipeg 2000.

Winnipeg no longer must rely on its role as the gateway to the west as its focal point for economic development. It no longer needs to depend solely on its

▲ *A gracious lifestyle is enjoyed by all who live in Wellington Crescent. Photo by George Siamandas.*

▲ Carol-Ann Borody, 1997-98 chairperson of the Winnipeg Chamber of Commerce. Photo courtesy of the Winnipeg Chamber of Commerce.

position as the commercial centre for the grain trade for its economic viability and growth.

Winnipeg now relies on its people–their skill, enterprise, innovativeness and industriousness–in order to grow and prosper.

A comparative study of the workforces in Winnipeg, Calgary and Kansas City, conducted as this book was being completed, revealed a surprisingly upbeat attitude that exists among workers in Winnipeg. They are happy, content, willing to learn new things, believe they are contributing and generally think of their work in a positive way.

Klaus Thiessen, chief executive officer of Winnipeg 2000, the city's economic development agency, sincerely believes the people in Winnipeg are the most successful marketing feature the city has when it comes to economic development.

"Our biggest strength in the future will be our people, our workforce," he said. "It's not just the work ethic, but also the stability and ethnic diversity contained within the workforce in this city. That's important when we engage in international trade."

Carol-Ann Borody owns an insurance and real estate brokerage firm in Winnipeg and was the chairperson of the Winnipeg Chamber of Commerce in 1997-98. "My experience as an employer is that the loyalty, integrity and commitment of the employees in Winnipeg is really quite overwhelming," she said.

Back to the opening of the Phillips & Temro plant and Siegfried Buschmann. Speaking with a pronounced German accent, he said, "It's nice to be in

Winnipeg where they don't look at you funny when you speak with an accent because everyone here has an accent."

While Buschmann was slightly overstating the case, for a city of its size Winnipeg does have a remarkable mix of more than 40 ethnic groups including the largest Francophone community in Canada outside Quebec.

To some it may seem like everyone speaks with an accent. It may also seem as if everyone speaks the language of business. From the rugged individualism that is natural in the farming community to the thousand-plus independent truckers based in Winnipeg, to the trading pit of the Winnipeg Commodity Exchange and the trading desk of the largest mutual fund company in the country, Investors Group Inc. . . . Winnipeg means business.

At the turn of the century the who's who of Winnipeg business was the who's who of Winnipeg. It is no different now.

Only now the city's power brokers are a mix of the modern financial services professionals, old money grain families and members of the large coterie of established family-owned firms like Palliser Furniture, Pollard Banknote, CanWest Global Communications and James Richardson International.

Winnipeg's business interests never had to overthrow the former aristocracy or curry favour with the social elite to gain entrance to power as was the case for the business communities of many other regions. The city was started by business people for the purpose of doing business–first the fur trade, then to outfit and supply the new settlements to the west, then to trade and manage agricultural production. Throughout the city's

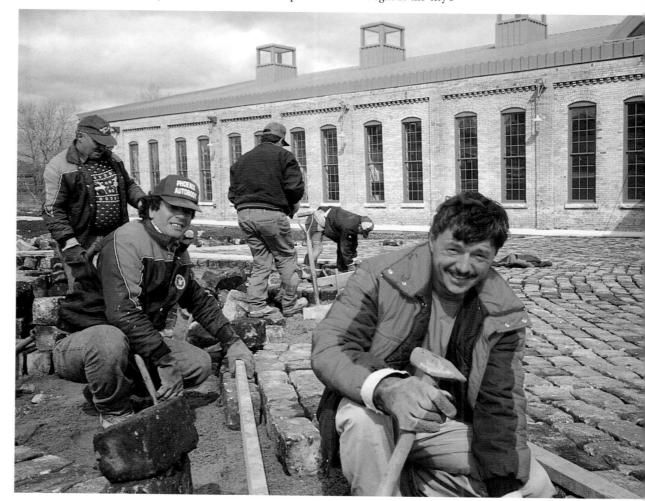

▲ Winnipeg relies on its people—their skill, enterprise, innovativeness and industriousness—in order to grow and prosper. Photo by George Siamandas.

Winnipeg's most valuable asset—the people who make up the workforce of this great city. Photos by George Siamandas.

formative and boom years, business people were its natural leaders.

Names like Ashdown, Bannatyne, McDermot, Nanton, Searle, Sifton, Riley, Asper and Richardson continue to live on, some only as the names of streets now, others as continuing leaders in the business community. All of the city's first mayors came from the business class.

Winnipeg's two-term mayor of the 1990s, Susan Thompson, ran a family retail business and was a long-time small business advocate before she became mayor.

That's not to say that the development of what is now a busy Prairie metropolis of 667,000 has been exclusively to serve the profit-motive of the business class, but it certainly has inculcated the community with a "can-do" attitude that has served the city well through the ups and downs of social and economic cycles.

▲ Buying grain. Photo by George Siamandas.

Winnipeg is in the midst of celebrating its 125th anniversary with a handful of projects in the works that demonstrates the city has plenty of know-how and the guts to take a chance or two.

In the late 1980s all three levels of government took a chance on reclaiming The Forks. The exact spot from which the city derives its heritage had become a 56-acre industrial ghetto. Miles and miles of railroad tracks and repair shops had made the area completely undesirable and out-of-bounds to the public.

Now the land at the confluence of the Red and Assiniboine is alive with public events, shopping, restaurants and entertainment. It functions once again as the meeting place it had been for thousands of years. As much as anything else in the city, The Forks is a symbol of Winnipeg's heritage and its future.

A public/private partnership is also responsible for Winnport Logistics Inc. About to commence its initial airlift to China at press time, Winnport has received a $5 million public sector investment and the corporation is laying the groundwork in establishing the Winnipeg International Airport as an air and multi-modal cargo hub.

While Winnport will take some number of years to develop, the city does

▲ Photo by George Siamandas.

▶ *Assiniboine Park Pavilion. Photo by George Siamandas.*

have a sure thing lined up—it will host the XIIIth Pan American Games in July and August, 1999. It is being billed as the third largest sporting event in North America after the 1984 Olympics in Los Angeles and 1996 Atlanta Olympics. The $122 million budget is only possible because organizers expect about 15,000 volunteers to lend a hand.

Projects like that and the city's well-thought out foray into high tech and telecommunications industries are examples of the commitment and energy that exist in Winnipeg for the future.

The Canadian Federation of Indepen-

dent Business says Manitoba is the most small business-friendly province in the country mainly because of an income tax freeze that, in 1997, was in its 10th year. Winnipeg, the capital city, has about 60 per cent of the province's population and accounts for about 80 per cent of its manufacturing. As Winnipeg goes, so goes the province.

Not only is Manitoba good for small business, but the province's fiscal record is the envy of the country. The 1997 budget of the Progressive Conservative government of Premier Gary Filmon, who has been in power since 1988, projected a

third consecutive budget surplus. That's something that has not been seen in Manitoba for 25 years.

This fiscal prudence is paying off in economic activity. In 1996 there was a 14 per cent increase in capital investment in the province, two times the national average and the fifth annual increase in a row—something no other province has seen.

It's not just businesses that are investing, but consumers are spending at a healthy clip in the province as well, posting a 6.1 per cent increase in retail sales in 1996, double the national increase for the second year in a row.

▲ *Winnipeggers enjoying a sunny day at Grand Beach. Photo by Mike Grandmaison.*

▲ The white lights of Broadway. Photo by George Siamandas.

◀ Dog sledding at the annual Festival du Voyageur. Photo by George Siamandas.

► This pair of bison, the provincial symbol of Manitoba, stands as silent sentinels in the Manitoba Legislative building. Photo by Mike Grandmaison.

(It's worth noting that the increase in retail spending is happening in a city of particularly clever and thrifty shoppers where great pride is taken in bargains uncovered.)

Winnipeg is not one of the media capitals of the country and sometimes the good news, like its recent all-star economic statistics, doesn't get the attention it deserves.

As a consequence, Mayor Thompson has sometimes been accused of boosterism. But in fact, knowingly or not, she is following a tradition that has been around since Winnipeg's earliest days when the mayor's office was a promotional organ for business development of the city.

And the city's business community certainly has a proud tradition. The Winnipeg Chamber of Commerce was actually formed six months before the city itself in 1873. It started as the Board of Trade, was federally incorporated in 1879 and changed its name to The Winnipeg Chamber of Commerce in 1948. In 1994 The Chamber started a fund in the name of the original president of the Chamber, Andrew G.B. Bannatyne. Endowed with $100,000 in donations from senior business leaders, the fund will help finance Chamber-initiated research.

That the city's business community actually incorporated before the city itself (which did so at the end of 1873) is an indication of the level of enterprise that permeates the city.

Although Winnipeg was hit hard during the Depression of the 1930s, it was partly because of an overly-optimistic prognosis on the future growth of the city based on the unprecedented growth prior to the outbreak of World War I.

It meant Winnipeg had to re-invent itself as a more stable, self-sufficient, multi-cultural entity. Since the end of World War II until today, the pace of Winnipeg's economic development can be characterized as *slow and steady*.

▲ Winnipeg Mayor Susan Thompson. Photo by George Siamandas.

▲ Manitoba Premier the Honourable Gary Filmon. Photo courtesy of Premier Filmon's communications office.

◀ *Designed by Etienne Gaboury, one of the city's most prominent architects of the late 20th century, the Royal Canadian Mint has produced 30 billion coins for Canada and 60 other countries since it opened in 1975. Photo by Mike Grandmaison.*

Dr. Barry Prentice, of the University of Manitoba's Transport Institute, said, "You can't sustain the kind of boom growth you have during the frontier era in perpetuity. But you can still have a growth rate that is very healthy especially as technology changes and creates new opportunities."

Winnipeg is now the eighth largest city in the country but, perhaps because of its history as an over-achiever, Winnipeg is one of the most cosmopolitan cities of its size in the world. For instance, Winnipeg has more performing-arts activity per capita and more major arts institutions than any other city its size in North America.

While it was Winnipeg's Ontario and British stock who instilled the attitude that Winnipeg is a great city, it is the city's ethnic diversity that is sustaining that greatness.

In many ways slow and steady growth suits people fine. But a growing stream of professionals are moving to Winnipeg to fill an increasing number of high tech jobs at places like Health Canada's Centre for Disease Control (the Virology Lab), Broadband Networks Inc., Bristol Aerospace and Faneuil ISG Inc—they risk exposing the well-kept secret that not only does Winnipeg mean business, but it is a wonderful and inexpensive place to live. ■

Portage Place attracts Winnipeggers and visitors alike to downtown Winnipeg. Photos by George Siamandas.

▲ Photo by Mike Grandmaison.

Winnipeg offers a quality of life second to none.

▶ Photo by George Siamandas.

▲ Photo by Mike Grandmaison.

3

Winnipeg, A City of Traders

Photos by Mike Grandmaison.

▶ *Photo by Mike Grandmaison.*

Winnipeg is about 2,000 kilometres from the west coast, 1,500 kilometres from Toronto and 600 kilometres from Minneapolis-St. Paul. It's a good 1,000 kilometres to the Port of Churchill, on Manitoba's shoreline of Hudson Bay, but much longer than that by train.

It truly is in the middle of the continent, about as far from tidewater as a city can get in North America.

In spite of that reality—in fact because of it—Winnipeg's current, past and future prosperity comes from its ability to trade.

The Red River settlement began as a fur trading centre. Then as the frontier spread west Winnipeg became a distribution and supply centre for the rest of western Canada. The Winnipeg Commodity Exchange was formed in 1887 and since

then Winnipeg has been at the centre of Canada's lucrative grain trade.

An on-going trade relationship has existed with its neighbours in the U.S. since the 1840s. High import tariffs imposed by the first Canadian governments in the late 1800s skewed Winnipeg's trading patterns east-west. But the region's natural inclination is to look to the larger population base immediately south in the U.S. midwest.

Now that the continental free trade environment is emerging and those tariffs are coming off, Winnipeg businesses are proving they can compete. Industries like the city's bus and tractor manufacturers that struggled in the late '80s are now thriving. The city's plucky garment industry is slowly but surely breaking into the U.S. market and companies like Standard Knitting are doing most of their business there.

And trade doesn't begin and end with the huge market to the south. Winnipeg's agri-food, software, telecommunications and equipment suppliers are now finding customers in Mexico, South America and Asia. Winnipeg-based television broadcasting company, CanWest Global Communications Corp., is now a major player in Australian and New Zealand television broadcasting and it is the largest partner in a new television network being formed in Ireland.

With the province's manufacturing sector almost tripling the Canadian growth rate in 1996, exports have also boomed and Winnipeg accounts for about 80 per cent of the province's manufacturing output.

In 1996, Manitoba's manufacturing output was more than $9 billion, almost a 50 per cent increase from 1991. For the first time, Manitoba's shipments outside the country were greater than its trade with the other provinces in 1996. Exports to the U.S., for instance, have grown by about 160 per cent between 1990 and 1996 to $4.47 billion in 1996. Provincial exports to non-U.S. destinations in 1996 were $1.52 billion.

It may be a medium-sized city in the middle of the continent but the city's underdog status creates a distinct pride and competitiveness. Winnipeg's mayor Susan Thompson has taken the lead in promoting the idea of a designated Mid-Continental Trade Corridor from Winnipeg along the U.S. interstate highway system through Kansas City, Dallas and down into Mexico to Guadalajara.

Winnipeg has world-class capabilities in aerospace, agri-business, construction, garment manufacturing, health industries, information and telecommunications and printing and publishing. Virtually all of them depend to varying degrees on export markets for their success. The city has a burgeoning information technology industry and is rapidly becoming an important centre for telephone call centres with more than 6,000 jobs created since 1992.

MID-CONTINENT TRADE CORRIDOR

...AND THE WORLD

CANADA

MANITOBA

UNITED STATES

MEXICO

▲ *Winnipeg is located at the center of the mid-continent trade corridor. Courtesy of the Manitoba Trade & Investment Corporation.*

Considering that Winnipeg started as a relatively isolated settlement, its early residents had to find ways to get the job done by themselves. That dynamic of isolation that first made Winnipeg a diversified economic centre is still at play.

Like many other places, Winnipeg's relative success has come from its business community's ability to capitalize on market opportunities.

But unlike many other places, Winnipeg has no regional market to speak of. It must find customers further-afield. That's why its economy is more than just Prairie grain, trains and a gateway to the west.

Plants in and around Winnipeg now produce a host of value-added niche products that are in demand around the world. For example: frozen french fries-Manitoba is now the second largest potato producer in Canada with two major frozen french fry plants in the region; busses-Winnipeg is the largest bus manufacturing centre in North America shipping both urban busses and inter-city coaches; scratch-off lottery tickets-Pollard Banknote Ltd. is one of the three largest printers of its type in the world; wireless transmission systems-Broadband Networks Inc. has sold its wireless voice/data/television transmission and receiving technology around the world (the 250-employee company was sold to Northern Telecom at the end of 1997 for an astounding $586 million); medical software-OpTx 2000 and Momentum Software are both establishing themselves in the U.S. as suppliers of important niche products; and agricultural growth chambers—Controlled Environments Ltd. is the world's largest supplier of high-tech growth chambers for agricultural research.

Manitoba has a $1.8 billion agri-food industry and there is significant new investment coming on stream including a $50 million J.M. Schneider Inc. hog processing plant that opened in St. Boniface in 1997. Schneider has already identified the Japanese market as the prime customers for the new Winnipeg plant.

Between 1995 and 1997 close to $325 million worth of investment in agri-food

or value-added agricultural production has been announced for Winnipeg and the agricultural area to the west and south of the city. It is a renaissance of sorts for the industrial/agricultural development in the region.

The Canada/U.S. border-crossing at Emerson, Man. is the busiest between Toronto and Vancouver, with more than 600 trucks per day heading north and south. From Winnipeg trucks can reach markets totalling 80 million people within 1,600 kilometers of the city in only 30 hours. The trucking industry employs about 5,000 people in Winnipeg with another 2,500 in the intra-city business.

Winnipeg is served by both Canadian transcontinental railroads, Canadian National and Canadian Pacific railroads, as well as the U.S.-based Burlington Northern Santa Fe Railroad. No other western Canadian city has that kind of access to rail service.

Winnport, the air and multi-modal cargo gateway being developed for the Winnipeg International Airport, will build on a major courier presence that already operates out of the airport. Purolator Courier Ltd. built a $6.6 million overnight sorting facility in 1996 and Federal Express and UPS both have substantial operations in Winnipeg.

The combination of truck, rail and air courier access into and out of Winnipeg is an important feature in the exporting success of the city's businesses.

After the agri-food and transportation industries the diversity of Winnipeg's manufacturing base is remarkable. For starters, it has the largest secondary manufacturing sector in the country with more than 1,800 firms employing about 45,000 people.

Winnipeg has a $650 million per year aerospace industry, the third largest in Canada next to Toronto and Montreal, employing about 4,250 people. About 1,200 people work at Boeing Canada Technology, Ltd., one of only two Boeing plants in Canada. It manufactures parts for the full line of Boeing commercial jets. Boeing's order book is filling so rapidly that the Seattle aerospace giant plans to

▲ The Winnipeg Commodity Exchange was formed in 1887 and since then Winnipeg has been at the centre of Canada's lucrative grain trade. Photo by George Siamandas.

▲ *J.M. Schneider, Inc., a $50 million hog processing plant opened in St. Boniface in 1997. Photo by George Siamandas.*

▲ *Winnipeg's hog processors maintain and adhere to strict sanitary codes. Courtesy of Manitoba Pork. Photo by Mike Grandmaison.*

increase its output to historic levels by 1998. That means the Winnipeg operation will also have to increase production and company officials believe its workforce will be up to 1,500 by then. The Winnipeg plant makes about 2,500 different parts mostly fabricated out of composite materials.

Bristol Aerospace and Standard Aero Ltd. are the other major components of the aerospace industry in Winnipeg, whose total export sales were about $360 million in 1996. Bristol is a multi-faceted company with manufacturing and repair and overhaul capabilities in both the civil and defence industries in fixed and rotary-wing aircraft. Standard Aero is one of the world's leading gas turbine engine repair and overhaul facilities. Both companies have long-standing track records as profitable units with customers all around the world.

Winnipeg is home to one of only five farm tractor manufacturing plants left on the continent. New Holland's Versatile farm equipment division makes large

▶ Winnipeg is home to the largest furniture manufacturer in the country, Palliser Furniture Ltd. Photo courtesy of Palliser Furniture Ltd.

front-wheel drive tractors that it ships all over the world with a workforce of close to 800 people and sales in 1996 of more than $700 million.

New Flyer Industries, owned by Winnipeg-based Dutch entrepreneur Jan Den Oudsten, is now making close to 1,000 busses per year. The former provincial crown corporation survived a competitive shake-out of the industry in the late '80s and emerged as leaders in a low-floor urban bus design. The company completed a $10.5 million expansion in 1997 that will add about 200 jobs to a workforce of about 1,000.

Across the city, Motor Coach Industries, owned by the Mexican industrial conglomerate, Consorcio Grupo Dina, announced a $39 million expansion in 1997 to establish an additional production line to build a newly-designed $500,000 luxury coach.

▲ Winnipeg-based television broadcasting company CanWest Global Communications Corp. is now a major player in Australian and New Zealand television broadcasting and it is the largest partner in a new television network being formed in Ireland. Photo courtesy of CanWest Global Communications Corp.

The expansion will add an additional 100 jobs to the workforce of 2,000. MCI controls about 60 per cent of the coach market in North America.

For the second year in a row the transportation equipment sector of the manufacturing industry produced more than $1 billion worth of product. Motor vehicles are now a more valuable export item for Manitoba than grain.

Unisys Canada Inc. has the only computer manufacturing plant in western Canada in Winnipeg. It is Unisys' only Canadian plant and the only one that makes memory storage drives. Back in 1984 the company had seven such plants around the world. But with technological and corporate changes the company only needs one plant and Winnipeg's was the one to survive.

Winnipeg is also home to the largest furniture manufacturer in the country, Palliser Furniture Ltd. Early in 1997 it announced a $14 million expansion at its suburban Transcona plant that will create up to 400 new jobs.

The western Canadian furniture industry was supposed to be decimated after the Free Trade Agreement with the U.S. But instead, Palliser closed its assembly plant in North Dakota, increased its Winnipeg workforce from 1,500 in 1993 to about 2,500 in 1997 and now exports more than 50 per cent of its production to the U.S.-up from about 10 per cent in 1988. Palliser now has annual sales of about $270 million worth of its stylish and contemporary pieces.

The Canadian garment industry was also not given much chance of competing against lower cost American and Mexican manufacturers in a continental free trade market. But the Winnipeg garment sector, the third largest in the country, has flourished and grown. The industry now employs about 8,000 and exports to the

▲ *Winnipeg International Airport. Photo by George Siamandas.*

▲ *Air Canada flies daily non-stop flights from Winnipeg to Chicago. Photo by George Siamandas.*

▶ From the fields to the trading floor, flax contributes
to Winnipeg's status as the nation's breadbasket.
Photo by Mike Grandmaison.

▲ Potatoes from beautiful fields like this will supply the growing french fry industry in the region. Photo by Mike Grandmaison.

U.S. have increased by tenfold during the first half of this decade.

Nygard International, one of the most technologically advanced garment manufacturers in the country, has more than 1,000 employees in Winnipeg, the central production site for the sprawling international ladies sportswear manufacturer.

Western Glove Works Ltd. is the one of the largest denim jean manufacturer in the country. Employing close to 1,000 people in Winnipeg, WGW makes its own Silver brand of blue jeans and private label brands for the likes of Calvin Klein. Winnipeg boasts a host of outerwear and sportswear manufacturers and is the home of the young entrepreneurs behind the stylish designer label, Mondetta.

Historically, Winnipeg has had a host of entrepreneurs who rise above the pack. For instance, Pollard Banknote is the major supplier of scratch-off and break-open lottery ticket to the Canadian, British and French national lotteries and has customers in eastern Europe and Asia and several large U.S. state lotteries with plants in Canada, the U.S. and France.

Westsun Inc. supplied the lighting system for Walt Disney's new musical stage extravaganza of the *Lion King* that opened on Broadway at the end of 1997.

Winnipeg may be a little off the beaten track but its business people are good at closing the gap. Marc Raymond, president of Westsun, has had to break into a highly specialized market against a very small

number of traditional suppliers based near New York.

But Raymond and his business are the epitome of a Winnipeg success story. Westsun was able to open on Broadway because of the skill of its Winnipeg workforce, relatively inexpensive operating costs, a mindset that said he had to find customers outside the region or the business would not be able to grow and a healthy dose of North End Winnipeg chutzpa.

Raymond said the same thing many other Winnipeggers who have been successful in foreign markets have said, "The customer doesn't really care where Winnipeg is." As long as they have all the other things going for them. ■

4

The City that Manages & Finances The Nation's Breadbasket

▲ Photo by George Siamandas.

◄ Photo by Mike Grandmaison.

▶ *Toronto Dominion Bank. Photo by Mike Grandmaison.*

Since before the turn of the century the grain barons have ruled Portage and Main. The economics of the Prairie agricultural industry still sets the pace at the corner of Portage Avenue and Main Street. Six of the province's 10 largest companies–Cargill Ltd., James Richardson International, XCAN Grain Pools Ltd., United Grain Growers Limited, Parrish & Heimbecker Limited and the tractor manufacturer, New Holland Canada–are agriculture-related.

Major international grain companies like Cargill, Louis Dreyfus, Bunge, Continental and ConAgra all run their Canadian operations at or near the famous corner. The Canadian Wheat Board (CWB) with its $6 billion worth of sales of Canadian wheat and barley is headquartered there.

The grain barons still operate at Portage and Main. But now they are found amidst the law offices, accounting firms, corporate head offices, banks and financial institutions of the high rise office towers that shoot up on each of the four corners of the famous intersection.

One of them–the 30-story Richardson Building–is named after the Winnipeg family whose grain business, James Richardson International, occupies the penthouse suite. It is the fourth largest privately-held, family-owned business in the country with revenue in 1996 of about $1.9 billion.

Another is called the Commodity Exchange Tower, even though the Winnipeg Commodity Exchange occupies only one of the building's 31 floors. The 80-lawyer law firm, Aikins MacAulay &

Thorvaldson, occupies the top floor of the Commodity Exchange Tower.

The other two high rises at Portage and Main are named after Canadian banks and the Big Five banks that don't have buildings named after them have very high profile locations at the famous corner.

The newest bank on the block is the Moscow Narodny Bank, a Russian-owned but London-based boutique bank specializing in trade financing. The bank's decision to make Winnipeg its base of operation in North America is testimony to the city's position as both a regional banking and a commodity trade centre.

A symbiotic relationship has developed over time between the banking industry and the Prairie agricultural industry.

For a long time in history a good part of that relationship was centred around the Winnipeg Commodity Exchange. Formed in 1887, it is the country's only commodity options and futures exchange and the only exchange in the world that trades canola futures contracts. Contracts for the oilseed crop are by far its most vigorously traded, representing close to 70 per cent of the trading volume of the exchange.

The Winnipeg Commodity Exchange was the prime market place for Prairie grain production until the creation of the Canadian Wheat Board in 1935. Now the CWB is responsible for marketing Canada's entire wheat and barley crop in Canada and around the world from its head office near Portage and Main. In the 1995-96 crop year the harvest was worth $5.8 billion.

▲ *The Canadian Wheat Board is responsible for marketing Canada's entire wheat and barley crop in Canada and around the world from its head office near Portage and Main. Photo by George Siamandas.*

The CWB, with its 500 head office staff, makes the key executive decisions that affect the movement of about 45 million tonnes of wheat and barley grown in western Canada every year. In doing so the CWB also controls about one-fifth of the world export market of wheat and wheat flour.

▲ Cargill, one of the countries largest grain companies, is very visible in actual prairie portrait of Winnipeg. Photo by Mike Grandmaison.

Winnipeg is the headquarters for several of the country's largest grain companies like Manitoba Pool Elevators, United Grain Growers and Cargill Canada. In 1996 those three companies alone accounted for profits of just under $100 million.

While these giants of Canada's grain industry continue to have an extraordinary impact on the regional economy, some of the dynamics in the industry are changing.

In 1995 the Canadian government ended long time rail transportation subsidies for grain—called the Crow Rate. This made Manitoba farmers and grain companies rethink their strategies. Now they must pay the full rail freight rate to ship their grain to port—either to Vancouver, Thunder Bay or Churchill—making profit margins for all grain shipments from Manitoba less attractive.

As a result of that investors are re-directing capital to various forms of value-added agricultural production in Manitoba so that the goods are worth more before they are shipped to market. Significant growth in industries like hog and other livestock production, specialty crops like potatoes for the growing frozen french fry industry in the region, and other sophisticated agri-businesses in Manitoba is already occurring.

As the financial, distribution and transportation centre of the region, not to mention the centre of intellectual and human resources, Winnipeg has managed to retain a central role in the $2 billion per year agri-food and beverage industry in the province. From 1993 to 1996 that industry has grown by about 23 percent annually and every indication suggests that it will continue to grow.

Total farm production in the province in 1996 was about $3 billion. About half of that total is exported and value-added food and beverage exports have doubled in the past five years to about $550 million.

From the beginning of 1996 to the end of 1997 about $437 million worth of capital investment had been committed to constructing and expanding food processing and other types of agri-business enterprises in Manitoba. All but two of these developments are within an hour's drive of Winnipeg.

In 1995 the food industry in Manitoba represented about 23 percent of the manufacturing industry in the province which is about the same level it has been at throughout the '90s. But the total volumes of agri-food products shipped out of plants in and around Winnipeg is expected to grow substantially over the next several years.

McCain Foods spent $70 million expanding its french fry plant in Portage la Prairie, an hour west of Winnipeg. MidWest Foods, the prime supplier of frozen french fries to McDonald's restaurants in the Chicago area, spent about $20 million expanding its french fry plant a little further southwest near Carberry. In addition to those facilities the Minneapolis-owned potato-chip company, Old Dutch Foods, has a plant in Winnipeg making Manitoba the second largest potato producer in the country behind Prince Edward Island.

Like the Winnipeg manufacturing industry, the agri-processing industry in Manitoba is also diversified. In the summer of 1997 several new plants opened or were under construction: Canadian Agra built a $55 million canola crushing plant in Ste. Agathe just south of Winnipeg; J.M. Schneider Inc. opened the first phase of what will eventually be a $50 million pork processing plant in Winnipeg; construction began on a $142 million strawboard plant in Elie, 20 minutes west of Winnipeg by a newly created company called Isobord Enterprises Inc.; a $5 million flour mill, the first new mill in Manitoba in 40 years, is also to be built near Elie; a $30 million ethanol and gluten extraction plant is expected to start construction by the end of 1997 near the Saskatchewan border; and near the end of 1997 Maple Leaf Foods announced it would build a $112 million pork processing plant in Brandon.

In 1995 there were about 39,000 Manitobans employed in primary agriculture and more than 9,000 additional jobs in the food and beverage production

▲ The 30-story Richardson Building is located on one of the four corners of the well known Portage and Main intersection. Photo by Mike Grandmaison.

industries, the majority of them in or near Winnipeg.

The convergence of activities in the agri-food sector has been phenomenal. The traditional crop of cereal grain is declining in its share of total cash receipts while oilseeds, specialty crops and livestock are going up. And investment in the agri-food industry is so strong that there is general consensus and well-founded optimism that there will be continued growth.

One indication of that is the continuing increase in hog production. With spin-offs to suppliers and the service sector, hog production contributes more than $1.2 billion to the provincial economy and directly employs about 13,000.

Doug Dodds, the chairman and CEO of

Kitchener, Ontario-based J.M. Schneider Inc., was in Winnipeg for the opening of his company's new 120,000 square foot pork processing plant in St. Boniface in June, 1997. He said there were several factors that helped the company decide to build its new plant in Winnipeg.

"We were encouraged and supported by the province's commitment to the growth of our industry and the concrete steps it had taken to put this commitment into action." Dodds said. "In fact, Winnipeg came out on top after being measured against a very tough set of economic, social and geographic considerations."

Officials with Isobord Enterprises Inc., are just as confident about their innovative Elie, Manitoba strawboard plant.

Isobord has developed a process of making a particle-board product with excellent tooling and handling characteristics using straw instead of wood particles as its raw material and a bonding formula that is formaldehyde-free.

Two large American manufacturers are committed to purchasing about 80 per cent of the plant's production for the first couple of years because they're concerned about declining availability and rising cost of timber and the increasing environmental concerns over the use of formaldehyde in traditional particleboard.

During the 1990s the capital markets in Winnipeg have blossomed so that there is now a handful of home-grown pools of investment capital, three of

▲ *Manitoba Pool Elevators, another giant of Canada's grain industry, is headquartered in Winnipeg. Photo by Mike Grandmaison.*

▲ *The Great West Life Assurance Co., started by Winnipeg businessmen in 1892, has been the city's largest corporation for many years. Photo by Mike Grandmaison.*

which invested in the Isobord deal: the Crocus Investment Fund has raised more than $62 million in RRSP-eligible investments from 13,000 Manitobans to invest in Manitoba companies; the $25 million Manitoba venture capital company, Vision Capital Fund; and the newly-created Manitoba Capital Fund with $25 million of Manitoba pension fund and institutional money to invest in Manitoba businesses in the form of subordinated debt.

They are all relatively new additions on the capital markets scene in Winnipeg. The Winnipeg Stock Exchange isn't new, but the smallest stock exchange in North

America—one of only five in Canada—now has electronic trading facilities, an aggressive new marketing campaign and new small business user-friendly regulations in Manitoba designed to make the exchange more responsive to the Prairie and Midwest market.

While the Winnipeg Stock Exchange is only now trying to re-establish itself, the Great-West Life Assurance Co. was started by Winnipeg businessmen in 1892 and has never stopped growing. It has been the city's largest corporation for many years and the one with the highest community profile. With its acquisition of

London Life in the fall of 1997 it became the largest insurance company in the country. Even before that deal, Great-West Life had revenues of $5.9 billion in 1996, and was one of the most profitable companies of any sector in Canada.

Winnipeg's second most powerful presence in the financial services industry is Investors Group Inc., part of the same corporate family as Great-West Life. It is the largest mutual fund company in Canada with assets under administration of more than $27 billion and annual revenue of close to $700 million in 1996.

The two companies combined employ

▶ United Grain Growers is one of the province's 10 largest companies. Photo by Mike Grandmaison.

close to 3,000 people in Winnipeg and provide a strong foundation for the kind of technical skills needed to compete in the competitive, high tech world of finance.

Manitoba's 75 independent credit unions are among the most successful in the country. With a total of 369,000 members, it means one-third of all Manitobans are credit union members. And with close to $4 billion on deposit they are a force on the financial service front.

There is no question that the agricultural industry remains the strategic sector that gives Winnipeg a lot of its promi-

nence. And it is that sector and its capital requirements that traditionally provide the underpinning for the city's financial services industry.

But Winnipeg's financial services companies are no longer dependent on agriculture or any other particular industry. Their customer base is as diverse as the city's economy and the service selection and product variety exhibits the kind of entrepreneurial flair for which Winnipeg is known. ■

▲ Investors Group, Inc., another powerful presence in the financial services industry, is the largest mutual fund company in Canada. Photo by Mike Grandmaison.

5

Planes, Trains & Semis

▲ Photo by George Siamandas.

◀ Winnipeg continues to thrive in its role as a transportation and distribution centre. Photo by Mike Grandmaison.

▼ *With the dawn of each new era in transportation and distribution technology, from rail to road to air cargo, Winnipeg entrepreneurs have made sure that the city gets its share of the action. Photo by Mike Grandmaison.*

Were it not for an expensive and risky act of will, Winnipeg might now be a small bedroom community with some light industry and a folksy connection to the river—much like the town of Selkirk that is about 75 kilometres north of Winnipeg.

In the early 1880s the construction of the transcontinental railroad was slowly heading west and Canadian Pacific Railroad engineers had identified Selkirk, Manitoba as the spot where the railroad would cross the Red River.

But the aggressive entrepreneurial business community in Winnipeg—a town of only 8,000 in 1881—knew what the railroad could mean to the city. Its business leaders had the ear of City Hall and convinced council to open the vaults to make sure Winnipeg was on the railroad's main transcontinental line.

And what a package of goodies they came up with! The city of Winnipeg gave the railroad exemption from municipal property taxes in perpetuity, provided free right-of-way for its lines and spurs and free land for the railroad's station and yards. In exchange the CPR promised to run its main line through the city and agreed to build its repair and overhaul shops in Winnipeg.

The decision, that included the construction of the Louise Bridge at a cost of $300,000 plus another $200,000 in cash, helped ensure that Winnipeg would be the dominant transportation centre of the region.

The property tax exemption expired in the 1970s but Winnipeg continues to have a strong presence from both the Canadian National Railroad and the Canadian Pacific Railroad and is the second largest rail centre in the country.

The impact of the decision to lure the railroad at any cost is still being felt a century later as Winnipeg continues to thrive on its role as a transportation and distribution centre. Winnipeg is still very much a railroad town.

But with the dawn of each new era in transportation and distribution technology, from rail to road to air cargo, Winnipeg entrepreneurs have made sure that the city gets its share of the action.

More than a century after the city and local business provided lucrative incentives to attract the railroad, Winnipeg's private and public sector are once again teaming up in a venture called Winnport Logistics Ltd.

Winnport's goal is to establish a circum-polar 747 air cargo route from Asia

to Winnipeg with a multi-modal distribution centre based at the Winnipeg International Airport. About $5 million from a federal-provincial-municipal government program has funded the development of the project to date along with an additional $1 million from more than two dozen private sector partners.

The idea behind Winnport is to use the Winnipeg International Airport, with its 24-hour per day operations, to create an alternative destination to the congested U.S. centres of Chicago or Los Angeles. The creation of a multi-modal distribution

site for air cargo traffic between Asia and the North American Midwest is Winnport's first goal. Ultimately it hopes to develop value-added manufacturing, processing, assembly and warehousing operations all located on abundant and inexpensive land adjacent to the airport.

From Winnipeg, shippers will have access to about 23 per cent of the U.S. air cargo business within a day's truck travel. When it gets up and running, Winnport's Forwarder Direct air freight business will be the only Canadian air cargo service flying Boeing 747s.

The manufacturing and distribution centre will probably require about $100 million in infrastructure spending to service that land, but it is that kind of industrial development that Winnport's proponents believe could eventually create 6,000 jobs and add $600 million in annual contributions to the local economy.

The transportation and distribution industry in the province still accounts for about 30,000 jobs, most of them in Winnipeg. It is the highest per capita concentration in the country. As Winnport develops it will go a long way towards maintaining the city's role as a transportation centre.

So too will the further development of the idea of a Mid-Continent Trade Corridor. Winnipeg mayor Susan Thompson has made Winnipeg one of the leading advocates for the creation of a designated North American Free Trade Agreement (NAFTA) trucking route whose

northern terminus is Winnipeg and bisects the U.S. along interstates 29 and 35.

With the signing of NAFTA in 1994 the number of trucks that pass through the Emerson, Manitoba/Pembina, N.D. border crossing, 75 kilometers south of Winnipeg, now surpasses the truck traffic passing between Manitoba and Ontario.

"Any goods coming up east of the Mississippi and from the south will want to travel through Winnipeg because our transportation routes are the best," said Barry Prentice of the Transport Institute of the University of Manitoba.

More than 600 semi-trailers head north

▲ Further concentration of traffic along the Mid-Continent Trade Corridor—the route south from Winnipeg all the way to Kansas City then south through Dallas/Fort Worth crossing the border into Mexico at Laredo, TX—will mean strategic growth potential for all the communities up and down the corridor. Photo by Mike Grandmaison.

▲ *Canadian National Railroad's high-tech computer/telephony integration centre in downtown Winnipeg handles about 45,000 customer support calls per week. Photo by Mike Grandmaison.*

and south across that border every day, carrying a total of about $4 billion worth of goods every year. It is the fourth busiest border crossing in the country.

Further concentration of traffic along the Mid-Continent Trade Corridor—the route south from Winnipeg all the way to Kansas City then south through Dallas/Fort Worth crossing the border into Mexico at Laredo, TX—will mean strategic growth potential for all the communities up and down the corridor.

There may or may not ever be a designated NAFTA superhighway or Mid-Continent Trade Corridor as such, but the pooling of common interests among the Canadian, American and Mexican interests along the route is serving to heighten knowledge and interest among the regions.

The promotion of Winnipeg as the northern terminus for a North American trucking route makes a lot of sense because Winnipeg has been home to one

of Canada's largest trucking industries for a number of years.

Winnipeg's trucking industry employs close to 7,500 people and represents about five per cent of the province's gross domestic product generating about $500 million in sales and about $400 million in wages.

At least three of them—Reimer Express Lines Ltd., TransX Ltd. and Paul's Hauling Ltd. and its related operations—are among the top 10 trucking companies in the country and close to 10 more are among the 100 largest trucking firms in the country.

There are now more people who work in the trucking industry in Winnipeg than there are in the railroad industry. Canadian National Railroad employs about 2,500 in Manitoba, with about 500 of them working at the railroad's customer support centre that opened in Winnipeg in the fall of 1996. It is a high-tech computer/telephony integration centre in downtown Winnipeg that handles about

45,000 customer support calls per week.

There are still about 840 CN trains per week through Winnipeg. At its Transcona shops, where 900 people are employed, CN workers repair and overhaul locomotives. At its Symington yard, another 600 are employed at CN's car shop and perform some additional power supply work. An arrangement signed with GE Transportation Systems in May, 1997, means GE will supervise the maintenance of 118 of CN's high-powered GE-built locomotives. Winnipeg is also home to the railroad's grain marketing business.

Winnipeg has always had a disproportionate share of railway jobs. Canadian Pacific Railroad still has a staff of about 2,000 in Winnipeg. Both CP and CN have large multi-modal facilities in Winnipeg—CN's handled more than 77,000 units in 1996—and both have direct connections south of Winnipeg with their respective American subsidiaries. Winnipeg is also serviced by Burlington Northern Santa Fe

Railroad. It is the only city between Vancouver and Toronto with that kind of rail service.

During the 1990s the Canadian federal government was in the process of divesting its ownership of airports across the country. On January 3, 1997 ownership of the Winnipeg International Airport was transferred to a non-share community-owned corporation called the Winnipeg Airports Authority Inc.

Located a mere 15-minute drive from downtown, it was Canada's first international airport when it opened in 1928. It averages about 200 scheduled take-offs and landings of passenger planes per day and in 1996 handled 130,000 tonnes of cargo and 2.7 million passengers.

Passenger numbers went up every month for the 30 months prior to the transfer to the local airport authority.

Daily flights out of Winnipeg provide service to every major city in Canada. Northwest Airlines provides daily return service from Winnipeg to its hub in Minneapolis and Air Canada also flies daily non-stop return flights from Winnipeg to Chicago.

Another 40 cargo planes land and take off every night from Winnipeg International, one of the only 24-hour daily international airports in Canada. Those night flights are servicing the courier business, a strategically important part of the airport's $22 million per year operation. With the vocal support of the

Chamber, great care has been taken in the zoning of land around the airport and on the flight paths to preclude opposition to night flights that might arise if there were new residential developments in the area.

Federal Express, UPS and Purolator each fly into Winnipeg about four nights per week. Federal Express spent $2.5 million on a new sorting facility in Winnipeg in 1995 and Purolator finished constructing an 84,000 square foot, $6.6 million facility near the airport in the spring of 1997.

There is a strong presence on the Winnipeg aviation scene from the Canadian air force. Canadian Forces Base Winnipeg or 17 Wing Winnipeg, employs about 4,000 people in Winnipeg,

▲ Federal Express spent $2.5 million on a new sorting facility in Winnipeg in 1995. Photo by George Siamandas.

including 1,000 civilians, and injects about $400 million into the local economy.

Seventeen Wing Winnipeg had been the home of Air Command, the Canadian Air Force Headquarters for several years until the Department of National Defence made a decision in 1996 to fold command-level headquarters of the army, navy and air force into more efficient operational level commands.

Although Air Command is to be dismantled, the Winnipeg base will become the centre of the air force's operational responsibilities. As such, Canada's NORAD region headquarters is to be relocated from North Bay, Ontario to Winnipeg.

Among other things Winnipeg is one of the Canadian Force's major academic and technical training centres. The Canadian Forces School of Survival and Rescue is to be transferred to Winnipeg in the late '90s. Winnipeg is also the national site of five other Canadian Forces training centres for flying, navigation, aerospace, meteorology and language training.

The significance of the transportation business to the Winnipeg economy does not stop with the actual service and movement of people and goods. Three of the city's largest manufacturing operations are transportation related—two bus manufacturers (New Flyer and Motor Coach Industries) and a tractor manufacturer (New Holland). The city's aerospace sector also boasts three companies—

Boeing Canada Technology Ltd., Bristol Aerospace Limited and Standard Aero Limited—with close to 1,000 employees each and there is a thriving secondary manufacturing sector that has developed supplying parts and services to those large original equipment manufacturers and service operations.

Even the secondary manufacturers are significant in the transportation industry. For instance, Vansco Electronics Ltd. makes instrumentation and electronics components for New Holland's tractors that are made across the street from Vansco's Fort Garry plant. The company also supplies electronics components on busses made by Motor Coach Industries.

In the fall of 1996 Vansco announced

▲ New Flyer busses are a vital part of the city's transportation network. Photo courtesy of New Flyer Industries.

▲ Many of Winnipeg's original old trains have been refurbished and are on display throughout the city. Photo by George Siamandas.

an $11.3 million expansion at the same time that Motor Coach Industries announced an expansion of its own. And even though Vansco is a supplier to a couple of important Winnipeg customers it expects to grow its business by more than 50 per cent through exports.

It only follows that since Winnipeg is a transportation centre, its industries are geared for the export market and the two elements of Winnipeg commercial life continue to evolve with each other. ■

The beautiful Norwood Bridge provides a safe crossing over the Red River for vehicles as well as bikers and pedestrians. Photos by Mike Grandmaison.

6

Education, A Pursuit of Excellence

▲ The Ukranian Cultural and Educational Centre. Photo by Mike Grandmaison.

◄ The University of Manitoba Agricultural College. Photo by Mike Grandmaison.

Winnipeg earned its reputation as a self-sufficient regional centre early in its history. Long before it was incorporated as a city in 1873 when there were only about 3,000 residents, sophisticated social institutions had already been established that continue to exist today.

The Roman Catholic church's presence in the Red River settlement, for instance, is almost as old as the settlement itself. The first mission church in St. Boniface—named after the German saint admired by Bishop Provencher, the first head of the dioceses—was established in 1818, only six years after the first of the Selkirk settlers had arrived. It has been destroyed by fire and re-built five times. The St. Boniface Basilica that stands today on the east side of the Red River across from the Forks was completed in 1972.

The church's presence in the early days of the community was directly associated with the French-speaking community who were dominant in the settlement through the first three-quarters of the 19th century. Because of the church's involvement in education in those days—and with the help of committed advocates through several rounds of heated debate in the Manitoba legislature throughout the 20th century—Manitoba remains an officially

▲ University of Winnipeg's stately Wesley Hall on Portage Avenue is one of downtown Winnipeg's most striking architectural sights. Photo by Mike Grandmaison.

bi-lingual province with education from kindergarten to grade 12 available in English and French across the province.

Manitoba is a small province with a population in 1996 of only 1.1 million people (667,000 of them who live in Winnipeg), but the commitment to and excellence of its educational system belies the relatively small population base.

In 1997-98 the provincial government committed to spend a little more than $1 billion on education, almost $300 million more than was allocated in the 1987 fiscal year. Included in that total was $214.6 million to the three universities in Manitoba and $57 million to the three community colleges.

Early settlers and church officials started St. Boniface College, the precursor to the University of Manitoba, in the 1820s. By 1877 there were two other denomina-

tional colleges in the Winnipeg area—the Anglican St. John's College and the Presbyterian Manitoba College. The three of them convinced the province to establish an examination and degree-granting body and in 1877 the University of Manitoba Act was passed, turning the three colleges into the first university in western Canada.

Today the University of Manitoba has a budget of a quarter of a billion dollars and a total staff of more than 6,000. Close to 22,000 students were enrolled in degree programs in the 1996-97 academic year including graduate students and more than 20,000 additional students were enrolled in degree and certificate programs through the university's continuing education division.

As a multi-disciplinary research and education centre, the university's presence

in the community is even more substantial than the sizable seven per cent of the city's population that it represents.

In the words of Dr. Arnold Naimark, the president of the university from 1981-to-1996, "The staff members of the University of Manitoba constitute the largest pool of highly trained and educated people in the province and contribute in countless ways to social, cultural and economic development here and abroad."

The U of M may be the most substantial post-secondary institution in the city but it is not the only one. The University of Winnipeg was formed in 1967 from the former United College which itself was formed from the merger of Manitoba College and Wesley College. Before 1967 it had been part of the University of Manitoba.

The stately profile of 100 year-old

▶ St. Boniface College, the precursor to the University of Manitoba, was founded by early settlers and church officials in the 1820s. Photo by George Siamandas.

Wesley Hall on Portage Avenue is one of downtown Winnipeg's most striking architectural sights. The University of Winnipeg's 7,000 students and 1,500 full and part-time employees believe they have an important role in the life of the downtown of the city and take that responsibility seriously.

The University of Winnipeg is primarily an undergraduate institution with masters degrees offered in marriage and family therapy, divinity and sacred theology and as well as joint masters programs with the University of Manitoba in history, religious studies and public administration. The school offers a broad range of undergraduate arts and science degrees with business computing, administrative studies and justice and law enforcement among the more popular programs.

The University of Winnipeg Collegiate offers high school education in a campus setting. In the 1996-97 school year there were 530 students enrolled. Grade 10 classes are expected to be added in 1997-98. The university also runs a thriving continuing education division out of additional space downtown.

In *Maclean's* magazine's annual ranking of Canadian universities, the University of Winnipeg ranked seventh in overall excellence in 1996 (up from 10th in 1995) out of 19 primarily undergraduate schools. The school has the second-smallest sized classes in third and fourth year studies and it gets more than its share of academic awards and faculty recognitions.

Among other things, the school has a successful inter-university sports program particularly in men's and women's basketball and volleyball. The U of W's Lady Wesmen basketball team tied a North

American record with 88 consecutive victories—a streak that was ended one short of the record by cross-town rivals University of Manitoba Bisons on Dec. 2, 1994.

The University of Winnipeg's academic successes are out of proportion to its size. For instance in 1996 U of W classics student Mark Matz was one of only 11 Canadian students to win Rhodes scholarships; the school received 13 undergraduate student research awards in 1996 from the Natural Science and Engineering Research Council (NSERC), more than any other school in the country; and U of W history professor, Robert Young, was named the Canadian professor of the year in 1996 by the Council for the Advancement and Support of Education (CASE), an international education organization.

Also established in 1967, Red River Community College (RRCC) has about

▲ Red River Community College has about 1100 full and part-time staff and 30,000 students enrolled in a host of certificate, diploma and continuing education programs as well as degree programs that are part of joint ventures with both the University of Manitoba and the University of Winnipeg. Photo by Mike Grandmaison.

1,100 full and part-time staff and 30,000 students enrolled in a host of certificate, diploma and continuing education programs as well as degree programs that are part of joint ventures with the two Winnipeg universities. RRCC has been particularly effective in responding to new and distinctive training needs in the commercial marketplace.

The college offers more than 90 different diploma, certificates and joint baccalaureate programs as well as training for apprentices in 20 different trades. Its students have an 80 per cent success rate in finding work within nine months of graduation and 75 per cent of them are working in fields related to their study.

Through its market driven training centre, RRCC provides customized training for some of the city's largest and most technologically advanced employers. In

1995-96 it earned $4.7 million in fees from those corporate clients, 12 percent more than the previous year and it is expected that the program will grow by about 18 per cent again in 1996-97.

The college has regional centres in five smaller southern Manitoba towns—Arborg, Winkler, Portage la Prairie, Selkirk and Steinbach—with about 3,500 students enrolled and another 1,000 who take courses through distance education. In 1995-96, for the first time, the college offered a course using video correspondence and another delivered via the Internet.

Red River Community College's success in working with new technologies and new clients is a strategy that the University of Manitoba employs as well. The U of M now has research tentacles in a surprising number of private sector

technology development and marketing enterprises in the province.

The University of Manitoba operates from a sprawling 274-hectare site in Fort Garry, on the southwest side of the city, as well as 10 buildings adjacent to the Winnipeg Health Sciences Centre near downtown Winnipeg where its faculties of medicine and dentistry are located. It has property and equipment that is valued at more than $775 million.

The College universitaire de St. Boniface (St. Boniface College) continues its association with the U of M from its original location beside the St. Boniface Basilica, offering instruction in French towards degrees in arts, science, education and translation. St. Andrew's College offers courses in Ukrainian studies and theology, the Jesuit-run St. Paul's College offers a Roman Catholic focus on

▲ *The University of Manitoba's Wallace Geological Sciences building. Photo by Mike Grandmaison.*

► The Asper Jewish Community Campus has Jewish community organizations, a Jewish high school and a state-of-the-art fitness centre. Photo by Mike Grandmaison.

education and St. John's College offers training for ordained and lay ministry in the Anglican church.

Credit courses for the U of M can also be taken at the Canadian Mennonite Bible College, Prairie Theatre Exchange and the Catherine Booth Bible College.

The U of M offers 78 different degrees including professional faculties of architecture, dentistry, engineering, law and medicine. Post-graduate degrees are available in all disciplines.

The university has several research centres throughout the province, including the 440-hectare Glenlea agricultural station and astronomical observatory; an agricultural research centre near Carman; a biological field station at Delta Marsh north of Portage la Prairie; Star Lake geological field station in the Whiteshell area of the province east of the city; and the Taiga Biological Station north of Wallace Lake in eastern Manitoba.

The U of M is home to more than 20 research centres and institutes ranging in scope from applied ethics, aging, cell biology, transportation and higher education to cardiovascular sciences, health policy, earth observation science and theoretical physics.

The University of Manitoba is also home to the federal government's Freshwater Institute, Agriculture Canada's research station and the Cadham Provincial Lab. Several research bodies are closely related to the U of M like the High Voltage Direct Current (HVDC) Research Centre, the Manitoba Cancer Treatment and Research Foundation, Telecommunications Research Laboratories (TRLabs), the National Research Council's Institute for Biodiagnostics and Wildlife Habitat Canada.

The university's fund-raising efforts have generated close to $10 million in each of 1995 and 1996 and the university attracted $68 million in research grants in 1995-96, $10 million more than the previous year.

While it is not among the largest schools in the country, its researchers continue to be disproportionately active. A study by the Philadelphia Institute for

Science Information found that U of M scientists were the second most often-cited as contributing to published research in the medical science field among all universities in the country.

In 1996 the university was made headquarters for a new Canadian Network of Centres of Excellence called Intelligent Sensing for Innovative Structures (ISIS). The $19 million, three-and-a-half year research program will study and develop standards and codes on light, non-corrosive composite materials that are 10-times stronger than steel that eventually can be used in engineering structures like bridges and buildings. Wiring the material with fibre optics means the structure's integrity can be monitored remotely.

In 1995-96 University of Manitoba professors received grants to study a variety of fields including the molecular basis of metastatic progression of cancer and the administration of and strategies to deliver health care to the aged; and the university's community health services became part of a Centre of Excellence based out of McMaster University, called HEALNet,

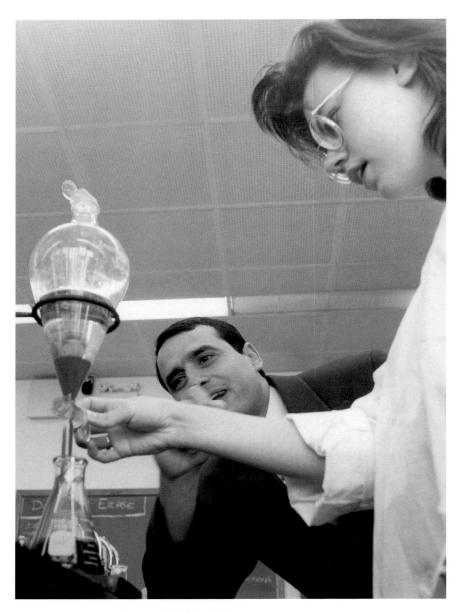

▲ University of Winnipeg professors often provide individual attention in the lab. Photo courtesy of the University of Winnipeg.

▲ The University of Winnipeg's Lady Wesmen basketball team tied a North American record with 88 consecutive victories—a streak that was ended one short of the record by cross-town rivals University of Manitoba Bisons on Dec. 2, 1994. Photo courtesy of the University of Winnipeg.

examining ways in which computer technology can improve the quality and efficiency of the health care system.

All three of Winnipeg's post-secondary institutions have had good success in attracting foreign students. One of the reasons for that, though not the only one, is that all three schools have relatively low tuition fees.

Winnipeg's elementary and secondary schools have a long history of multi-cultural and multi-lingual schools. French is not the only language other than English in which the children can be taught. Of the 235 schools in Winnipeg 10 are heritage language schools providing instruction in Hebrew, Ukrainian and German. There are a total of 60 elementary and secondary schools that offer either French immersion or full French environments.

Close to 96,000 students attended elementary and secondary schools in Winnipeg in 1996-97. An additional 13,500 attended private schools throughout the province, the largest being the schools of the Winnipeg Board of Jewish Education as well as St. John's Ravenscourt, Mennonite Brethern Collegiate, Balmoral Hall, St. Paul's High School and St. Mary's Academy.

Winnipeg's schools and its educational leaders have an enviable track record of recognitions and awards. In the 1996-97 year alone teachers and students from Winnipeg's largest school division won no less than 11 national and international awards.

Like several other of Winnipeg's rich cultural traditions, the educational system prides itself on excellence that surpasses expectations. ■

▲ Students at Whyte Ridge Elementary School enjoying the fresh air and sunshine. Photo by Mike Grandmaison.

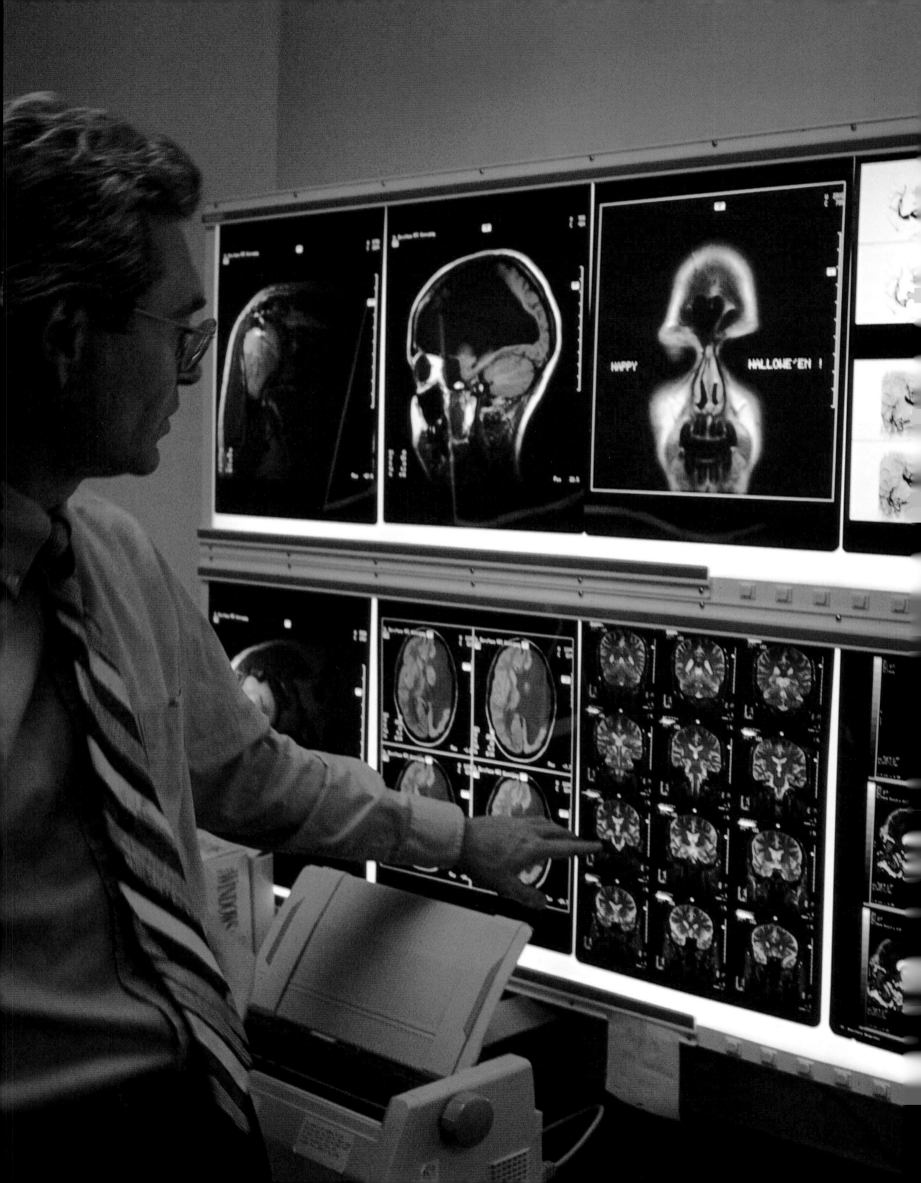

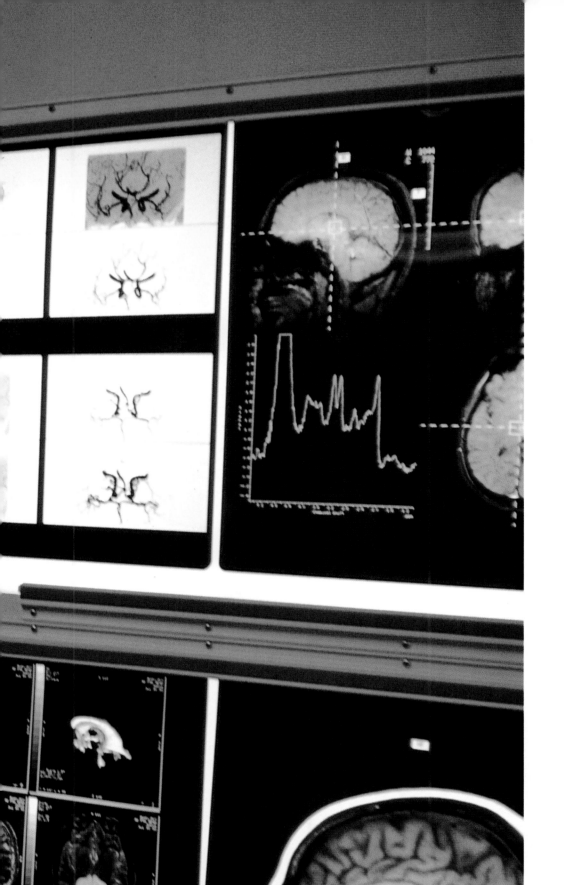

7

Health Care & Technology, From Fibre Optics to Biodiagnostics

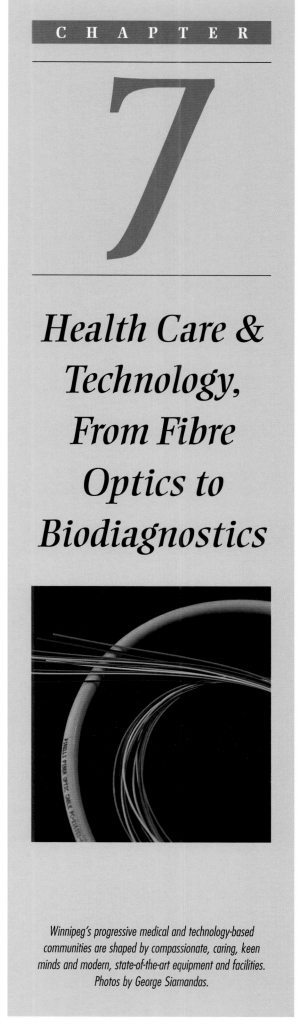

Winnipeg's progressive medical and technology-based communities are shaped by compassionate, caring, keen minds and modern, state-of-the-art equipment and facilities. Photos by George Siamandas.

91

▶ The National Research Council's $21 million Institute for Biodiagnostics. Photo by Mike Grandmaison.

Except for the arrival of the railroad in the 1880s, Winnipeg's history has always been more affected by natural social evolution—the fur-trade, the buffalo hunt, the development of commercial agriculture—than from outside pressures of the larger North American community.

The frontier self-sufficiency of the 19th century served the community well when do-it-yourself know-how meant the difference between living comfortably and just surviving. Winnipeg's future prosperity depends on the city's ability to maintain that can-do attitude in the face of a new world that includes high-speed digital communications. In that world, Winnipeg's strategic geographic location in the middle of the continent is secondary to the talent and skill of its people.

For a relatively isolated city whose underlying business dynamic is strongly linked to agricultural production and transportation, Winnipeg has developed a remarkable amount of expertise in several important high technology pursuits particularly in the fields of health care and telecommunications.

Much of the health care research is centred around the city's two major teaching hospitals—the Health Sciences Centre and St. Boniface General Hospital. There is a total of 1,800 beds between them, and both have sprawling research activities with active fund-raising foundations attached to them.

In its 1997-98 budget the province of Manitoba committed $1.8 billion, or 34 per cent of its budget, towards health care delivery throughout the province. While greater efficiencies are being squeezed out of health care budgets everywhere in Canada—for example, clinical and administrative functions at Winnipeg's seven hospitals are being integrated—the province still spent $500 million more on health care in 1997 than it did 10 years prior.

During that same 10-year period the private sector has invested another $500 million developing commercial enterprises in the health industries field. What is remarkable about that level of investment is that in the mid-'80s that there really wasn't much of a health care industry to speak of in Manitoba.

In 1997 there were about 100 companies, more than 2,000 employees and $300 million in annual sales in both the pharmaceutical and medical devices industries in Winnipeg. In 1984, for instance, there were only four companies with annual sales of no more than $25 million.

After a conscious decision was made in the late '80s by the provincial government to attempt to encourage investment and develop expertise in health care-related industries, Winnipeg has become the centre of the third largest cluster of such companies in the country. Low-interest financing is available through government programming and banking partnerships and the province's Health Industries Development Initiative provides support in various ways for industry participants.

That atmosphere of industry support is not exclusive to the health care industries. Winnipeg 2000 president Klaus Thiessen believes that support from the greater business community is an important reason for Winnipeg's rising reputation as a good place in which to do business.

"If you're starting a business in Winnipeg, there are an awful lot of resources that can be accessed," Thiessen said. "If you want to meet a government cabinet minister, you can. If you want to meet with a senior business person in town, many of them will gladly make the time. That's extremely important."

Winnipeg has become a significant centre for research and production for Canada's two large generic drug manufacturers. There is also a growing critical mass of university-related, leading edge health research and administrative and diagnostic software.

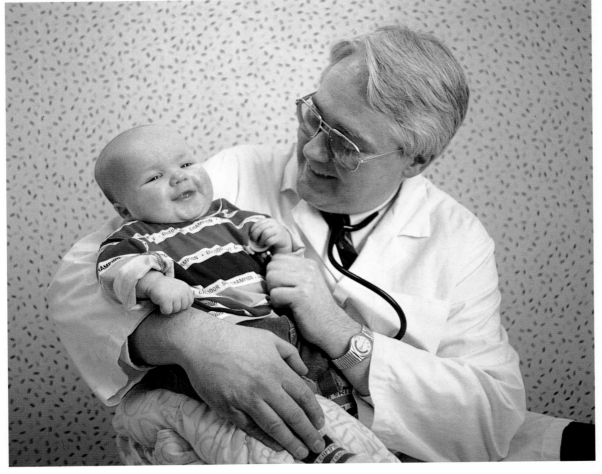

▲ Winnipeg is proud of the bedside manners of its doctors and health care professionals. Photo by George Siamandas.

The health research and technology industry in Winnipeg is expecting a strong boost as the most advanced human and animal disease control laboratory in the world opened in the fall of 1997, Health Canada and Agriculture Canada's $143 million Virology Lab.

Winnipeg researchers are involved in three of the four National Centres of Excellence in biomedical research. Medical scientists at the combined Children's Hospital Research Foundation (CHRF) and the Health Sciences Centre Foundation (HSCF) receive about $30 million worth of research grants annually. The St. Boniface General Hospital Research Centre has another $10 million annual research budget of its own. Those facilities as well as the Manitoba Cancer Treatment and Research Foundation through its Institute for Cell Biology have a total of more than 400 research scientists on staff.

At the Health Sciences Centre, medical researchers are doing work on infectious diseases, respirology and clinical neuro-science including spinal cord injuries. Child health researchers at the CHRF concentrate on breathing disorders; growth disorders and diabetes; infectious diseases such as AIDS; genetics, including screening for Down's syndrome and muscular dystrophy; leukemia and other childhood cancers; blood disorders; kidney disease; as well as fetal and neo-natal research.

The St. Boniface General Hospital Research Centre has the premier heart research program in the country and one of only two Medical Research Council-designated centres for cardiovascular sciences. Among other things, the centre conducts research and patient assessment work with magnetic resonance imaging and in the late '90s started a major program studying degenerative disorders associated with aging.

Both of those facilities, along with the National Research Council's $21 million Institute for Biodiagnostics, are focused on the potential commercialization of their specific research endeavors.

Research connected to the Health Sciences Centre alone creates about 1,000 direct jobs and applying a modest multiplier effect probably means more than $150 million per year to the city's economy.

One of the Winnipeg medical research community's most enduring and successful commercial applications is WinRho SD. Produced from human plasma, it is used for the prevention of hemolytic disease of the newborn (blue baby syndrome) and other blood irregularities. WinRho was developed by doctors at the Health Sciences Centre and licensed for use in Canada in 1980. In the late '80s Mississauga-based Apotex Inc. acquired the university's WinRho operation and renamed it Rh Pharmaceuticals. In 1995 Rh Pharmaceuticals merged with Cangene Corp. Cangene is now the publicly-traded research division of Apotex, one of Canada's two large generic drug manufacturers. Cangene's operations are primarily based in Winnipeg with WinRho SD the major source of revenue for the company, which in 1996 was about $12.3 million.

Another Apotex division operates a specialized pharmaceutical production facility in Winnipeg where it makes the generic cholesterol-lowering drug lovastatin. Apotex has invested about $100 million and employs more than 100 people many of them with post-graduate degrees at that facility.

Winnipeg is also an important base of operation for the publicly-traded research division of the other major Canadian generic drug company, Novopharm Ltd. of Scarborough, Ontario. Novopharm Biotech Inc. merged with Winnipeg biotechnology company Genesys Pharma in 1997 and has a combined staff of about 50

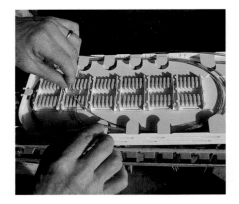

▲ *Photo by George Siamandas.*

researchers and technicians in Winnipeg with several bio-medical products in development. That company began clinical trials in Winnipeg in the summer of 1997 on an encouraging new drug for the treatment of AIDS.

Biovail Corporation International, another Toronto-based pharmaceutical company, has its manufacturing operation in nearby Steinbach where it employs about 50 people making time-released pharmaceutical formulations that are shipped and sold around the world.

Other players in the pharmaceutical

industry include Vita-Health Co. which makes specialty nutritional supplements, vitamins and other over-the-counter pharmaceuticals and STC Laboratories which extracts enzymes and proteins from horseradish and eggs for sale to pharmaceutical and medical product companies.

One of the best examples of Winnipeg's success in attracting new players in the health industries is National Healthcare Manufacturing Corp. NHMC owns and operates the world's first and only automated robotic production facility capable of assembling and packaging various trays and kits for medical and surgical procedures.

Winnipeg is also becoming a centre for medical and hospital administration software. OpTx 2000 has developed a sophisticated interactive oncology treatment software that is gaining a growing

▲ *Vita-Health Co., a prominent player in the pharmaceutical industry, makes specialty nutritional supplements, vitamins and other over-the-counter pharmaceuticals. Photo by Mike Grandmaison.*

▶ *The Manitoba Marathon attracts health-conscious individuals from miles around to participate in this annual event. Photo by George Siamandas.*

following among cancer clinics in the U.S. Other Winnipeg software companies like Momentum Software Corp., CareWare Software Systems Inc. and MedEasy have developed software for the management and administration of various types of hospital and medical clinics.

The development of this type of high tech industry would not be possible were there not adequate telecommunications facilities in place—and there are. Manitoba has one of the most extensive fibre optic networks in the country with more than 46,000 kilometres in the ground including 5,000 kilometres in Winnipeg.

Manitoba Telecom Services Inc., the former provincial Crown corporation that was privatized in January, 1997, is the fifth largest telecommunications company in the country. Its Winnipeg network is served by a fully digital switching platform all connected by fibre optic cables.

The company has been investing heavily in modernizing its network over the past several years with $165 million budgeted to be spent on capital projects in 1997. The city is also served by a growing number of telecommunications

competitors like AT&T, Sprint Canada, Fonorola, London Telecom and a handful of long distance re-sellers.

With a technologically-sound infrastructure in place the city has become a growing centre for the telecommunications

▲ *Videon Cable Systems, Inc. Photo by George Siamandas.*

service industry—or call centres. In 1997, after only three years in the business the city has attracted about 5,000 jobs and created a whole new industry in the city.

The city's reliable, stable workforce, telephone rates that are at the low end of the spectrum and availability of office space that is also among the least expensive in the country is attracting service centre operators like AT&T Transtech Canada, Faneuil ISG Inc. and TeleSpectrum Worldwide Inc. as well as national service centres for Canadian National and Canadian Pacific.

Like its economy in general, the high tech field is nicely diversified in Winnipeg. Air Canada runs its sophisticated centralized reservation network out of Winnipeg and computer out-sourcer, ISM Information System Management Corp. has a large Winnipeg operation.

Brand name computer manufacturer,

Unisys Corp., makes disk-drives in Winnipeg. It is Unisys' only Canadian plant and the only computer manufacturing facility in all of western Canada. Winnipeg-owned Mind Computer Products assembles high quality business and personal computers selling to a growing marketplace in western Canada and more recently into the northern Plains states.

There are a growing number of home-grown, innovative computer solution providers like OnLine Business Systems which now exports its expertise with offices in Minneapolis and Calgary.

Winnipeg is home to some of the top independent software companies in the country like Infocorp Computer Solutions Ltd., makers of point-of-sale software for retail chains and Emerging Information Systems Inc., which has developed software for the mutual fund brokers. Both companies have customers and on-going

marketing activities around the world.

Broadband Networks Inc. is one of the city's most exciting new entries in the telecommunications field. The company designs and manufactures digital wireless transmission and receiver systems that are used in Canada's first two wireless cable television operations out of Brandon, Manitoba and Yorkton, Saskatchewan; and Broadband Networks already sold systems in Japan and South Korea.

Winnipeg has become somewhat of a centre for microwave technologies with work being done by a couple of other Winnipeg companies in the field of distance education and novel applications like the traffic light control system for the city of Las Vegas.

Winnipeg's secondary manufacturing companies provide high tech components for the electronics industry. Vansco Electronics, Kraus Industries and C-MAC

▲ *A CITY WITHIN A CITY—Beyond the doors of Health Sciences Centre lies a community as complex as any city, a community made up of people dedicated to using the very best in medical practice to bring hope to those in need. Photo courtesy of Health Sciences Centre.*

▲ The curiosity and dedication of physicians and researchers at the St. Boniface Hospital and Research Centre have led to new discoveries in the treatment of many diseases. Photo courtesy of St. Boniface Hospital.

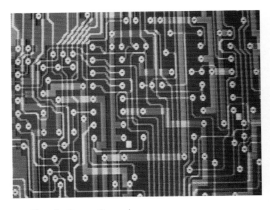

▲ *Photo by George Siamandas.*

Electronic Systems all have printed circuit board manufacturing capabilities and all make a wide range of high quality, specialized custom and proprietary electronics components.

The city is also home to other innovative enterprises that depend on intellectual capital as much as investment capital. Pollard Banknote Limited makes instant-win lottery and game tickets for customers and government-run lotteries around the world. In 1996-97 Pollard acquired a Michigan company and another in Paris, France so that it is now among the three largest printers of its kind in the world.

The International Institute for Sustainable Development (IISD), one of the world's leading think tanks that studies ways to integrate environmental and economic decision-making around the world, is based in Winnipeg. The IISD is another occasion for strategic international attention to be focused on Winnipeg. Maurice Strong, a senior official with the United Nations who grew up just outside of Winnipeg, is one of the IISD's board members.

The ability, confidence and organization with which Winnipeg enterprises are developing industries using leading edge technologies, particularly in the field of health care, is testimony to the bright future the city has in the 21st century and beyond. ■

▲ *Health Canada and Agriculture Canada's $143 million Virology Lab, the most advanced human and animal disease control laboratory in the world, opened in Winnipeg in the fall of 1997. Photo by Mike Grandmaison.*

▶ *Infocorp is one of the top independent software companies in the country. Photo courtesy of Infocorp Computer Solutions Ltd.*

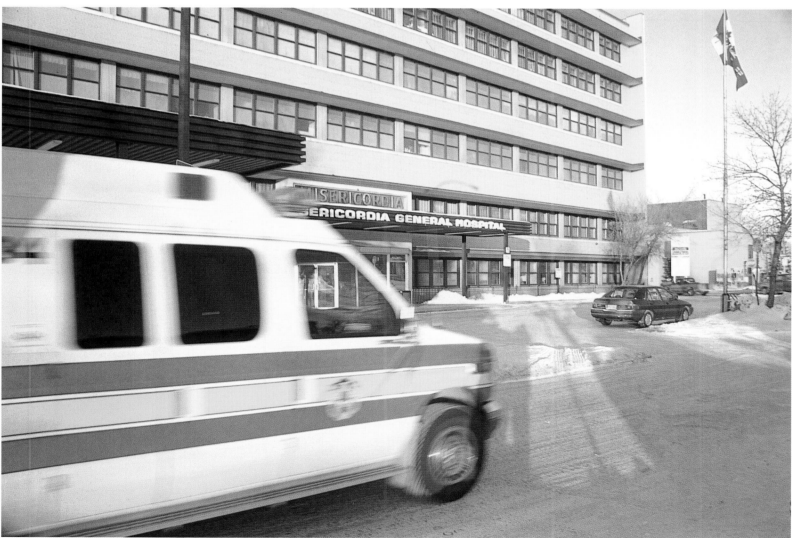

▲ *Winnipeg's hospitals provide prompt and reliable emergency services. Photo by George Siamandas.*

8

The Whole City's A Stage

▲ *Maestro Bramwell Tovey, artistic director of the Winnipeg Symphony Orchestra. Courtesy of the Winnipeg Symphony Orchestra. Photo by Paul Martens.*

◄ *The Winnipeg Folk Festival, held at Bird's Hill Park, began in 1974 and is considered the largest folk festival in North America. Photo by Mike Grandmaison.*

▶ Evelyn Hart, Principal Dancer and indisputable star of the Royal Winnipeg Ballet, in Swan Lake. Courtesy of the Royal Winnipeg Ballet. Photo by Paul Martens.

It was particularly cold and snowy even for Winnipeg in the weeks following Christmas, 1996. It is hard to imagine that this would have been an advantageous time for Winnipeg concert or event promoters to sell tickets for challenging New Music concerts or outdoor heritage festivals.

Yet between January 6 and February 10, 1997, the Winnipeg Symphony Orchestra, the Festival du Voyageur, the Manitoba Theatre Centre, and a handful of other not-for-profit cultural organizations sold about 125,000 tickets to concerts, plays and festivals. They attracted more than one out of every five Winnipeggers to a cultural or entertainment event of one kind or another during that one winter month alone.

Both the Winnipeg Symphony Orches-tra's New Music Festival, the largest of its kind in North America, and the Festival du Voyageur, the city's annual celebration of its French heritage, are held annually during the depths of winter's grip.

But one shouldn't think that just because Winnipeg is a winter city that January is the high season for arts and cultural events. A municipal task force that released a report on cultural policy in mid-'97 compiled the above-mentioned attendance statistics to point out that the arts thrive in Winnipeg, even during the coldest weeks of winter.

Not only do the arts thrive in Winnipeg, the variety and sheer number of performances are so plentiful that the arts have become one of the featured elements in the pitch that economic development officials use to attract new businesses or professionals to the city.

Casual visitors have long marvelled at the proliferation of professional plays, concerts and festivals in Winnipeg. Toronto arts consultants Genovese Vanderhoof & Associates recently concluded that there are more performing arts events in Winnipeg per capita than anywhere else in Canada, perhaps in North America.

Despite Winnipeggers' legendary reputation for modesty, thrift and indifference to glamour, we give more money per capita to the arts than do Torontonians.

Winnipeg is the home to three large performing arts companies—the Royal Winnipeg Ballet, the Winnipeg Symphony Orchestra and the Manitoba Theatre Centre. Most North American cities of Winnipeg's size are hard-pressed to support even one such major company.

As well as those three major performing companies, the Winnipeg Art Gallery and the Manitoba Museum of Man and Nature (one of only three attractions in all of Canada to receive a three-star rating from the Michelin Green Guide) have annual budgets of close to $5 million each and both attract about 250,000 visitors per year.

In total there are more than 130 not-for-profit cultural organizations in Winnipeg who employ about 2,000 people and whose operating budgets surpass the $50 million mark. The arts scene has long been a source of pride for many people in the city. It is also an undeniable economic generator and an

▲ Downtown Winnipeg at Christmas. Photo by George Siamandas.

▲ *Keanu Reeves in Manitoba Theatre Centre's 1995 production of* Hamlet. *Courtesy of Manitoba Theatre Centre. Photo by Bruce Monk.*

important magnet for some of the city's most creative sons and daughters.

For some reason Winnipeg continues to be home to more than its fair share of writers, film makers and musicians like Carol Shields, who won the 1996 Pulitzer Prize for her novel, *The Stone Diaries*; art-film director Guy Maddin; and the Crash Test Dummies, whose pop music CD's sell in the millions around the world.

That the city should be such a hot-bed for artistic and cultural expression has been the subject of a fair bit of conjecture over the years. Neil Young, Burton Cummings and the Guess Who, comedian David Steinberg, Academy Award nominated cartoonists Richard Condie and Cordell Barker as well as the creator of Bugs Bunny, Charles Thorason all came from Winnipeg. A new crop of performers like movie director and television auteur Ken Finkleman, pop-singer Chantal Kreviazuk and Miss Saigon herself, Ma-Anne Dionisio are also from Winnipeg perpetuating the phenomenon that this city produces more

performers and entertainers than it has any business doing.

The remarkable Royal Winnipeg Ballet (RWB) is perhaps the city's proudest cultural achievement. It is the oldest professional ballet in Canada and the second oldest in North America. In 1999 it celebrates its 60th anniversary. It is one of the most toured ballets in North America, presenting about 100 performances every year to about 100,000 people with tours in the mid-'90s to such far-off locales as Japan and South America.

Known for its elegant mix of the classics and innovative contemporary ballet, the RWB has a tradition of appealing to the community as a whole and not just to ballet lovers. It is one of the truly lovely Winnipeg experiences to see an RWB performance of *Nutcracker* on a crisp winter afternoon during Christmas holidays.

Evelyn Hart, who joined the RWB in 1976 and became its principal dancer in 1979, is the company's resident guest artist and its indisputable star.

The Royal Winnipeg Ballet runs an internationally recognized professional school and a popular general division with more than 1,000 students.

The city is also home to the oldest modern dance company in the country, Contemporary Dancers. It too runs a busy dance school, adding to the extraordinary mix of classic and modern dance productions that take place in Winnipeg.

The Manitoba Theatre Centre (MTC) is the oldest regional theatre in North America and in 1997 celebrated its 40th anniversary. The success of MTC has made it a model for many other regional theatres in North America.

MTC has a proud tradition that includes the production of stage classics and daring experiments. Artistic director Steven Schipper said the theatre is committed to a mixed repertoire. "Not just contemporary, not just musicals, but a celebration of the widest variety of theatre art," he said. Its 1995 production of *Hamlet* with Toronto-born Hollywood

▲ *These young musicians may one day perform in the Winnipeg Symphony Orchestra. Photo by George Siamandas.*

movie star Keanu Reeves, was a wonderful example of the ambition and expertise that reside at the MTC and just what it is capable of producing.

Schipper, an ex-Montrealer, said, "In order for MTC to thrive artistically we need to nourish the local talent pool. What is unique about Winnipeg is that there are a number of wonderful theatres. I always think when another theatre does well it looks good on us. I don't want to take the shine off any others, but if there were no other theatre it would be a sign that MTC was doing something really wrong."

Schipper has nothing to worry about. There is an amazing range of theatres in Winnipeg from the French-language Le Cercle Moliere, the oldest continuously performing theatre company in the country, to Shakespeare in the Ruins, the most recent addition to the summer must-see schedule of Winnipeg events. Each year the small company stages outdoor presentations of a work by the Bard complete with full production values at the site of an abandoned Trappist monastery just south of the city.

Prairie Theatre Exchange, in a modern and unlikely location on the upper floor of the downtown shopping mall Portage Place, has a mandate to produce Canadian plays and over the years has been the champion of many local playwrights. Rainbow Stage is the oldest continuously

▲ *The Winnipeg Symphony Orchestra enjoys a very high profile in the city and performs a popular annual program of 60 concerts. Courtesy of the Winnipeg Symphony Orchestra. Photo by Paul Martens.*

▶ The Manitoba Children's Museum is located in a completely rebuilt 19th century industrial building at the Forks National Historic site and annually attracts children (and adults) by the thousands. Photo by George Siamandas.

running outdoor summer theatre company that operates from an amphitheatre in Kildonan Park, the city's lovely North End park alongside the Red River. Rainbow Stage packs them in with productions of musical favorites like *South Pacific, Oklahoma, Guys and Dolls* and the *Wizard of Oz.*

More experimental theatre from a handful of independent companies and the popular Manitoba Theatre for Young People make the city an important centre for the Canadian theatre world.

As well as the MTC's wonderful mainstage and warehouse stage, the city is blessed with the excellent performance spaces including the Walker Theatre, a former vaudeville theatre that was turned into a movie theatre and is once again hosting live performances.

The Centennial Concert Hall is home to the RWB and the Winnipeg Symphony Orchestra (WSO). The 67-piece WSO is a popular local institution and one of the best managed symphonies in the country.

The Winnipeg Symphony Orchestra performs with the Royal Winipeg Ballet and the Manitoba Chamber Orchestra draws its members from the WSO. Maestro Bramwell Tovey helps give the orchestra a very high profile in the city with a popular annual program of 60 concerts. The Winnipeg Symphony Orchestra is one of the only orchestras in Canada with a resident composer who is focused on the symphony's annual New Music Festival.

Summer in Winnipeg now means one performance festival after another. The oldest and the biggest is Folklorama, Winnipeg's annual celebration of multiculturalism in Winnipeg and Canada. With 42 different pavilions, the popular two-week festival in the middle of August attracts about 500,000 people and is ranked as the number one event in Canada by the American Bus Association.

The Winnipeg Folk Festival at Bird's Hill Park just north of the city began in 1974 and is considered the largest folk festival in North America. One of the newest summer events, and now the largest in terms of audience size, is the MTC-sponsored Winnipeg Fringe Festival, the second largest fringe theatre festival in the country. Throughout the rest of the summer there are Caribbean, Aboriginal, Latino, reggae and jazz music festivals.

Winnipeg also has its share of nightclubs and discos. The downtown Exchange District was transformed into the de facto

▲ Rainbow Stage is the oldest continuously running outdoor summer theatre company that operates from an amphitheatre in Kildonan Park. Photo by George Siamandas.

◄ With its 1.7 million-piece collection, including the recently acquired 6000-piece collection of the Husdon's Bay Co. collection, the Museum of Man and Nature, established in 1970, continues to be the city's largest and best-attended cultural organization. Photo by Mike Grandmaison.

▲ *The Winnipeg Jazz Festival. Photo by George Siamandas.*

nightclub district in the late '80s. In the '90s the city has also been included on the itinerary of major touring rock and pop shows like Pink Floyd, the Rolling Stones, Garth Brooks, U2, Bush, and the Tragically Hip's annual Another Roadside Attraction concert.

The Winnipeg International Children's Festival is one of the largest and best of its kind. One of the festival directors is Winnipeg's own Fred Penner, one of the most popular children's entertainers of the day.

One of the reasons arts and cultural organizations continue to grow and thrive in the city is their fairly consistent commitment to community—more particularly, family—involvement. Virtually every arts and cultural organization in the city includes programming for children or casual family participation.

The Manitoba Children's Museum is the apotheosis of that attitude. Located in a completely rebuilt 19th century industrial building at the Forks National Historic site, there are six interactive galleries where children can climb through a tree identifying the birds and animals that inhabit it, pretend they are back in 1910 in a passenger train complete with station house, or produce a television newscast in a fully-functioning in-house television studio.

The children's museum would not be possible if the Manitoba Museum of Man and Nature was not so well established. The museum complex, that includes the interactive science centre Touch the Universe and the Manitoba Planetarium, started a $17 million capital campaign in 1997 to expand and renovate the facility.

With its 1.7 million piece collection, including the recently acquired 6,000 piece collection of the Hudson's Bay Co. collection, the Museum of Man and Nature, established in 1970, continues to be the city's largest and best-attended cultural organization.

The Winnipeg Art Gallery (WAG) is the city's other major full-time cultural institution. Built in 1971, the Winnipeg Art Gallery's dramatic Tyndall stone triangular bunker is the contemporary counter-point

▲ Izzy Asper, CanWest Global Communications Corp. founder. Photo courtesy of CanWest Global Communications Corp.

to the Victorian brilliance of the Manitoba Legislative building just south of the art gallery on Memorial Boulevard.

With permanent holdings of more than 20,000 pieces, including one of the largest collections of Inuit art in the world, the WAG's eight galleries, auditorium, rooftop sculpture garden, public spaces and family programming is another example of a cultural institution thriving in Winnipeg and going out of its way to be as welcoming as it can to the whole community.

The latest cultural pursuit to emerge onto a more commercial environment in Winnipeg is the film and television production industry. While still far from claiming the national stature that the city's theatre and dance community has, the film industry has grown from little more than a hobby scene in 1990 to a $30 million annual industry with proponents predicting it will triple in size by early in the 21st century.

The Credo Group is responsible for about half of the industry's volume of production. Among other things the energetic Winnipeg company produces the popular children's mystery series, *The Adventures of Shirely Holmes*, shot at various locations throughout Winnipeg.

Winnipeg has four local television stations—CBC, the CTV affiliate CKY, Global Winnipeg and the independent MTN, owned by Craig Broadcast System of Brandon. It is also the home of the cable station WTN (Women's Television

▲ The Winnipeg Art Gallery contains permanent holdings of more than 20,000 pieces—including one of the largest collections of Inuit art in the world. Photo by Mike Grandmaison.

▶ *Assiniboine Park. Photo by George Siamandas.*

Network), owned by Moffat Communications, the Winnipeg company that also owns CKY and regional cable television operations.

CKND's parent company, CanWest Global Communications Corp., is also Winnipeg-based. Formed by Izzy Asper in 1977, CanWest Global now owns stations in British Columbia, Saskatchewan, Manitoba, Ontario, Quebec and the Maritimes and has profitable broadcast investments in Australia and New Zealand with combined revenue in 1996 of $628 million.

Winnipeg has two daily newspapers-the *Winnipeg Free Press* with a daily circulation of about 150,000, celebrated its 125th anniversary in 1997; and the *Winnipeg Sun* which began operation in 1981, has a daily circulation of about 50,000.

The municipal task force on cultural policy found that one of the reasons for Winnipeg's success as a centre for the cultural and entertainment industries is that it is an urban community where artists can afford to buy homes and live off the proceeds of their art.

And, as luck would have it, Winnipeggers love a good show. In 1996 more than 3.2 million people attended shows or cultural events in Winnipeg. Winnipeggers love of the arts and the artists' love of Winnipeg is one of those serendipitous situations that helps make a city great. ■

▲ *A full house at the Walker Theatre—originally a vaudeville theatre that was turned into a movie theatre and is once again hosting live performances. Photo by George Siamandas.*

▲ Winnipeg's smiling youth. Photo by George Siamandas.

▲ Colorful clowns attract children and adults alike at the Fringe Festival. Photo by George Siamandas.

▶ Making toffee at the Festival du Voyageur. Photo by Mike Grandmaison.

▲ Folklorama, Winnipeg's annual celebration of multiculturalism, is held in the middle of August and attracts about 500,000 people. Photo by George Siamandas.

9

Winnipeg At Play, One Great City

Whether one heads to Gimli Harbour (left) in the spring or summer or loves tobogganing in the winter (above), Winnipeg provides a very broad array of recreational opportunities and activities. Photos by Mike Grandmaison.

There is a frame of mind that overcomes you in Winnipeg that makes you believe, without really thinking about it, that anything is possible.

It's not a dreamy, fantasy state but a clear-headed understanding that living in Winnipeg allows you to have access to a range of opportunities, activities, information, recreation and as many career paths as a city twice the size.

Temperatures get up to 30 degrees Celsius in the summer and down to -30 °C degrees in the winter. But it is sunny virtually all year long with about 2,300 hours of sunshine per year making it the sunniest city in the country.

It is also among the cleanest cities in North America according to an organiza-tion called Keep America Beautiful. It is a great city to raise a family in witnessed by, among other things, the fact that Winnipeg has one of the busiest networks of neighborhood community clubs in all of North America.

Enrollment in hockey, soccer, baseball and softball leagues—for boys and girls—are always full across the city. All of the public institutions like the Assiniboine Zoo, the Winnipeg Art Gallery, the Museum of Man and Nature, even the pro-fessional sports teams—the Blue Bombers, the Moose, the Goldeyes and the basket-ball Cyclone—have high-profile organized activities directed at children and families.

Winnipeggers are extremely industri-ous and there is increasing evidence, both anecdotal and scientific, that there is a great work ethic in Winnipeg. But that's not to say Winnipeggers don't know how to have fun.

There is a collective recognition that we all deserve a reward once the summer arrives and it's hard to imagine a more beautiful climate than the sunny, hot, breezy summers of southern Manitoba.

And because of that fine weather, it can sometimes be hard reaching business associates in the summer. Chances are they're at the golf course or at the lake.

Winnipeggers are golf crazy. There are 118 golf courses in the province, only eight of which are private. There are more than 40 golf courses either in the city or less than an hour's drive away including five city-owned courses.

There are literally hundreds of lakes to enjoy within a one-to-two-hour drive of the city. Going to the lake in southern Manitoba means every manner of cottage country experience. Manitoba lakes are what fishermen dream of with 28 species of fish waiting to be caught and plenty of outfitters to show you where to find them.

Winnipeggers say they are going to "the lake" regardless of whether they are going to a cottage, a beach, or a fishing, camping or boating excursion. Going to "the lake" may have once referred exclu-sively to Lake Winnipeg, the sixth largest freshwater lake in the country whose southern tip with its sandy beaches at Grand Beach, Victoria Beach, Winnipeg Beach and points in between are less than an hour's drive from the city.

Now however, when people say they're going to "the lake" they might just as well mean the lakes of Whiteshell Provincial Park like Falcon, West Hawk and Caddy lakes; the beautiful Clear Lake at Riding Mountain National Park, north-west of Winnipeg; Lake Manitoba or Lake Winnipegosis; or the lakes of North-western Ontario, a mere two-hour drive away.

Summer weekends in southern Manitoba also mean one country fair after another. And the fairs are as charming as they sound... the Emerson International Theatre Festival, the Manitoba Stampede and Exhibition in Morris, the Strawberry

▲ There are hundreds of lakes to enjoy within a one-to-two hour drive of the city. Photo by Mike Grandmaison.

Festival in Portage la Prairie, the Manitoba Threshermen's Reunion and Stampede in Austin, the Manitoba Sunflower Festival in Altona, the Winkler Harvest Festival, the Morden Corn and Apple Festival, the Frog Follies National Frog Jumping Championship in St. Pierre-Jolys, Pioneer Days at the Mennonite Heritage Village in Steinbach, the Kleefeld Honey Festival, the Triple S Fair and Rodeo in Selkirk, and the Islendingadagurinn Icelandic Festival in Gimli, often attended by the president of Iceland.

Winnipeg not only represents more than half the population of the province, but it's also situated at the centre of the fertile Red River valley. That puts the city within easy driving distance of all the Red River towns south to the U.S. border, the interlake towns north of the city between Lake Winnipeg and Lake Manitoba, the hill country around Riding Mountain National Park, the towns and beaches along the south end of Lake Winnipeg as well as the Whiteshell region to the east to the Ontario border.

Winnipeg has long been one of the strongholds for the Canadian Football League. The city's beloved Blue Bombers have won the Grey Cup 10 times since 1925, most recently in 1984, '88 and '90. Winnipeg hosted the Grey Cup in 1991 and that remains one of the city's biggest and best celebrations of recent history and is scheduled to host 1998's version.

That being said, Winnipeg is a hockey town through and through. It is home to the International Hockey League's Manitoba Moose, and recreational and competitive leagues abound throughout the city. Anyone who questions the future of the game in Canada should attend a

▲ Winnipeg has long been one of the strongholds for the Canadian Football League as witnessed by the tremendous attendance to one of their own beloved Blue Bomber's game. Photo by George Siamandas.

▲ Soccer leagues are popular among Winnipeg's youth. Photo by George Siamandas.

▲ This indoor facility will be the site of the swimming competition when Winnipeg hosts the 1999 Pan American Games. Photo by George Siamandas.

recreational league game at an outdoor rink on a clear Winnipeg evening of crisp -20 degree Celsius weather and they will witness the heart of the game. Winnipeg, along with Portage la Prairie, Selkirk and Brandon are hosting the 1998-1999 World Junior hockey championships.

Professional baseball returned to Winnipeg in 1994 in the form of the Winnipeg Goldeyes of the independent AA Northern League. Owned by former rock concert and entertainment impresario, Sam Katz, the Goldeyes have also proved to be fan favorites.

In the summer of 1997 Katz and a group of partners received zoning and land lease approvals to turn a vacant chunk of land east of Portage and Main and just north of the Forks into a charming little minor league baseball park.

That stadium will become one of the major legacies for Winnipeg after it hosts the 1999 Pan American Games. The $140 million games are expected to be the largest sports and cultural event ever in Canada and the third largest sports event ever in North America, surpassed only by the 1996 Atlanta Olympics and the 1984 Los Angeles Olympics in terms of the number of athletes competing.

Pan Am Games organizers are expecting 7,000 athletes and officials from 42 countries with about 15,000 local volunteers lending a hand for the games that will be held in and around Winnipeg from July 24 to August 8, 1999. More than 100,000 visitors to the city are expected for the 15-day games that will include cultural and entertainment events and a major trade show.

Winnipeg's 6,000 hotel rooms will certainly all be spoken for during those two weeks. The city has more than 1,500 hotel rooms downtown—many providing the kind of top-notch service and accommodations that North American travellers demand including The Lombard (a Canadian Pacific hotel), the Crowne Plaza, the Place Louis Riel All-Suite Hotel and the finely restored Hotel Fort Garry.

Winnipeg is one of the curling capitals of the world, home-town to two different world champions in the '90s—Kerry

▲ A very familiar and popular winter sight—ice-skating on the pond at Assiniboine Park. Photo by George Siamandas.

Burtnyk and Jeff Stoughton. In the summer Winnipeggers golf and in the winter they curl. Winter bonspiels are annual events of impressive scale.

Maybe it's because the pace of day-to-day life is a little more relaxed in Winnipeg that there is more attention paid to leisure pursuits. There are about 850 parks in the city with baseball diamonds, soccer pitches, elaborate play structures, and plenty of cross-country skiing trails. Winnipeg is also a great cycling city, an undeniable attraction being the fact that it really is a flat city.

Tourism Winnipeg, the city's tourism

▲ Enjoying a moment of peaceful solitude at Victoria Beach. Photo by George Siamandas.

promotion agency, figures the city hosts about 2.5 million visitors per year, 12 per cent of whom are from the U.S., and four per cent from overseas.

The 78,000 square foot Winnipeg

▲ Building a sand castle at one of Winnipeg's most popular beaches, Grand Beach. Photo by Mike Grandmaison.

Convention Centre sees about one million people per year at 600 events including around 30 conventions per year. Among the top convention centres in the country, its flexible facilities can hold a banquet for a few thousand people, large-scale trade shows, professional basketball games (it is the home of the International Basketball Association's Winnipeg Cyclones), as well as intimate events catered by award-winning chefs.

In the early '90s the provincial government got into the gambling business in Winnipeg and there are now three full-service casinos in the city—the Crystal Casino offers European-style gaming with blackjack, roulette, baccarat, la boule and slot machines, and the McPhillips Street Station and Club Regent are state-of-the art gaming facilities with various types of bingo and slot machines open every day. Video lottery terminals are available to patronize at taverns and hotels throughout the province.

Old fashioned river boats ply the Red and Assiniboine Rivers like a kind of floating social hall. The Assiniboia Downs is as fun as any horse-racing experience in the country. The Western Canadian Aviation Museum has an amazing display

of vintage planes of every size and shape in a coverted hangar near the airport.

There are many ways to enjoy the wildlife and natural environment of the region. Fort Whyte Centre is a 200 acre reserve of natural habitat and wildlife at the southwest side of the city with plenty of workshops and interactive activities run by a non-profit organization. Oak Hammock Marsh, a 36 square kilometre wildlife management area run by Ducks Unlimited includes an interpretative centre and an excellent spot to observe about 280 species of birds. It is located about a one-half hour drive north of the city.

The Assiniboine Park is the jewel of the city's 850 parks. It is 376 acres of bicycle paths, English gardens, a botanical conservatory, a sculpture garden—featuring the works of internationally renowned sculptor and Winnipeg resident Leo Mol—and beautiful picnic areas. It is also the site of recreational sporting events as exotic as cricket and ultimate frisbee.

The Assiniboine Park Zoo features more than 80 species of animals including huge Siberian tigers, polar bears and grizzly bears and animals in their own environment in the delightful Kinsmen Discovery Centre.

By any account, the Forks National Historic Site is the favorite attraction in the city. The meeting place at the confluence of the Red and Assiniboine rivers has served as such for more than 6,000 years and now is the place where close to seven million people visit every year. They come to the shops and restaurants of the Public Market and Johnston Terminal, the Manitoba Children's Museum, the skating and tobogganing facilities in the winter, almost daily festivals and concerts in the summer, or just to have a stroll on the river walk.

Winnipeg owes much of its visual charm to the stock of exquisite turn-of-the-century architecture that is a testimony to its boom years from 1880 to 1920. Several examples are open to the public including the magnificent Manitoba Legislative building with its guardian, the Golden Boy, clasping his lighted wheatsheaf atop the building's dome; the downtown neighbourhood known as the

Exchange District features one of the largest collections of 19th century commercial buildings in North America; the St. Boniface Museum is the oldest building in Winnipeg and the largest oak-log building in North America; Seven Oaks House is one of the oldest surviving homes in Manitoba; Riel House on River Road in St. Vital was the home of Louis Riel's parents and the place where he laid in state after his hanging in Regina.

One of the most distinctive pieces of

▲ *This picture is worth a thousand words! Photo by Mike Grandmaison.*

◀ ▼ *Assiniboine Park Zoo. Photos by George Siamandas.*

modern architecture in the city is the Royal Canadian Mint building in St. Vital. It is one of the first sights of the city greeting travellers driving in from the east with its pinkish glass and steel pyramid. Designed by Etienne Gaboury, one of the city's most prominent architects of the late 20th century, the mint has produced 30 billion coins for Canada and 60 other countries since it opened in 1975.

There are plenty of attractions and events to attend in Winnipeg. For many Winnipeggers the most enjoyable ones might just be getting together with friends for cappucino and Italian ice at a Corydon Avenue cafe, or raising a glass or two of locally brewed ale at a sports bar downtown.

Winnipeg may not have a sea-side view or fresh mountain air or a particularly fast-paced commercial scene, but it is a clean, safe city that is increasingly becoming known as one of the most livable cities of North America. ∎

◄ *Winnipeggers enjoy the simple pleasure of getting together with friends at a Corydon Avenue café. Photo by George Siamandas.*

▲ *Winnipeggers are avid golfers. Photo by Mike Grandmaison.*

◀ Manitoba lakes are what fishermen dream of with 28 species of fish waiting to be caught. Photo by Mike Grandmaison.

▲ The Ducks Unlimited interpretive centre at Oak Hammock Marsh. Photo by Mike Grandmaison.

◄ This family is enjoying Fort Whyte Centre, a 200 acre reserve of natural habitat and wildlife at the southwest side of the city. Photo by Mike Grandmaison.

▲ *The St. Boniface Museum is the oldest building in Winnipeg and the largest oak-log building in North America. Photo by Mike Grandmaison.*

▲ Not all learning takes place in the classroom. Photo by George Siamandas.

▶ The Exchange District in downtown Winnipeg features one of the largest collections of 19th century commercial buildings in North America. Photo by George Siamandas.

129

Photos by George Siamandas.

▲ *Elim Chapel. Photo by Mike Grandmaison.*

The license plates say Friendly Manitoba. It's very simple and straightforward and any place might think it's a nice epithet for their own province or region.

But it may not really make sense in another place. In Manitoba it does.

When the water of the Red River spilled over its hard clay banks in the spring of 1997 like it hadn't done for 150 years, thousands of Winnipeggers pitched in wherever the sandbag hot-line directed them and it turned out the city was full of expert sandbaggers.

While no one would wish to go through the events of the spring of '97 again, the experience galvanized Winnipeggers. A crisis occurred that required people to act in the community's best interests—and the people of Winnipeg responded brilliantly.

The city's ability to coordinate its defenses made everyone proud. As determined as people were to hold off the raging Red River it probably wouldn't have made a difference had there not been the foresight and courage shown by the city and provincial governments in the 1960s to spend $67 million to build the Winnipeg Floodway.

The unsettling images of the kilometres-wide "Red Sea" stretching as far as the eye could see will be hard to erase. But for many Winnipeggers the flood of '97 is more likely to leave an impression as an event that really brought the people of Winnipeg together.

Such community bonding is full of emotion in Winnipeg. There are so many Winnipeggers whose ancestry is so differ-

ent that those kind of events become something greater than just civic pride.

Since its early days, Winnipeg's multicultural fibres have been important elements of the city fabric. Now, according to Statistics Canada, Manitoba is the most ethnically diverse province in the country and Winnipeg reflects that with large Ukrainian, German, Polish, Icelandic, Filipino and Chinese communities. It has the largest French-speaking community west of Quebec where francophones can enjoy a host of services and rich lifestyle in French.

▲ *Since its early days, Winnipeg's multicultural fibres have been important elements of the city fabric. Photo by George Siamandas.*

▲ ▶ *The Flood of 1997 brought all of the people of Winnipeg together in the united effort help their neighbours and make their city proud. Photos by George Siamandas.*

▲ Ukranian Cathedral. Photo by Mike Grandmaison.

◄ Colorful Ukranian dancer celebrating her heritage. Photo by George Siamandas.

Winnipeg's aboriginal community is one of the most substantial in the country.

The city's multicultural heritage is responsible for many things we now take for granted in Winnipeg, like the famous Manitoba social, for instance. It is now a pan-cultural event in Winnipeg—meaning just about everyone has a social regardless of one's ethnic background. They are most commonly held in church basements or so-called "social halls." Most often, but not necessarily, these dance/party/banquets are held as a fund-raising event for a soon-to-be-wed couple.

Even though all communities have socials, it's impossible to have one without a Ukrainian deli-spread that includes perogies, holobchi (cabbage rolls), kielbasa (garlic sausage) and cheddar cheese cubes. At some point during the course of the evening everyone who attends will be greeted by the guests of honour with a shake of the hand and a heartfelt, "Thank you for coming to my social."

The Ukrainian community emigrated to Canada in two waves—around the turn of the century and then between the two world wars. Besides the popularity of the Manitoba social, the depth of that community's roots in Winnipeg, is illustrated by the presence of Oseredok: Ukrainian Cultural and Education Centre. The downtown museum and cultural centre has the largest collection of Ukrainian books, historic and cultural articles outside of Ukraine.

The Ukrainian community, as well as the original German, Polish and Jewish immigrant communities, settled in the city's famed North End—north of the Canadian Pacific Railroad's original trans-Canada line through Winnipeg. Before WWII it was an imaginary boundary in the city between the more established—and well off—English and French communities and the newcomers who spoke different languages, worshiped at different churches and dressed a little differently.

Now the well-educated second and third generations of those European immigrants have taken their places as part of the mainstream of Canadian society. More recent immigrants from the Philippines, and southeast Asia are now just as likely to call the North End home.

There are good sized communities in Winnipeg from India; recent immigrants from east Africa; an increasing presence from Latin and South American countries; and solid representation from most European cultures living in Winnipeg.

A little-Italy blossomed in the late '80s along Corydon Avenue in Fort Rouge and is now the site of the most wonderful collection of cafes and restaurants in the city. A chapter of the international Italian Chamber of Commerce was established in the city in the late '90s.

Winnipeg's Aboriginal community, also a growing part of the colourful social landscape of the North End, make up close to 10 per cent of the city's population and because of its growing size is having an increasingly significant impact on civic affairs. Winnipeg is home for the current president of the Assembly of First Nations, Phil Fontaine, and his predecessor, Ovide Mercredi.

Winnipeg's Jewish community is active

▲ *Chinese Pavilion. Photo by Mike Grandmaison.*

▲ *The leaders of the Jewish community succeeded in raising several million dollars to develop the beautiful Asper Jewish Community Campus. Photo by George Siamandas.*

▲ *Photo by Mike Grandmaison.*

◄ *Photo by George Siamandas.*

▼ *Photo by Mike Grandmaison.*

in every aspect of Winnipeg life. The local community, whose ancestors came to Winnipeg from eastern Europe escaping religious persecution throughout the 20th century, has been one of the strongest and most dynamic Jewish communities in Canada. In the late 1990's leaders of the Jewish community succeeded in raising several million dollars and developed the beautiful Asper Jewish Community Campus at the site of a former army barracks. The complex includes Jewish community organizations, a Jewish high school and a state-of-the-art fitness centre.

Icelanders and Mennonites from Germany and Russia were the two earliest groups of European immigrants to the city dating back to the 1870s. Their ancestors are now among the leaders of every aspect of social, cultural and political life in Winnipeg. The Icelanders originally settled in Gimli on the south end of Lake Winnipeg and their ancestors in the region represent the largest Icelandic community outside the north Atlantic island nation itself.

The city is full of beautiful churches. There are old and new Jewish synagogues, Byzantine Ukrainian Orthodox churches with dome-shaped belltowers and a fine collection of Gothic revival and Romanesque revival Protestant and Catholic churches found throughout the Core Area and the city's North End. The rebuilt St. Boniface Basilica and the Etienne Gaboury-designed Precious Blood Catholic Church in St. Boniface are a couple of modern churches in Winnipeg of exceptional design.

Winnipeg's layout as a city is described by the rivers—the Red running south to north bisecting the city into its eastern and western halves and the Assiniboine flowing from the west into the Red at the Forks cutting the city into north and south sides. The Seine River flows down the length of St. Boniface into the Red. The city's neighbourhoods and road grid yield to the rivers.

But even those neighbourhoods in the northern reaches of the city are still only a 20-minute drive to Portage and Main as are those in Charleswood south of the

▲ Winnipeg's aboriginal community is one of the most substantial in the country. Photo by George Siamandas.

▲ Another colorful parade and celebration in Winnipeg! Photo by George Siamandas.

▲ ▶ *Families and children are Winnipeg's greatest treasures. Photos by Mike Grandmaison.*

Assiniboine on the western edge of the city, Fort Richmond and St. Norbert in the south and Transcona in the far eastern end of the city limits.

Although there are no freeways through Winnipeg—except for the Perimeter Highway, which defines the city limits—just about every neighbourhood is within easy access to downtown. People who are used to grueling daily commutes in other cities are relieved to learn that Winnipeg is virtually rush-hour free save for about a 12-block radius around Portage and Main between 4:30 and 5:30 P.M.

Visitors from other cities are also pleased with the shopping opportunities in Winnipeg. Winnipeggers are known to go to extraordinary lengths to find a bargain and retailers attempt to respond to that particularly demanding approach from consumers.

Winnipeggers' thrift is more than just urban myth. The city has long been considered an effective test market because, as merchandisers say, "If it sells in Winnipeg, it'll sell anywhere."

That being said, the city is well retailed with large regional malls like the mega malls Polo Park and St. Vital Centre and a great collection of big-box retailers. Winnipeg has a good selection of North American chains and some outstanding local retailers like McNally Robinson Booksellers and Advance Electronics. Winnipeg is the head office for national chains like Cotter True Valu, Saan Stores, the North West Company and Ben Moss Jewellers.

Winnipeg's downtown sky-walk network is a development dating back only to the late '80s that makes getting around to the shops, businesses, service and theatres in downtown Winnipeg convenient all year long. One can travel all the way from Portage Avenue and Memorial Boulevard to Portage and Main through the 1.8 million square foot climate-controlled walk-way system. Along the way there is access to more than 200 shops, more than 60 restaurants and snack bars, four movie theatres, about 700 apartment units and 10 different office buildings.

Like every other city in North America, Winnipeg civic officials are concerned that they do the right things to ensure the future vitality of the city's downtown core. Maintaining an active commercial scene as well as encouraging arts and entertainment entrepreneurs to operate downtown is a direction many believe the city should take. The construction of a baseball stadium near the Forks and continuing development of the Forks site

▲ Winnipeg is the head office for outstanding local retailer, the North West Company. Photo by Mike Grandmaison.

▲ Winnipeg will continue to celebrate when it meets at the Forks once again for the 1999 Pan American Games. Photo by Mike Grandmaison.

◄ Winnipeg's finely restored Hotel Fort Garry. Photo by George Siamandas.

▲ *A true prairie portrait… Photo by George Siamandas.*

Winnipeg's Enterprises

Photos by George Siamandas.

11

Agriculture & Food Processing

Photo by Mike Grandmaison.

The Canadian Wheat Board

Located in the centre of Canada's grain trade, in Winnipeg, Manitoba, the Canadian Wheat Board (CWB) markets Prairie-grown wheat and barley to grain buyers around the world. Selling farmers' grain to more than 70 countries worldwide, the CWB is Canada's fifth largest exporter and the largest net earner of foreign exchange.

Canada's supply of wheat and barley is mostly grown on the western Canadian Prairie, which stretches over 1,600 kilometres and accounts for almost 40 million hectares of productive agricultural land. Wheat, first planted in Canada some 400 years ago, is the main crop grown on the Prairies, and barley is the second largest crop. The first shipment of wheat was exported from Western Canada in 1878, launching what is now a multi-billion-dollar industry, employing thousands of Canadians.

The Prairies currently produce about 25 million tonnes of wheat and 12 tonnes of barley per year, despite a short growing season that averages 110 frost-free days. Of those production totals, Western

The CWB is the Prairie farmers' marketing partner. Photograph by Dave Reede.

Canada annually exports about 20 million tonnes of wheat and durum wheat, and between 3 to 6 million tonnes of malting and feeding barley. Although it is a relatively small producer, Canada is one of the world's largest suppliers of wheat and barley. Canada produces only 5 per cent of the world's wheat and 7 per cent of the world's barley, yet it holds 21 per cent of the world wheat trade and about 22 per cent of the world barley trade.

The Canadian Wheat Board is the sole exporter of Prairie-grown wheat and barley, with the goal of attaining the best possible price for farmers. It is also responsible for the sale of wheat and barley within Canada for human consumption.

The CWB's annual sales revenue ranges from $4 billion to $6 billion, depending on prices and the amount of deliveries by farmers. This makes the CWB the largest single wheat and barley marketing corporation in the world. All proceeds from sales, less CWB marketing costs, are returned to farmers. In this sense, western Canadian farmers are the CWB's only shareholders.

As the Prairie farmers' marketing partner, the CWB's main business activity is marketing. Ensuring quality products, quality service and paying close attention to customer needs are the cornerstones of

Western Canadian wheat and barley are used in food products around the world. Photograph by Jerry Grajewski, Custom Images.

The CWB's head office is the hub of the grain industry in Winnipeg, Manitoba. Photograph by Robert Tinker.

the CWB's marketing efforts. This involves being seller, banker and shipper of many classes and grades of western Canadian wheat and barley. The CWB is involved in every stage of the grain trade, from delivery from the farm to customer end-use.

At the core of maximizing returns to farmers are the CWB's three corporate pillars. These pillars are single-desk selling, price pooling and the partnership with the federal government.

Single-desk selling, or the monopoly on sales, is the backbone of the CWB, and it continues to give strength and marketing power to Prairie farmers. As the sole exporter of Canadian wheat and barley, the CWB is able to command premium prices for Canada's high quality grain and its excellent customer service.

Through price pooling, Prairie farmers enjoy an effective risk management tool. Pooling smooths out the seasonal fluctuations in the prices and reflects values that are achieved over the course of the marketing year. It provides farmers access to both the high-priced and low-priced markets.

The link between farmers and the federal government offers three distinct economic advantages. First, the federal government guarantees initial payments to farmers when they deliver their grain. Second, the CWB is able to compete in higher risk markets and make sales on credit with federal government backing. Finally, the government guarantees its borrowings, which allows the CWB to borrow at lower rates of interest than a comparably sized, private-sector company. These financial savings are passed back

to farmers.

Based in Winnipeg, the CWB has branch offices in Vancouver, Tokyo and Beijing, as well as a network of staff across the Prairies. It also works closely with the Canadian International Grains Institute, its educational and technical arm, to bring international buyers to Winnipeg to learn more about Canadian

The CWB's Asia-Pacific marketing team. Photograph by Robert Tinker.

grain. By working with both current and potential customers to show them how to best use western Canadian wheat and barley, the CWB and its partners in the grain industry can increase demand for Prairie grain. Since 1972, over 13,000 people from over 100 countries have taken part in courses at the Institute.

As with its overseas customers, the CWB works hard to establish solid relations with the millers and maltsters in Canada. Canadian mills are the CWB's second largest customer group for malting barley. The CWB strives to ensure that farmers receive the best possible price for their wheat and barley, while at the same time balancing the need of processors to compete in the finished product market.

The key to providing excellent service rests with the CWB's highly qualified, well-trained staff. Changes in the international market, new computer technology and fast-moving interest rates and money markets require people with specialized training. CWB staff are well versed in the

international aspects of the grain business, many of them fluent in foreign languages to better meet the needs of customers around the world. A high percentage of the staff also have strong links to the farm community and the farmers they serve.

Working with the farmers of Western Canada and its industry partners, the CWB is pivotal in Canada's approach to marketing wheat and barley. It is this approach—combined with a commitment to excellence and a strong attachment to the farmers of Western Canada—that ensures the CWB will remain the world's preferred supplier of grain. ■

Ridley Canada Limited

There's a major transformation underway in the world's food markets these days, and Ridley Canada, based in Winnipeg, Manitoba, is at the leading edge of that transformation. Fuelled by social change, rising affluence and increasing populations, international demand for meat and dairy products is soaring. Helping to satisfy that demand with its scientifically formulated feed rations is Ridley Canada Ltd., an integral part of Manitoba agriculture since 1939, trading as Feed-Rite Ltd. Feed-Rite joined forces with Australian-based Ridley Corporation Limited in 1994, in a corporate marriage that brought Ridley into North America.

The merger marked an initial foothold from which Ridley in North America rapidly levered remarkable growth—development that placed Ridley in the vanguard of North American stockfeed and animal nutrition. And Ridley's finely honed technology, innovative research and development, and marketing savvy supplied renewed vigour to the solid, historically proven product lines of the Winnipeg-based Feed-Rite Ltd.

In its first three years of operation since the merger, Ridley Canada has expanded rapidly and now has 35 feed production facilities throughout the livestock and grain-growing areas of Canada and the United States.

Rapidly rising international consumer demand shows in recent export numbers: pork exports to Japan from Manitoba soared by some 35 per cent in 1997. Total North American exports of meat, poultry and dairy products rose by more than 50 per cent in the five years between 1992 and 1997.

Ridley plans to be an integral supplier for that demand. The company has forged strategic alliances with large-scale livestock producers and meat processors, and is working to significantly expand its top-quality herd of Cotswold pigs. Ridley has positioned itself through the Cotswold pig to handle the precise demands of rapidly growing export demand for pork products. These genetically advanced pigs offer the lean profile and consistent carcass traits

Ed Moloney, President and CEO, Ridley Canada Limited.

needed for the precision pork processing demands of local and export markets.

Ridley Canada has also positioned itself to satisfy the expanding requirements for livestock feed in the cattle and poultry markets in addition to swine herds. The company's feed manufacturing outlets offer a full range of proven brand names that include Feed-Rite, Hubbard, Zip Feeds, Vigorena, Protein Blenders, Farmix, Crystalyx, Green Valley Feeds, Quality Feeds and Daco Western Canada. Feed products are available for anything from swine to chinchillas; even pet food is made by Ridley.

Ridley Canada Ltd. has soared into the ranks of the ten largest animal feed manufacturers in North America.

With its 1997 purchase of the Hubbard feed business in the United States, Ridley Canada has become one of only three North American feed manufacturers with significant operations spanning the Canada/United States border, and the largest manufacturer of low moisture feed blocks on the continent. These feed blocks,

manufactured in a tightly controlled process, provide a unique form of regulated, consistent delivery of feed supplements for horses and beef and dairy cattle.

The company places strong emphasis on customer service. As part of that service, livestock operators can call on the expertise and leading-edge technical advice of Ridley's nutritional specialists, over a dozen of whom hold Ph.D.s, veterinary medicine doctoral degrees, or both.

The solid base provided by Ridley's North American acquisitions has been enhanced by the capacity of Ridley's Australian parent to provide valuable resources, including access to ongoing Australian research and development. As a result, Ridley products provide high-performance, value-added animal nutrition that's cost-effective where it counts: in weight gain, feed efficiency, yield and animal health.

The company also operates a network of retail farm supply stores, livestock equipment distribution, animal health supplies, pet food, engineering and design

Blake Gilmore (left), a Feed-Rite driver, delivers another consignment of feed to Joe Maendel, Manager, Layer Operations, at Forest River Colony, Fordville, North Dakota.

production industries. Ridley aims to continue acquiring strategically located feed businesses across North America and integrating them into the overall Ridley organization.

With its eye on expansion, Ridley will continue to emphasize quality and service—hallmarks of its North American and Australian operations. Ridley Canada's Feed-Rite Winnipeg plant was the first animal feed company in North America to achieve ISO 9001 registration, and the Cotswold breeding facility the first in North America to be ISO 9002 registered. The company aims to have all plants similarly designated. This energetic Australian-North American corporate combination is ready and eager for the challenges of the 21st century, and proud of its Winnipeg heritage. ∎

services for livestock and feed manufacturing facilities, and research poultry farms, and has the exclusive right in Canada to market the genetically advanced line of Cotswold pigs, handled through wholly owned subsidiary Cotswold Canada Limited.

The Cotswold pig answers growing processor and consumer demand for consistent, top-quality pork, through a genetically advanced animal that provides fast growth and large litters. The animal's excellent feed efficiency appeals to growers, and desirable carcass traits of consistent size and leanness are attractive to pork processors.

Cotswold Canada's nucleus herd provides breeding replacements into multiplication herds, of which some are owned by independent producers who grow the animals under Cotswold Canada's management guidance, and some owned by Ridley

Canada. From the multiplication herd, it's one more step to the commercial pig producers, who raise the market hogs that are sold to processors. Cotswold pigs, only introduced in the past few years in Canada, could in a few years supply up to eight per cent of the sows required by pig producers in Canada.

Since 1994, Ridley Canada, under the direction of Ed Moloney, its President and C.E.O., has seen its production capacity triple to approximately 1.5 million tonnes per annum and sales quadruple to over $400 million per annum. The company's many operations that contribute to this astonishing growth include 24 primary feed mills, five premix facilities, three grind and mix facilities and three low-moisture feed block manufacturing facilities.

This ambitious company plans to continue growth with North America's expanding feed, livestock and meat

Feed-Rite's Winnipeg plant, the first feed mill in North America to be ISO 9001 registered.

James Richardson & Sons, Limited

Founded in 1857 as a one-man operation in Kingston, Ontario, James Richardson & Sons, Limited has been nurtured by successive generations of the Richardson family, all of whom have exhibited a keen "success" instinct. Their drive, astuteness and confidence in meeting challenges head-on have made James Richardson & Sons, Limited and the Richardson family itself legends in Canadian business history.

Today, as a privately owned Canadian corporation involved in the international grain trade, oil and gas development and real estate, James Richardson & Sons, Limited operates under the leadership of George Taylor Richardson, Chairman and Managing Director, and Hartley Thorbjörn Richardson, President.

The 34-storey Richardson Building, which overlooks the historic corner of Portage and Main, in the heart of downtown Winnipeg, is home to the head office of James Richardson & Sons, as well as to the executive and administrative offices of many of its affiliated companies.

Going back to the mid-1800s, James Richardson & Sons got its start as a grain company, and has thrived on grain ever since. Ranking amongst this country's boldest business pioneers, the company's early grain merchants left a legacy of foresight and fortitude. It was through their efforts that Canada was ushered into the 20th century on a wave of prosperity. By applying traditional business values to trading and transporting grain, JR succeeded in contributing a healthy share to Canada's economy.

Hartley Thorbjörn Richardson and his father, George Taylor Richardson, are the power behind James Richardson & Sons, Limited and affiliated companies. The former is President, James Richardson & Sons, Limited and Chairman of the Board of its largest subsidiary, James Richardson International. George Richardson is Chairman & Managing Director, James Richardson & Sons, Limited.

Throughout its history, JR has not hesitated in taking the lead, being the first to blaze new ground. In 1882 in Kingston, Ontario, it built the first major elevator to handle Western Canadian grain. A year later, it shipped the first cargo of grain overseas from Western Canada by way of the Great Lakes. It also dispatched the first shipment of wheat from the Port of Churchill on Hudson's Bay to England, and arranged for the first grain shipment in 1932 through the new Welland Canal. JR companies were eager to embrace new technology and were the first in the Canadian grain business to use teletype machines to transmit orders and informa-

tion between all offices and the appropriate markets.

Drawing from more than 140 years of experience, JR's grain companies are today respected for their service, integrity and innovative approaches to marketing, which give them an edge in what has become a fiercely competitive grain trade environment.

Today, JR's combined grain operations make up the company's largest division. In 1996 all its grain industry companies were grouped under the banner of James Richardson International Limited. JRI maintains offices and facilities in six Canadian provinces, and actively participates in all phases of agriculture, including production, marketing and the provision of goods and services to farm and business customers, both here, at home and internationally.

Pioneer Grain Company Limited, a subsidiary of James Richardson International Limited, is Canada's largest privately owned grain company, and its orange-and-yellow grain elevators are landmarks across the Canadian prairies. The company has three large grain handling terminals, located on Vancouver's north shore and at Thunder Bay, Ontario, and Sorel, Quebec.

James Richardson & Sons, Limited is also involved in oil and gas, and has a 50 per cent interest in Tundra Oil and Gas Ltd., another private company. Tundra, which operates across the Prairie provinces, produces 1.5 million barrels of oil per year and has in excess of 150 million acres of mineral rights under its control.

As well, James Richardson & Sons, Limited has extensive real estate holdings

The 34-storey Richardson Building, at the historic corner of Portage & Main in downtown Winnipeg, serves as the head office of James Richardson & Sons, Limited, as well as the executive and administrative offices of many of its affiliated companies.

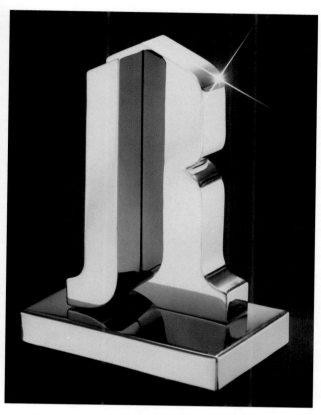

James Richardson & Sons, Limited's record of achievement has been made possible through the bond of confidence and cooperation that exists between it and its 2,000 personnel, along with the communities and industries it serves.

in Canada and the United States. Lombard Place was the first major real estate development project it undertook. Situated on 4 1/2 acres at Portage and Main, Lombard Place, completed in 1969, is comprised of the Richardson Building, The Lombard (a 21-storey, 350-room hotel managed by Canadian Pacific Hotels), the eight-storey Bank of Canada Building, an underground concourse of retail shopping and service providers and an 829-stall parking facility adjacent to the hotel. JR also undertook the construction and development in the United States of The Ridge Tahoe at Lake Tahoe, Nevada. It is a luxurious interval-ownership property, which has gained wide recognition as one of the finest of its kind in North America.

Together, the companies under James Richardson & Sons, Limited continue to foster new ideas and ways to better the times in which we live. Few business organizations have played such a diverse and interesting role. JR's record of achievement has been made possible through the bond of confidence and cooperation that

exists between it and its 2,000 personnel, along with the communities and industries it serves.

There is little resemblance between the grain dealer who served a single community back in 1857 and today's broad-based business with personnel criss-crossing the globe. Yet, there is an unmistakable thread that has run throughout James Richardson & Sons, Limited over the years. It links the new to the old in an ageless philosophy: "Our goal is to be the kind of organization in which people can place their trust."

This statement has been expressed, in essentially the same words, by every Richardson president since the first, and has formed a framework for decision-making, planning and success.

Throughout its history, JR's commitment to the timeless traditions of quality, honesty and hard work has positioned it well to look forward to the bright promise and the global business challenges of the twenty-first century. ■

12

Transportation, Manufacturing & Distribution

Photo courtesy of Standard Knitting Ltd.

Kitchen Craft

I n 1971 teacher Herb Buller traded in his chalk and ruler for a measuring tape and lumber. He and his partner, John Rademaker, along with a group of five investors, had noticed a need in the emerging housing industry in Winnipeg, and they planned to fill it. The need was for modular kitchen cabinets.

They started with 10,000 square feet, a few saws, two assembly tables, a shipping door, a handful of employees and a commitment to hard work and excellent quality. Today, as the second biggest cabinet manufacturer in Canada, Kitchen Craft employs over a thousand people, has a 300,000-square-foot factory, and annual sales of $85 million around the world. The remarkable, solid growth of this company is the product of entrepreneurial spirit blended with an old-fashioned commitment to service, quality and people.

Kitchen Craft shows its commitment to customer service in a variety of ways. The company prides itself on being responsive to consumer demand and the ever-changing trends of the marketplace. Kitchen Craft offers a wide variety of style options with a huge selection of woods, stains, painted finishes and melamines. Wood, however, appears to be the material of choice

with today's market. Oak and maple are traditional favourites with cherry, hickory and pine growing in popularity. With over 140 door styles and colours to choose from, the company is able to meet the needs of even the most discriminating consumer.

Kitchen Craft's sales force scattered throughout North America exemplifies outstanding customer service. Many of their salespeople are certified kitchen designers. This enables them to help customers who are new to the cabinet business to overcome difficulties with product and design. Kitchen Craft's own retail stores have given the sales team the experience to be able to provide advertising and marketing support for independent dealers.

Excellent service continues with the company's customer service representatives.

They are friendly and knowledgeable and respond promptly to any customer query. Their training and experience allows them to assist in product and design questions. Once the order has been placed, customer service continues in every department of the plant to ensure that the company's four-week delivery promise will be met.

It was this detailed attention to customer service that first attracted customers south of the border. They were impressed with Kitchen Craft's flexibility in adapting their product to meet regional preferences and to the four-week delivery time. In 1992, the American market made up 10 per cent of Kitchen Craft's sales. American sales rose to 50 per cent in less than five years, due to top quality merchandise and an aggressive marketing campaign.

Emerging Kitchen Craft markets include Japan, Germany, Puerto Rico, Russia and China. With all this international success, Kitchen Craft remains a local business with its head office, two showrooms, retail stores and manufacturing plants in Winnipeg. The choice to remain in Winnipeg was more than just a sentimental one. With its central location, Winnipeg is known as the distribution hub of North America, and is in fact the starting point of the North American Free Trade Corridor.

Quality is an integral part of Kitchen Craft's success. Kitchen Craft goes to great lengths to ensure that its raw materials and machinery are state-of-the-art. Their people travel throughout the world to find the best raw materials and the latest

share program encourages employees to be innovative with cost-control ideas as well. The end result is a blend of quality, beauty and durability at an affordable price.

Herb Buller stresses that relationships are a key ingredient of his company's success. "Throughout the years, a strong partnership was developed between the company, customers, employees and suppliers. I am very proud of these relationships. Long-term relationships such as we have always speak of commitment, loyalty and satisfaction. These good relationships humble me, especially when I see the success of our team." Excellent service, quality and relationships–for Kitchen Craft, it's been a blueprint for success. ■

designs, technology and machinery available and bring them back to Winnipeg. All cabinets are made of premium grade materials, and strict attention to detail is made a priority throughout the production process. Wood cabinets are treated with a special Craftguard finish. This process includes applying a stain, sealer and top coat. Once completed, it protects the cabinet from fading and has a high impact resistance. It's guaranteed to provide the customer with long-term satisfaction.

The people who make up Kitchen Craft enhance the best in technology and materials. The Buller family now runs Kitchen Craft with a loyal group of executives and senior managers who have proven their expertise and ability through many years of service to the company. Kitchen Craft has many long-term employees who have helped to develop the systems and finishing techniques that are unique to the company. With this sense of ownership, employees take pride in ensuring the quality of Kitchen Craft products. A profit-

Winnipeg Airports Authority Inc.

Winnipeg International Airport is truly a community asset, and in January 1997, Winnipeg Airports Authority Inc. (WAA), a local not-for-profit private-sector corporation, took over the management and operation of the airport from the federal government. It is currently Canada's sixth busiest airport in terms of passenger and cargo movement, and has set its sights at joining the top five within the next few years. The four cornerstones to achieving that goal are:

- Developing the airport as a 24-hour intermodal transportation gateway and hub;
- Enhancing customer service and value;
- Utilizing the airport to develop tourism and economic development; and
- Involving community resources to the maximum.

In 1997, roughly 3 million passengers got on and off planes in Winnipeg. The strong economy in Winnipeg and

New front entrance sign erected September 1997.

Manitoba coupled with the introduction of "low-fare" carriers in Canada has had a significant impact, encouraging people who wouldn't normally travel to do so. Part of the airport's growth strategy is to become a significant regional gateway with great service connections to domestic and international destinations.

Discussions are on-going with several air carriers regarding the development of expanded routes and better access into the U.S. As well, WAA is endeavoring to get scheduled year-round direct service to Europe, now available only during the summer months.

Winnipeg Airports Authority Inc. doesn't just deal with passengers, though. These days, a herd of elk is just as likely to be taking off from Winnipeg International Airport as is a group of tourists or business executives. Because of its unrestricted 24-hour status and geographic centrality in North America, Winnipeg International Airport is strategically positioned to become a transportation and distribution hub for the cargo and courier markets. Whether it's flying live hogs and chilled pork to Asia, or farm combines to developing nations, there's tremendous potential. As the northern terminus of the Mid-continent Highway Corridor, Winnipeg also stands to benefit from the growing north-south flow of goods. Winnport, a private-sector initiative, would establish Winnipeg International Airport as an international intermodal transportation distribution centre and free-trade zone, capitalizing on Manitoba's transportation infrastructure. Seventeen airlines, including five freight, cargo and courier carriers, operate daily out of the airport. The province also has two national rail systems, an excellent highway system, vibrant trucking industry and access to ocean ports.

But the equation for success also factors in another variable—community support. It's a delicate balance to have the

The Goldwing Ambassadors, the airport's community volunteer service.

airport operate round-the-clock and yet maintain a good relationship with its residential neighbors. Therefore, an extensive noise management program has been put in place, as well as a process of ongoing community consultation and zoning restrictions to prevent incompatible development near any flight path.

In taking over the 69-year-old airport from the federal government, WAA recognized the need for a new corporate culture and subsequently set about establishing a more friendly, customer-driven, commercially oriented organization, sensitive to the community and the public it serves. WAA immediately eliminated a charge for baggage carts for international passengers and implemented a community volunteer program. The Goldwing Ambassadors, identified by their distinctive gold vests, are community volunteers who provide assistance and can answer questions ranging from where to pick up rental vehicles or grab a quick bite to eat to where to stay in Winnipeg and what there is to see and do.

For passengers and those waiting for their arrival, the airport's mezzanine level provides several boutiques where they can shop and browse. The philosophy is

WAA's entry in the 1997 Dragon Boat races, a fundraising event.

simple—to showcase Manitoba products, lending "a bit of flavor" of the city and the province. There's everything from Mondetta sweatshirts and Jeanne cakes to aboriginal arts and crafts. But that's not to forget other brand-name items, which provide proof of the retailers' commitment to "street"-pricing. Whether at the airport or at a store downtown, travellers can expect to pay the same. It's an invitation for tourists to pick up those gifts and memories before they depart or for the busy traveller to shop when they have a few moments.

On-site food and beverage services also rely on the same philosophy of street-pricing and capturing the spirit of Winnipeg's unique food establishments. WAA strongly believes in exposing local companies to national and international business opportunities by having a presence at the airport.

With the opening in 1998 of the enclosed "New Horizons" observation lounge, visitors to the airport will be able to relax and watch the planes take off and land. A glassed-in elevator takes visitors to the rooftop, where they can sit inside, have a coffee or something to eat and look out across the tarmac. Or if they'd rather, they can read a book in the comfort of an armchair.

Change is what it's all about. The airport would like to explore relocation of the downtown bus terminal to the airport, providing the unique opportunity to be one of the first in Canada to provide intermodal passenger service. Along with the bus terminal, plans are being made to look into constructing a parkade for customer comfort and convenience.

Other exciting initiatives which involve community partnerships include an agreement with Manitoba's Transport Institute to have students conduct research and provide support such as economic modelling, performance indicators and route development. Take Pride Winnipeg has worked with the airport to provide landscaping—trees and entranceway signs. Increasingly, Winnipeg sees itself as a gateway to the northern communities, especially with the economic shift that has divided the Northwest Territories into two regions, east and west. An Arctic Centre, which would focus on providing a sensitivity to travel in the Arctic from a cultural, social and economic standpoint would fit right in.

Winnipeg and Manitoba have both cultural diversity and economic strengths as the economy prepares for the next millennium by looking outward to export markets as local industry gains confidence in its ability to compete. Winnipeg Airport Authority Inc.'s slogan embraces this balance of community and growth: *"Community Character... Global Reach."* ■

WAA logo snow sculpture—done in January 1997, during the transfer process to launch WAA's corporate identity.

Palliser Furniture, Ltd.

I n 1944, Abram Albert DeFehr sold his car for $500 so he could open his own woodworking shop—building step ladders, ironing boards and clothes drying racks in the basement of his north-end Winnipeg home. He loved working with wood, and one of his unique designs—a half-moon end table—caught the attention of Eaton's department store. Soon, he was producing a line of wooden furniture out of a converted chicken barn, which he rented for $12 a month. Today, that business has been transformed into Canada's largest manufacturer of household furniture. Covering more than two-million square feet, Palliser Furniture produces everything from leather sofas, loveseats and chairs to occasional tables, wall and entertainment units, bedroom suites and furniture for the home office. Its nearly 3,000 employees are responsible for more than 7,000 pieces of furniture each day, and annual revenues in excess of $300 million.

Just as A.A. DeFehr's strong values—hard work, persistence and dedication—influenced such growth, his choice of Winnipeg as home positioned the company well for the future. The development of free trade turned Winnipeg into

Art DeFehr, President of Palliser Furniture Ltd., sits on the Trillium Award-winning sofa, the Tara.

a strategic distribution hub, and today, the company exports into the United States and Latin America, as well as Europe, Asia and the Middle East. Distanced from traditional suppliers in Ontario and Quebec, Palliser looked to a vertically integrated model of production. Unlike most other furniture manufacturers, Palliser manages the entire process from the sawmill to the finished product. The company produces its own particle board in Winnipeg from recycled wastes and has a part interest in a lumber operation in Wisconsin to produce its own wood components. By investing in the education and training of its employees, many of whom came to Canada as immigrants, Palliser has also developed its own "brain trust" and anyone would be hard-pressed to find such a strong labor force elsewhere.

Change is almost synonymous with Palliser. It's a very dynamic company. It's not the same company it was five years ago, let alone 50-plus years ago. In tribute to its humble beginnings, the chicken barn where it all began is now a museum, tucked in amongst the buildings off Gateway Road that now accommodate the company's corporate office, as well as its wood casegood (bedroom and home office

furniture, wall and entertainment units), leather upholstery and leather chair divisions. Several kilometres away, in Transcona, are its particle board and panel casegood divisions as well as its distribution centre. It also operates two upholstery plants outside the province, in Airdrie, Alberta, and Troutman, N.C.

Over the years, Palliser has stayed true to its roots—focusing on quality, value and service. Yet, in an industry that's extremely competitive, there's strong motivation to think outside the box and create new benchmarks. An innovative thinker, Art DeFehr has followed in his father's footsteps, and now serves as company President. He embraces change and has pushed for technological advancements which have kept costs down and differentiated its products, while maintaining a high quality.

Much of the equipment has been imported from Germany and Italy, but the company has scoured the world looking for technology that will give it a competitive edge. Palliser was among the first to utilize numerically controlled computerized equipment to assure accuracy and reduce costs. It pioneered laminating technology for the North American furniture industry. The development of specialized

Raw material for the production of particle board which Palliser produces at its Particle Board Plant.

papers and chemical finishes resulted in Palliser being able to inventively combine panel and wood technologies to create new and interesting products at affordable prices. Palliser has consistently tried to position itself in the mid-price range, and has gained a reputation for creating products with exceptional value.

That outlook very much reflects what the company is all about, and in June 1997, it was incorporated in its mission statement: "To be a community of people dedicated to leadership in design, service and customer value in the furniture industry."

However, the mission statement goes further, addressing the values upon which the company is built. Those values find their origin in the faith and experience of the company's founder, A.A. DeFehr, but are not limited to a single religious tradition or ethnic origin. The mission statement says:

"Building on a heritage of faith, we aspire to:
· Demonstrate integrity in all relationships.
· Promote the dignity and value of each other.
· Respect the environment.
· Support our community.
· Strive for excellence in all we do."

Long before its mission statement, the company had been putting those words into practise through the DeFehr Foundation, a philanthropic foundation which funds Christian education and third world development, as well as providing community support, whether to the arts, charities or health organizations. From the company's earliest days, people

Upholstering a leather sofa.

with special needs—the hearing impaired, those with mental or physical handicaps and people reentering society after a period of personal difficulty—have been integrated into Palliser's workplace.

Along with its mission statement, Palliser has come up with a plan to take it into the new millennium. The focus is on capturing a larger marketshare, doubling sales and increasing exports outside of the U.S. to at least 10 per cent of its business.

In countries like those in Scandinavia, there is a growing interest in North American products, especially traditional and country-styled furniture, including motion sofas and recliners.

In looking at its home market, Palliser decided in the spring of 1997 to stop producing a full line of fabric upholstery and focus entirely on leather, a market that had grown significantly. Palliser currently supplies more than 1,300 retailers across North America. ∎

The Series 282 Master Bedroom.

Standard Knitting Ltd.

Standard Knitting Ltd. was founded in 1926. This privately held knitwear manufacturer has since built a solid retail customer base that expands to over five continents throughout the world. The foundation for this growth has centered around three very important tenets to Standard Knitting Ltd.: Fashion, Quality and Service.

In developing highly fashionable apparel products, Standard has committed tremendous amounts of resources in its research and development area. Designers in Italy, New York and Winnipeg work throughout the year to create the designs that will literally be turned into "works of art" through colorful imagery and three-dimensional texture of its knitted fabrics.

The creative spirit is evident every day in the year. All major designs are highly valued and protected by copyright. Through the use of a computer-assisted-design (CAD) system, a software program is written to provide knitting instructions for the state-of-the-art electronic knitting machines. These knitting machines make it possible to produce intricate designs that would once have been impossible by hand.

Standard's manufacturing facility is situated on five acres of land located in Winnipeg's Inkster Industrial Park. With a capacity of close to 1,000,000 units per year, the factory is fully integrated to handle everything from the storage of raw materials to the manufacture, packaging and distribution of a wide selection of garments. However, it is also a business based on people, and Winnipeg, a city that has seen many immigrants settle here, has provided a highly skilled labor force. These people brought with them the skills, the creativity and the culture of their homelands, and they have played an important role in the apparel industry. They are dedicated workers, which has resulted in Standard Knitting being in the enviable position of having a low staff turnover. That has contributed significantly in the maintenance of high quality standards and in the efficiency of the operation. To ensure that quality products are produced, Standard Knitting has instituted various quality inspection points throughout the production process

starting from selecting reliable suppliers for yarn, to inspection of the fabric while it is being knitted and after it has been knitted, right through the cutting, sewing and finishing stages of the production process.

There are many different lines that make up the Standard Knitting group of products. The different labels include TUNDRA, T2, ATG and Tundra Sport. The most well known of these lines is the TUNDRA label. This label represents Standard Knitting's men's sportswear collection. Some of the products sold under this label include sweaters, cardigans, knitted and silk vests, outerwear, knitted and woven shirts, silk neckties, scarves, socks, dress slacks, casual pants, casual shorts and loungewear. This range of products can be found in better quality men's stores. Although many different age groups wear the TUNDRA label products, the line itself is geared more for the

mature adult male. For the younger men's market, Standard Knitting developed a more fashion-forward line under the label T2. The main focus of this label is tops. Under the ATG label, Standard produces all-terrain gear, including ski and other outdoor sportswear. ATG products can be found in some of the most renowned ski resorts in North America. Through Tundra Sport, its licensed product division, Standard has carried licenses for Major League Baseball, the National Football League, National Hockey League and colleges in the National Collegiate Athletic Association (NCAA). In the fall of 1997, through a licensing arrangement with John Elway of the Denver Broncos, Standard also released the John Elway

in the United States extends to the attendance of all the major trade shows such as the MAGIC show, the Chicago Collective, the PGA show and the BATMAN show, to name a few. In order to ensure that they can provide the best of service, they offer their customers the choice of either contacting their sales agent, the New York office or the customer service department located in Winnipeg, through a toll-free number. Standard Knitting is also looking to do business in the global marketplace. It has established distribution networks into Europe, Asia, South America and Australia.

of access to a broad array of markets. Often referred to as The Gateway to the West, Winnipeg is developing into the northern distribution and transportation terminus of the "NAFTA highway," which extends down through the United States and into Mexico. Winnipeg International Airport plays an equally key role, providing reliable, affordable transportation for Standard's finished products to be delivered to world markets. The city is also the hub of a well-developed railroad and highway network, making for the efficient movement of goods throughout Canada and the United States.

Standard Knitting has its eye on the future, and is still fully committed to growth. It's looking to expand by developing TUNDRA retail outlets, a move that will ensure it maintains its leadership role in the industry. ■

sportswear collection. It has a proud association with sports and is also a sponsor of the Canadian and U.S. national alpine ski teams and the Canadian national hockey teams.

Standard's largest market is easily the United States, where it operates through a wholly owned subsidiary, Tundra Knitwear, Ltd. Established in 1972 and based in New York, Tundra Knitwear has developed a network of agents representing every state of the union. Its presence

It is no secret that its success has been built upon its "quality, high-value clothing," clothing that has distinctive flair and appeals to the fashion-conscious. In recognition of its efforts to expand its global markets, Standard was awarded a Canada Export Award for 1995, presented by the federal government's international trade department.

One of the advantages of being situated in Winnipeg, the geographic centre of North America, is quite simply the ease

Premier Printing Ltd.

Winnipeg has one of the highest concentrations of commercial printing companies in urban settings in Canada, but a small printer that began more than thirty years ago in a tiny shop has been among the city's most successful. Premier Printing's survival and expansion in such a competitive environment is tribute to this company's business philosophy—the commitment to providing dependable quality and service, based on principles of fairness, trust and reliability. Premier Printing clients are valued as "professional partners," and long-term business relationships, based on integrity and good value, are this company's goals for the customers it serves.

(seated, left to right) Jake Kuik, Gerry Kuik and W. (Bill) Gortemaker. (standing, left to right) Bill Raap, John Toet, Lawrence Toet and Ben Kuik.

Premier Printing began in 1962 as a one-man shop, the size of a small office, and quickly grew from a small, dedicated group of skilled craftsmen into one of Manitoba's largest and most respected printers. Today, the company operates from a production facility of over 60,000 square feet, and it employs 80 full-time staff, with upwards of 200 in peak summer months. The company provides "all-in-one" printing services, including state-of-the-art design using the latest computer technology, scanning and imaging services, and printing services with computerized bindery equipment and modern multicolour presses. Premier began operations in the Winnipeg working-class suburb of Transcona, with its sole original employee also its founder and owner. Gerry Kuik had immigrated from the Netherlands as a master printing tradesman, in a trade where precision, accuracy and painstaking attention to fine detail have always been critical to the quality of the final product.

The small company did well immediately. A year later Mr. Kuik moved his operation a block away from its original location, expanding the business. After ten years, in 1972, the bold step was taken to build a bigger facility on Plessis Road, again staying in Transcona, and drawing on the encouragement of Winnipeg's business community for support to help the small company prosper and grow. With that support, Premier Printing has been able to expand the Plessis facility four times until that location, too, was outgrown.

Looking to settle elsewhere in this community, the company found a site in St. Boniface Industrial Park on the corner of Dugald Road and Beghin Avenue. In August 1987 Premier Printing moved to a brand new facility, but it soon became apparent that further expansion was necessary to fulfill the increasing level of service demanded from the Winnipeg business community, as well as rapidly growing national business. Having been at this location for ten years now, and having completed three expansions, Premier Printing constantly aims to satisfy the printing needs of its clients—and has continued its growth.

In 1996, a sister company was established in Grimsby, Ontario. Premier Impressions Inc., with a 25,000-square-foot facility and 18 employees, operates under the same management as its Winnipeg parent; the companies are family-run. Gerry Kuik, the founder of the company, retired from active daily participation a few years ago, but still takes a keen interest in the business, serving as Chairman of the Board. The present partners are President W. (Bill) Gortemaker, General Manager Bill Raap, Pricing/Computer Manager Jake Kuik, PrePress Manager Ben Kuik, Maintenance Manager John Toet and Lawrence Toet, Plant Manager of Grimsby's Premier Impressions.

Some of Premier Printing's presses in the 60,000-square-foot Winnipeg plant.

Holding to a business philosophy where the principles of fairness, trust and reliability are paramount, Premier and its people have succeeded in building sound business relationships with clients as valued partners. Many of these professional partnerships have spanned decades of dependable printing services. While the printing industry has undergone remarkable technological changes, from the old linotype and manual processes to today's computerized and digital technologies, the need for insistence on detail, precision and accuracy has not changed. While the metamorphosis of applications in the printing world will continue, these basic constants will remain.

Premier Printing and Premier Impressions have their busy seasons in the summertime, when they produce together over 3.3 million Premier School Agendas. The product was originally developed by Premier Printing, similar to the school time management products available for both students and teachers in Europe. Entering the North American market in 1983 with this combination calendar, daytimer, homework-recorder and appointment book, Premier quickly found further development of Premier School Agendas was warranted. Refining

the product over the next seven years, the company's unique offering became so successful that a separate company was founded in 1991 with two other partners. In 1996 that company, Premier School Agendas, was sold to Franklin Quest Co. in the U.S.A., and by 1997 would reach total North American sales of over 11 million units. More than two million units of these customized daily assignment books are manufactured at Premier Printing during the peak summer months. An additional 130 students, from high school and university levels, are employed in the manufacturing process. Like their full-time counterparts, many are from the east Winnipeg area; Premier Printing's people are a close-knit group, a community both geographically and in common goals.

Premier's strength is its people. Their ability to turn around a job quickly, and their willingness to place multifaceted talents at the client's disposal result in years of trusting business relationships, as well as many letters of commendation. The employees participate in a profit-sharing plan, in which profits they help earn are invested on the employees' behalf, toward the day they leave or retire from the company.

Premier also aims to be first in relationships, whether that be among staff members or with business clients. Success measured in these terms gives great satisfaction. As a company, Premier acknowledges the individual gifts brought to bear on the work done, and the Creator who provides for us so generously. ■

Premier employs 80 full-time staff, with upwards of 200 in peak summer months.

Guertin Bros.

Celebrating 50 years of excellence in business, original founding brothers Antoine and Norbert pose with second generation Charlie and Phil (left to right).

Guertin Bros. saw the future and changed. Up against tough new environmental regulations, the Winnipeg paint manufacturer acted quickly, investing in the early '90s in research and development aimed at eliminating solvents in the manufacture and application of paint. Today, it is one of only seven Canadian manufacturers of powder paint, considered an "environmentally benign" technology. For more than half a century, Guertin Bros. has consistently responded to the challenges and demands of a changing market.

The company was founded in 1947 by two brothers, Antoine and Norbert Guertin, who initially sold housepaint. The brothers started their business out of a two-car garage at the rear of 506 St. Jean Baptiste St. in St. Boniface. After the war, construction was booming and it was an expanding market. But to survive, they eventually felt they had to manufacture their own housepaints. For them, the trick was to hire people who knew what they were doing. In 1957 they journeyed to Ottawa, where they hired a chemist and convinced him to come to Winnipeg. In the early '60s, Guertin Bros. started manufacturing liquid industrial finishes, and in 1976, it was decided to get out of housepaint altogether. About the same time, the company went in a new direction, expanding to include a specialty line of caulking, sealants and adhesive materials for the transportation, construction and agriculture markets.

In 1993, the company hired a powder chemist from the United Kingdom not only to work for them, but to train other chemists in what was then a relatively new field. Today, powder paint is widely used by manufacturing companies on their production lines. Everything from agricultural equipment to electrical transformers, lawn and garden equipment and

automotive components is sprayed with the powder, then passed through a bake oven which melts and cures the paint. Guertin Bros. is also developing a new water-based single and two-part paint, which would further eliminate the use of solvents in their liquid paint lines.

In the mid-'90s, Guertin Bros. started selling resin, a base used in liquid paint, to other paint companies. Up until this point, it manufactured 60 to 70 per cent of the resin it needed for its own paints. Even at that, it had an excess capacity, and opted to hire a sales force to promote resin sales to outside users. It now develops resins in its labs for select users, based on specific performance characteristics they want in a finished product. It can take between six months and two years to develop a resin. This ability to customize the product differentiates Guertin Bros. from other North American paint companies its size and shows a healthy growth potential. It has established a separate company, Guertin Bros. Polymers, to concentrate on this market.

Guertin Bros. remains a family-owned business today with Antoine's sons, Phil and Charlie, now at the helm. With the

hiring of one of Charlie's sons, a third generation is already in place. However, Guertin Bros. has grown considerably over the years. Today, it employs 72 people, 16 of whom are chemists working strictly in research and development. After several plant relocations, including Assiniboine Avenue near the Main Street bridge, the plant now is situated on 5.8 acres of land on Panet Road, which has access to a rail spur. Guertin Bros. does all its manufacturing and research and development in Winnipeg, but has a distribution network of nine warehouses–six in Canada and three in the United States. The Winnipeg facility is 78,000 square feet, which includes 10,000 square feet of labs.

As an ISO 9001 registered company, Guertin Bros. puts a heavy emphasis on meeting quality standards and technical requirements. It has six labs, which work toward this end. Its analytical lab fingerprints or identifies raw materials to make sure they meet quality and purity standards. Most of the chemicals are imported from the U.S. and offshore. In its liquid and powder coatings lab, computerized modeling is used to optimize formulations. Liquids are tested for such qualities as viscosity,

Environmentally friendly powder paint extrusion and cooling production line put the company at the forefront of the new compliant technologies for the coatings industry. Chuck, a third generation Guertin, monitors the manufacturing process.

sag, hiding, specific gravity, moisture content and conductivity. Dry products are tested for things as hiding, flexibility, impact, humidity, chemical resistance, hardness and abrasion. The labs are also equipped with accelerated test equipment to conduct tests for corrosion, using a salt spray cabinet, and for color fading, in which ultraviolet light is used to simulate sunlight. The other labs include sealants and polymer labs, a quality control lab and a pilot and applications lab.

Guertin's objective is to ensure its customers "receive the highest possible level of service, with consistently superior quality products, at competitive pricing, with on-time delivery and batch-to-batch consistency."

The plant itself is designed to meet those objectives. It is extremely efficient and modern. A new computer system was installed for production control. It allows data to be collected on production processes and to analyse that statistically, reducing errors and minimizing deviations from established standards, part of ISO requirements.

In continuing to look to the future, Guertin Bros. is focusing its growth into export markets, and is specifically fostering north-south trade. Exports currently represent a small percentage of its sales,

Paul Chan, Manager, Resin Development, uses molecular modeling to speed up new polymeric development projects, shortening time and reducing cost to market.

but are expected to grow substantially in the future. It has already developed many products compliant with new U.S. environmental regulations. ■

Arnold Bros. Transport Ltd.

I t's the people who make the difference at Arnold Bros. Transport, a progressive transportation company that has made Winnipeg its headquarters since 1960. With its roots firmly entrenched in the solid, hardworking traditions of rural Manitoba, Arnold Bros. was founded by Frank and Gerald Arnold in the early '50s, in the small town of Oakbank near Winnipeg.

The fast-growing company was formally incorporated in 1958, and the head office soon moved to Winnipeg, eventually to encompass locations across Canada, in Chicago, Illinois, and in Emporia, Kansas. Over the years, Arnold Bros. has carried materials ranging from airplane tails and fragile perishables, to a set of genuine world-famous hamburger chain "Golden Arches" and a shipment of mining equipment destined for the Yukon.

Today, with a staff numbering roughly 600, almost 400 trucks, over 800 trailers, state-of-the-art satellite communication, computer technology and various tractor

Arnold Bros. is a reliable, experienced carrier along the international North-South transportation corridor stretching between Winnipeg and the southern United States.

Arnold Bros. was founded by Frank and Gerald Arnold in the early '50s, in the small town of Oakbank near Winnipeg.

trailer configurations, Arnold Bros. services the entire North American market, and counts among its satisfied, long-term customers a wide range of manufacturers of retail goods, food products and industrial equipment.

As the company celebrates its fortieth anniversary in 1998, it looks back on its official beginnings in 1958 with great pride. Back then, Frank and Gerald Arnold specialized in the movement of feed ingredients, steel and machinery across the Prairie provinces. As the brothers' list of products and customers grew, so did the company.

The people who work with Arnold Bros., and the community that has supported the

company during those forty years of growth, have contributed to the company's record of steady growth. Winnipeg has offered Arnold Bros. a secure, stable and healthy economic home, a solid foundation upon which to build a thriving, nationwide business. Good people, with a strong sense of community and a heads-up work ethic, have allowed for a major network of road carriers based in this centrally located Prairie city.

The Arnold Bros. employees form a family that extends past the name Arnold, to a committed workforce of well-trained, responsible employees. This experienced team of fleet managers, drivers, area controllers, sales representatives and administrative staff shares a common mission: to meet the customers' needs with the steady, solid reliability that's typical of Winnipeg and its citizens.

A strong focus on training and safety with ongoing training to develop professional drivers and to upgrade training to existing professionals, enables the maintenance of a high standard of excellence in customer service. The safety and compliance of both drivers and facilities is regularly audited internally.

Technology plays a vital role in keeping the far-flung system in contact, through the tracking, measuring and recording of relevant information. Using trucks equipped with satellite communications, service is constantly monitored and reported back to customers, through a fully computerized Central Control that keeps track of hundreds of daily shipments.

Customers can choose to link up with the company through this Electronic Data Interchange system, which utilizes the latest computer technology to connect customers to Central Dispatch. Here, clients can input their own delivery orders and direct them instantly to the Central Dispatch facility. Customers can also keep

Using trucks equipped with satellite communications, Arnold Bros.' service is constantly monitored and reported back to customers through a fully computerized Central Control that keeps track of hundreds of daily shipments.

track of their own deliveries onscreen, and can receive instant updates and current information about their shipments.

The Arnold Bros. team prides itself on the establishment of long-term, mutual beneficial partnerships with customers, by knowing and understanding their needs. And Arnold Bros. employees strive for the same kind of relationship with

the company's suppliers–relying on consistent, stable performers who provide competitive pricing and quality equipment–to ensure the company can continue to offer customers the best service possible.

As a result of this corporate commitment to quality service, a very safe driving record is achieved, along with a high level of customer satisfaction, with a rate of more than 97 per cent of completed delivery as requested. Going that extra mile is an integral part of the Arnold Bros. customer service policy, and the result is that the Arnold Bros. client list seldom sees names leave it.

But although much has changed in the past forty years of remarkable growth, both for the trucking industry and for the city of Winnipeg, two things have remained as constants: Winnipeg has continued in its role as a major transportation hub in Canada, and it has been the people who make the difference in successful transportation. Customer service means more than expensive technology and modern trucks. It means having the best people available to do the job.

As Winnipeg anticipates a rosy economic future– forming a significant link in the fast-growing North-South highway transportation corridor, a road ribbon that will run from this city all the way to the U.S.-Mexico border and beyond into Central America– Arnold Bros. is proud to be a part of this next stage of international transportation. The company recently initiated a U.S.A. domestic operation, M&M Trucking Inc., and has seen growth in its associated storage trailer rental business, Western Transport Ltd.

A strong background in shipment of agricultural commodities and food products

Arnold Bros. serves the entire North American market, and counts among its satisfied, long-term customers a wide range of manufacturers of retail goods, food products and industrial equipment.

will position Arnold Bros. as a reliable, experienced carrier along the international North-South transportation corridor stretching between Winnipeg and the southern United States, and into points even further south. So, as the Winnipeg Chamber of Commerce and Arnold Bros. both celebrate significant milestone anniversaries in 1998, both can look forward to the future with great hope, and with pride in the past, and in the people who have built this city. ■

Prolific Group

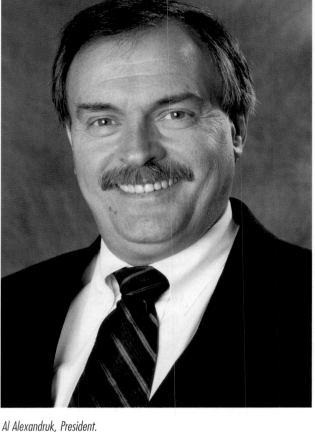

Al Alexandruk, President.

From two people and a couple of small offset printing presses, working 100-hour weeks in Al Alexandruk's basement 23 years ago, the Prolific Group has grown into a 43,000-square-foot facility in a Winnipeg industrial park. Employing 72 people and working with the latest in print and computer technology, the Prolific Group now operates the most diversified print services shop in the city. Five divisions span the full range of offerings, from concept to completion, of business letterhead to fine art reproduction, brochures and direct mail pieces.

It's a phenomenal success story, but company President Al Alexandruk, still at the helm, credits the city and people of Winnipeg for their contributions to the living and working environment that enabled Prolific to become a major printing firm. Alexandruk believes Prolific has taken its operative cue from traditional Prairie philosophies of hard work, integrity, honesty and respect for your neighbours that are exemplified in this sprawling, energetic Prairie city.

The little printing company grew quickly from its basement beginnings, building, as it developed, a loyal, local customer base that goes back to that start in 1975, when Al Alexandruk and partner Tom Wilton began Prolific as a labour of love. Within a year, they had to expand from the basement, in response to demand. They rented space near the Winnipeg International Airport, and then some four moves later, in 1987, the Prolific Group expanded once more, to move to its current location in northwest Winnipeg's Inkster Industrial Park area.

The Prolific Group has blossomed into five divisions, which umbrella Prolific Graphics Inc., a general commercial printer specializing in high-quality, full-color printing; Regent Press, for custom index tabbing; Display Printing Services, with specialty and screen printing, retail signage and truck fleet marketing and equipment manufacturers decal marketing; Target Direct Mail, inserting and addressing mass mailings based upon Canada Post specifications; and Prolific Digital, which, in keeping with progress, has created on-demand printing service of one-colour, with spot colour, or full four-colour reproduction.

Many of Prolific's current clients have been with the company since its humble beginning. Even though the printer's solid reputation has attracted customers from locations as distant as Vancouver, Thunder Bay and the United States, those local clients, with their continued business, receive the same dedication to service from Prolific as they did in the early days. From short-run, single-colour jobs, to multi-colour runs in the thousands, Prolific provides whatever is needed through its full range of services. This includes in-house state-of-the-art prepress and small and large printing presses, complemented by a complete bindery.

One of Prolific's operating principles revolves around ensuring the company is able to offer the latest in technological applications for clients' printing needs, as well as upgrading and purchasing of new equipment that represents the state-of-the-art, whenever genuine technological advances have been made. In addition to the superior service that the state-of-the-art equipment provides to clients, that

Reviewing computerized image for film output prior to printing.

same principle enables Prolific employees to layer additional skills onto their already-solid base of experienced craftsmanship.

The long-term staff, along with the company, have a commitment to quality work. Those customers whose needs are well served will become permanent clients, knowing that they can rely on Prolific to come through on-time, at the correct price and with proper attention to quality. The top-drawer workmanship within Prolific's print products can achieve a level of genuine fine art. Prolific's account base reads like the top 500 companies "Who's Who," along with noted Canadian artists for limited-edition prints, plus the Winnipeg Art Gallery's catalogue, which accompanies their art exhibition for many artists from around the world.

Whether the company handles commercial tasks, such as busboards or letterheads, each is given the identical dedication to fine workmanship. Prolific's commitment to quality has been recognized by an ISO (International Standards Organization) 9001 certification for quality standards, which means they

consistently produce top quality work, no matter how large or small the order.

Winnipeg's stable and steady economic growth, its varied and vibrant cultural community, the city's highly competent and diversified workforce and the atmosphere of support and encouragement from the local, close-knit business community have all helped to foster the growth and development of successful companies like Prolific. It's not surprising, then, to see that Prolific offers support in return.

The company received a 1995 Premier's Volunteer Service Award nomination because of the company's regular contributions to cultural organizations, research groups

Press operator reviews colour and image registration of printed product.

and charities. The Royal Winnipeg Ballet, Winnipeg Symphony Orchestra, St. Boniface Hospital Research Centre, The Manitoba Cancer Treatment and Research Foundation, The Children's Hospital, Assiniboine Community College, Manitoba Cancer Society, the Shriners and The Manitoba Schizophrenia Society are some of the recipients of Prolific's support, along with many smaller associations.

That support stems from another deeply ingrained Prairie tradition: neighbours help each other out and give each other support. The Prolific Group may have established a reputation that has crossed both provincial and international borders to attract new clients, but its Prairie roots are Winnipeg-based and will continue to be grounded in the city that helped enable it to grow. ∎

Printed product is assembled and finished to trimmed size.

The Willmar Group of Companies

The rigors of living in Winnipeg's harsh winter climate have not been lost on the Willmar Group of Companies. When it comes to manufacturing windows and doors, the Willmar Group—Willmar Windows and Hi-Therm Windows & Doors—is about quality without compromise, thanks to its leading-edge cold weather technology.

With temperature extremes ranging from -30 degrees Celsius in winter to 30 degrees Celsius in summer, Winnipeg has proven an excellent test market for its energy-efficient products. Its engineers, together with a complete research and development team, have worked hard to ensure energy efficiency and comfort aren't compromised by the creativity and style of its windows, designed to welcome in the natural light and beauty of the outdoors.

From its traditional, elegantly styled wood window to its Synergy window—a marriage of wood and vinyl—Willmar Windows caters to the needs of the new construction market. Hi-Therm Windows and Doors serves primarily the renovation market, with a uPVC line of windows, which offer low-maintenance durability.

All window lines are made in Winnipeg, where the company has more than 260,000 square feet of manufacturing space, including a door plant which produces a full line of front entrance, garden, patio, terrace and French doors. Its window line includes a solid Wood Window, a Metalclad, low maintenance wood exterior window, a uPVC window and a Synergy window, which combines wood on the interior and uPVC on the exterior.

The facilities in Winnipeg produce roughly 1,100 units—windows and doors—per day and employ about 880 people. During peak periods, the plants operate with three shifts a day.

Willmar started as a family-owned business in 1962. In March 1997, it was acquired by another family-owned enterprise, JELD-WEN Canada, which has grown into a large conglomerate, owning more than 160 companies. Yet, the strong, solid values that have traditionally set family-owned businesses apart still remain.

JELD-WEN is committed to Winnipeg. Not only did it decide to expand its Winnipeg operation, it opted to move the JELD-WEN head office to the city. Winnipeg is a natural choice, with its excellent tax structure and central location from which to build and distribute its products across Canada, into the U.S. and overseas.

Willmar has it own fleet of trucks, giving it complete control from the time its products are manufactured to the time they are delivered to customers throughout North America.

Export is the key to future growth for Willmar. It already exports into Japan and Saudi Arabia, and is considering exporting to Germany. It is a participant in Export House, a home built near the Winnipeg Convention Centre to showcase Manitoba builders and building products. ■

When it comes to manufacturing windows and doors, the Willmar Group—Willmar Windows and Hi-Therm Windows & Doors—is about quality without compromise, thanks to its leading-edge cold weather technology.

Empire Iron Works Ltd.

Empire Iron Works Ltd. of Winnipeg knows it's not gold, but steel that links Winnipeg's Royal Canadian Mint with the gold mines of Red Lake, Ontario. The Winnipeg-based steel fabricator supplied the 2,000 tonnes of steel that lines the mine shafts near the Ontario/Manitoba border and did the structural work on the Mint's celebrated pyramid.

Started in 1958 as an ornamental metal fabricator in a small garage in Middlechurch, Empire Iron Works today operates out of a 40,000-square-foot facility on Jarvis Avenue and focuses

heavily on industrial work–bridges and major projects such as Vancouver International Airport and the $200-million expansion of Simplot chemical plant in Brandon.

Although much of the raw material must be imported from the United States–Algoma Steel is the only mill in Canada–there is a high demand in the Manitoba and Prairie region for steel fabrication because of the area's large industrial base and, in particular, its mines and paper mills.

Each year, nearly 5,000 tonnes of steel go through the Winnipeg plant, where the steel is custom fabricated and painted to meet the specifications on a particular project. However, Empire Iron Works' role doesn't end there. The parts are shipped to the construction site, where employees erect the structure.

There is little repetition in the types of products produced by the Winnipeg firm. Most work is tendered or negotiated on an individual basis with company owners or general contractors.

Empire Iron Works, which also has plants in Alberta and British Columbia, employs between 80 and 100 people in Winnipeg. The city has always provided a competitive advantage because it's a good source of labor. Many graduates of Red River Community College have been hired as tradesmen. The city's mid-continent location also makes it ideal for shipping products east, west, south and occasionally north.

The Winnipeg plant is somewhat unique in that it has a sophisticated paint facility, which allows it to use the exotic paints necessary for a variety of highly corrosive environments such as pulp mills and potash mines. It also has a state-of-the-art, computerized, numerically-controlled beam and column line.

Because structural steel work tends to be cyclical, based on the economy, Empire Iron Work has also branched out to include a construction services division, which undertakes mechanical and electrical projects, renovations, plant shut-downs and maintenance.

At Empire Irons Works safety is of primary importance. The company has developed a shop and field safety orientation program, which is closely monitored along with compliance levels. ■

Reimer Express Lines

Within Canada, and everywhere there's a roadway, today's Reimer Express Lines Ltd. con—tinues its tradition of quality backed by more than 26,000 transportation professionals. Nineteen-ninety-seven saw the friendly acquisition by Roadway Express result in a fully integrated, seamless trans-

the United States. The transportation of these products marked the beginning of Reimer Express.

Today, company founder Dr. D. S. Reimer remains Chairman of Reimer Express.

Winnipeg plays an important role in the Reimer system. It is home to approxi-mately 700 employees, including the bulk

Reimer Express Lines prides itself on offering quality service to customers, meeting and exceeding customer require-ments through continuous process improvement. Reimer received the Canada Award for Business Excellence in Quality, the first company in the transportation sector to be so recognized. The award, given by the federal govern-ment, acknowledges unmatched superior perfor-mance of every Reimer employee.

Since 1982, Reimer has set the pace for Canada's expedited service through its direct-to-customer *Fast as Flite* service, which helps major manufacturers and retailers eliminate costly interim ware-housing. Reimer is so proud and confident of this service that it offers an *On Time or Free* guarantee on major west-bound lanes.

The Reimer Express Driver Training Institute Inc. is also a vital part of Reimer Express's overall transport improvement. The school, a stand-alone entity, was created in the early 1970s to provide superior training for drivers at Reimer Express. As the pro-gram expanded, the training institute matured and now provides driver training to the entire trucking industry. It offers three programs, serv-ing a full range of skills development, and has been so

portation system like no other; Reimer's wide-ranging transportation services now include Canada, the United States, Mexico and 65 countries around the globe.

That's a long way from humble begin-nings dating back to 1952, when the father and grandfather of Dr. D. S. Reimer operated a general store and feed busi-ness in the southern Manitoba community of Steinbach. They used to purchase pack-ing house by-products used in animal feed production in Winnipeg, to sell them in

of Reimer's linehaul drivers, and is the location for the company's corporate and administrative head offices for Canada as well as the central Canadian breakbulk and maintenance facilities.

Reimer is not a traditional trucking company. For many years, Reimer Express has employed a full-time chaplain to offer counselling to staff members. Based in the Winnipeg head office, the chaplain and his wife travel across Canada visiting employees.

successful it has been accredited to deliv-er driver training programs by the Canadian Trucking Human Resources Council.

There's an exciting new chapter being written at Reimer. But the players haven't changed. Nor has their drive to succeed in every aspect of the transportation ser-vices they offer in Manitoba, within Canada, the United States . . . and every-where there's a roadway. ■

Vansco Electronics Ltd.

Vansco's specialty is the design and manufacture of custom electronic, electro-mechanical and electro-hydraulic products for original equipment manufacturers. The company serves the agricultural, truck, bus and construction equipment markets. Its customers span three continents and include companies such as New Holland, Motor Coach Industries, Caterpillar, AgChem, Champion, JCB and Komatsu.

Vansco supplies these customers with custom solutions to improve the performance of their heavy machines. Its products range from vehicular instrumentation, to systems for recording compaction levels on road paving machines, to the electronic controls and wire harnesses for Motor Coach Industries' Renaissance Coach. One example of the many unique products that

Vansco can get involved in new product designs as early as the conceptual development stage. Alternately, it can take a customer's idea and do the detailed design, or it can simply build products to customer drawings.

Vansco is registered to the ISO 9001 quality standard. The company's mission is to exceed customer expectations in every aspect of its business. To achieve this, it has an ongoing training program in quality, workmanship and customer service. Through meeting customer challenges head-on, Vansco has managed to grow at a rate of 40 per

Vansco's WHT Division builds harnesses in a wide range of sizes and complexities—from parts that fit in the palm of your hand to assemblies the length of a highway coach.

Fine pitch surface mount components are placed at high speed using laser centering and optical verification.

Vansco manufactures is a computerized site-specific farming system. This system allows fertilizer to be custom blended on the fly, based on computer maps of the field and GPS (global positioning system) satellite signals. Ninety per cent of Vansco's 1,500 products have been designed in-house by an engineering staff of 60 engineers.

To precisely meet its customers' needs,

cent per year since 1978, when Ed Van Humbeck and his wife, Therese, started the company. Today, the privately held company operates out of more than 90,000 square feet of manufacturing and office space in three adjacent buildings on Clarence Avenue.

In 1993, Vansco purchased a small local wire harness facility which it has now built into its successful Wire Harness

Technologies division (WHT). WHT's staff has now grown from its initial complement of 10 people to more than 150. Its harnesses and cables interconnect the electronic modules on heavy equipment, ranging from back hoes and bulldozers to farm seeding equipment, highway coaches, leisure vehicles and cooking equipment.

Vansco has gained a reputation in the industry for its product reliability, strong testing capability, cost-effective production and on-time delivery. This has resulted in a growing export market for its products. With sales in excess of $40 million, Vansco now does 50 per cent of its business in the United States, 10 per cent in Europe and 40 per cent in Canada.

"Nineteen-ninety-eight promises another 40 per cent increase, most of which will be export," says Van Humbeck. "Winnipeg has been a great place to grow the business. It offers a quality lifestyle with strong cultural diversity and amenities, low cost housing and good educational facilities—and Winnipeggers have a strong work ethic—it probably comes from their roots in the farm sector." ■

13

Communications, Energy & Technology

Photo by Mike Grandmaison.

Nygård International

Peter Nygård, founder of Nygård International, is a sought-after public speaker, with his galvanizing, energetic presence and his passion for excellence.

It may be a $300-million, worldwide women's apparel manufacturing firm, but Nygård International is really in the information technology business. That's the way the company's founder and owner, Peter Nygård, sees it—and his instincts have taken the company from humble 1967 beginnings as Tan Jay, a small garment manufacturer in Winnipeg, to far-flung status with international offices and production facilities from Shanghai and Sri Lanka, to New York, Los Angeles and Mexico.

Peter Nygård built the company by putting in seven-day work weeks of sixteen- to eighteen-hour days, a schedule

Peter Nygård with his daughter áliá, for whom the off-the-rack, moderate-price range áliá separates are named.

he maintains, while he moves from location to location—Winnipeg, California or his unique island home in the Bahamas, the design for which he is personally the architect, the engineer and the general contractor, just as he did the corporate headquarters in Toronto and in all key facilities worldwide.

The founder of the Manitoba Fashion Institute, which encourages and provides training for apparel manufacturing

employees and middle managers and fosters professionalism among Manitoba's garment manufacturers, Nygård was also the first Canadian apparel manufacturer to jump into the U.S. market more than 20 years ago, and argued persuasively in favour of North American free trade well before it was politically fashionable.

He has served as the Chairman of the national task force to recommend long-term strategies for Canada's textile and clothing industries, on the International Trade Advisory Committee, as President of the Canadian Ladies Fashion Institute, as a founding member of the Canada-USSR Business Council, a member of the Prime Minister's committee in the Bahamas for that country's quincentennial, with his designed fashions to be the country's official attire. He continues to be a sought-after public speaker, with his galvanizing, energetic presence and his passion for excellence.

The Nygård name now attaches to women's apparel lines ranging from the off-the-rack, moderate-price range áliá separates, to Tan Jay's coordinated fashions, the "upper-moderate" Nygård Collection, Bianca Nygård contemporary career dressing and the Peter Nygård Signature Collection—designer clothing at the "bridge" price point between off-the-rack and designer collectables.

Nygård International employs more than 2,500 people worldwide. While the company's international head office is now in Toronto, 1,600 of the Nygård employees remain in hometown Winnipeg; the founding factory has grown to three locations in Winnipeg, one of them a 60,000-square-foot, computerized production facility that turns out about 65,000 pairs of polyester pants every week. The company operates more than 170 retail locations of its own, as well as "soft shops" established with major retailers like Saks Fifth Avenue, featuring the Peter Nygård Signature Collection.

Finnish-born, Nygård emigrated to Winnipeg as a child with his parents, was first educated locally, and subsequently obtained his university degree abroad. Thereafter, he began his career in the fashion industry with the eminent Canadian department store chain of Eaton's, and joined Tan Jay in the late 1960s. It did not take long before the young man became CEO of the company, and then owner. The Nygård fashion empire took off, soaring from $800,000 in sales when he joined the company, to more than three hundred million by 1998.

Nygård is a habitual visionary whose instincts have led to remarkable success. So when Peter Nygård decided to invest in a custom-designed drive to push the technology envelope beyond paper and scissors and into hi-tech computer CAD/CAM technology, it's no wonder the decision was implemented with zeal by Nygård's senior managers.

The first try, a ten-million-dollar

Nygård and his daughter Bianca, the namesake of the Bianca Nygård contemporary career dressing line.

computer platform cobbled together between 1981 and 1992 did not work well. Sometimes visionaries are just a step too far ahead of the pack; the technology had not yet caught up to what Nygård felt it should ultimately be able to do. The second try, at $30 million, code-named NS2000, is working brilliantly, achieving computerization of the company right down to the total elimination of paper in 1998 as the medium of internal communication at Nygård International, and as far as using computer-controlled techniques to cut cloth, cutting fabric waste to 2 per cent from the 12 per cent that's wasted when material is cut by hand. That's a 10-per cent saving that can mean a good deal in the highly competitive international garment trade, especially when costs at the Nygård Canadian production facilities in Toronto, Montreal and Winnipeg must measure up—or down—to those in countries like China and Indonesia, where labour costs are considerably less. And because the unique CAD/CAM system also incorporates a process called A.R.T.S. 2 (automatic reorder to sale), which keeps a tight rein on production using an

inventory replacement method that supplies retailers on a just-in-time basis. In 1997 alone, some ten million dollars was saved through improved inventory control and product forecasting.

But business-building is not Peter

Nygård's only passion. He has been the North American Yachting Champion and a member of Canada's Olympic yachting team. His early years of hard work gave him keen awareness that not everyone is born to success, so he established the Nygård Endowment Fund at his University of North Dakota alma mater. He maintains close interests with the Juvenile Diabetes Foundation, and in 1995, threw the support of his fashion empire behind breast cancer awareness and prevention, continuing to be a major fundraiser through the annual "Magical Night of Fashion" gala in Winnipeg. Nygård has become the top contributor to the Misericordia General Hospital Foundation.

In his ancestral homeland, his "Finland Foundation" is being set up to honour the defense of Finland during the Winter War of 1939. And from Nygård Cay in the Bahamas, he plays a leading role as a conservationist, working to preserve and protect the oceans and coral reefs of the Bahamas. "Peter Nygård is without a doubt a nature lover." ■

Peter Nygård at one of his shows.

Centra Gas Manitoba Inc.

Christmas Eve of 1883 was brighter than any that the people in the small Prairie settlement of Winnipeg had seen before. That was the night the gas lights were turned on for the first time, fuelled with gas manufactured from coal and pumped through pipes of hollowed-out tree trunks laid along Winnipeg's major roads.

The technology used to deliver gas has gone from tree trunks in 1883 to a vast network of steel and plastic pipes that now deliver clean-burning natural gas to serve the energy needs of industry and homes in Manitoba. The company that began service that night has come a long way too.

Originally called the Manitoba Electric and Gas Light Company, the company remained comparatively small until 1958 when the new TransCanada Pipeline first delivered natural gas to Manitoba from the rich gas fields of Alberta. This direct access to natural gas fuelled quick growth for a number of gas distribution companies in Manitoba and that was followed by a series of mergers culminating in the formation of a single Manitoba natural gas utility.

Employing innovative technologies will help Centra reach many new customers in the years ahead.

Westcoast Energy purchased the company in 1990 and renamed it Centra Gas Manitoba Inc. in January of 1991. Westcoast Energy is an integrated energy company based in Vancouver. It ranks in the top 50 publicly traded Canadian corporations in terms of assets. The efficiencies and cost savings created by Centra's affiliation with Westcoast are a benefit that is passed on to Manitoba home and business owners.

Today, the more than 650 employees of Centra Gas serve 235,000 customers in approximately 100 communities across Manitoba. Centra delivers natural gas to homes and businesses through a system of more than 6,000 kilometres of pipelines.

Natural gas is the preferred choice of many consumers because it cuts energy costs to almost half those of electric heat or a third those of conventional fuel oil. In a climate where winter temperatures can routinely plunge to minus 30 degrees Celsius for weeks at a time, a dependable supply of heating fuel is something Manitobans know they can count on from Centra Gas.

Centra's mission is to improve the quality of life of Manitobans by providing outstanding value and superior service. The company offers a cost-efficient, clean-burning, environmentally sound energy choice. Natural gas is ideal for home heating, water heating, cooking, swimming pool heaters, barbecues and even patio lamps.

Centra is working aggressively to bring natural gas service to more rural agricultural areas which are not yet served by natural gas. A stable supply of low-cost energy will allow these communities to process more agricultural products locally, spurring further economic development. The company's 1995 expansion to 14 rural Manitoba communities demonstrated its willingness to work with federal, provincial and local officials to extend natural gas service. In the years ahead, innovative techniques will allow Centra to focus on delivering natural gas to an increasing number of rural areas in southern Manitoba.

In all the areas it serves, Centra Gas provides basic customer service with 100 service people available on 24-hour

Manitobans benefit from the expertise of Centra's customer service staff 24-hours a day.

emergency response, year round. Residential customers receive no-charge labour service, with problem diagnosis and repairs made with only the cost of replacement parts billed on the customer's monthly statement. But Centra Gas is more than just a reliable provider of clean, cost-efficient, safe energy services; the company and its employees are active participants in the communities they serve.

The company provides financial support for education, health and welfare and cultural and sport activities. In recent years, Centra has made significant contributions to the United Way in Winnipeg, the Royal Winnipeg Ballet, the Children's Hospital Foundation and the 1997 Canada Summer Games in Brandon.

The company regularly participates in rural fairs and parades, and steps in when there is a need for help in sadder circumstances. The record flood of 1997 in southern Manitoba saw the Red Cross and the Salvation Army's efforts bolstered by substantial donations to each organization, while Centra employees spearheaded nationwide fundraising for flood victims and were among the army of civilian Manitobans who helped sandbag threatened homes and communities.

Operation PAL (for Public Alert) began in 1995 as a way Centra employees could assist people in the communities they serve by using their mobile communications capabilities in emergency situations. Centra employees keep alert for emergency or potential criminal situations that require assistance and use the company's communication systems to get help fast.

Centra's Educator's Program, "Natural Gas in Canada," a support package for elementary school teachers to help educate youngsters about natural gas, has been recognized by several gas industry associations for its outstanding quality. More than a thousand of these educational kits have been delivered to Manitoba elementary schools.

Centra's head office is located in downtown Winnipeg. Centra is one of Manitoba's top 15 private-sector employers.

Centra is also committed to excellence, leadership and stewardship in protecting the environment. In 1996, the company instituted an ongoing Environmental Audit for all company facilities. The audit is another example of the commitment Centra Gas holds for the communities it serves.

Centra is committed to delivering quality service to all customers, to helping smaller Manitoba communities grow and prosper and to contributing to the social and cultural fabric of the communities it serves. Through these commitments, Centra Gas aims to not only serve, but also to help improve the quality of life in communities in which it does business. ■

Through telephone and computer networks, Centra's natural gas traders secure adequate supplies at the lowest possible price.

Monsanto

Monsanto began as a small company in 1901, a saccharin-manufacturing enterprise, founded by a high school dropout named John F. Queeny and given his wife's maiden name. Started with faith, hope and 5,000 dollars, it grew into a fast-moving, competitive, technology-driven, international giant, in chemistry and the life sciences.

In 1997, Monsanto became two, with a new company, Solutia, designed to function as an applied chemistry company, and the company which retains the original name moving to concentrate wholly on life sciences: linking the previously separate worlds of agriculture, nutrition, and consumer products, pharma, health and wellness and sustainability into an interconnected whole.

And Monsanto, the life sciences company with a commitment to provide better food, better health and better nutrition for all people, has defined and adopted a new set of values for business, a set of five themes that interconnect together as well.

Operational Excellence addresses the need to continue to find ways to do things better—ways in which the company can be flexible and reactive to customers' needs, can anticipate what will be needed in our world in the future, and be innovative in fulfilling those needs.

Globalization summarizes the need to decentralize responsibility and initiative, taking it throughout the world, because each culture, each people, each part of the world is valued for what it can contribute to innovation.

Growth is about taking risks, and not fearing failure, about trying new things to enable the discovery of the really big ideas, while the company continues to strive for excellence in the things it is already doing.

Sustainability recognizes that the resources and people of this world are finite, and that any business decision must consider the effect it will have on all of us and our children. The products we make must not use up all of a natural resource, or, worse, contaminate what is left behind.

Photo ©Michael Darter.

Photo by Sally Mayman. ©Tony Stone Images.

Culture means the working environment must be one of trust, honesty, openness, imagination, initiative and care, in order for Monsanto to be healthy, to grow and to prosper.

Monsanto is made up of business sectors, the organizations where products and services are developed, made and sold. Three of the sectors, Agricultural, Nutrition & Consumer Products and Pharmaceutical, are built around currently strong ongoing operations. Two others, Health & Wellness and Sustainable Development, pursue emerging opportunities.

The Agricultural Sector broadens and redefines agricultural niches by integrating the former Crop Protection, Ceregen and Protiva business units. Its objective is to transform the way food and fibre are produced everywhere in the world. By bringing foundation technologies, like herbicide use and breeding techniques, together with advanced biotechnology, the Agricultural Sector positions itself to provide abundant nutrition for the world's rapidly growing population.

In Manitoba, Monsanto's Winnipeg office houses the people who take care of the Western Canada agricultural component in the company.

And in Morden, Manitoba, the Monsanto plant started up in April 1994, producing surfactant-based, granular Roundup herbicide. Morden currently produces three different formulations that are sold in Canada, Asia Pacific and Latin America. Monsanto invented Roundup back in 1970, and it's now the world's leading multi-purpose, non-selective agricultural and industrial herbicide.

Roundup is just one of Monsanto's major products, and agricultural pesticides and herbicides only part of what the company does. People with insomnia can take Ambien, as a short-term treatment. Calan and Covera-HS calcium blockers help treat chest pain and hypertension. Daypro treats osteoarthritis and rheumatoid arthritis. Nutrasweet sweetens coffee, tea and hundreds of sugar-free food products. Bollgard, insect-protected, biotechnologically developed, cotton protects itself against specific insect pests, and Newleaf potatoes, developed similarly, protect themselves against the Colorado flea beetle.

Monsanto is dedicated to the development of breakthrough products like these—products that link agriculture, food and medicine, that create insect-resistant crops or find innovative treatments for life-threatening diseases.

And Monsanto's future is all about hope: fulfilling people's hopes—for environmentally sustainable solutions, and for a healthier planet. ■

Unisys-Winnipeg

Earning customer confidence in the highly competitive world of technology is a daunting performance task. For employees of Unisys-Winnipeg, Canada, it is the only way to conduct business.

During 20 years of operations, Winnipeg has received numerous business and community awards for performance and service. One of Winnipeg's proudest moments was when it received the highly coveted *Chairman's Total Quality Award* in 1995.

Unisys-Winnipeg manufacturing facility on Burmac Road, just off Lagimodiere Blvd.

Open Storage Module—Modular design allows user to easily increase storage for future growth.

"The performance criteria for this prestigious award are the same as those used for the Malcolm Baldridge Quality Award, which stresses leadership, planning, human resource development, process quality and customer satisfaction," says Tom Hartberger, Unisys-Winnipeg General Manager. "Based on rigorous audits, we were selected for our ability to exceed customer expectations."

This very judgment has been validated again and again by customers who also have recognized Unisys-Winnipeg's capability and performance.

Technology market leader Sun Microsystems has integrated Winnipeg's storage products into its own product line. In 1996, Sun rated Unisys-Winnipeg a *"Best in Class"* Supplier. In 1997, for the fifth consecutive year, Winnipeg was ranked the highest in customer achievement by customers from around the world, reported an independent customer satisfaction study.

The more than 300 employees at Unisys-Winnipeg stand for superior quality and teamwork. Emphasis within this technology-driven business is on employee involvement, continuous learning and the development of skills.

"For two decades, we provided great opportunities for new graduates with degrees in technology, engineering and business," points out Hartberger. "Our people produce and deliver cost competitive storage solutions and products to a worldwide market. We are proud to share that in Manitoba, Unisys-Winnipeg is known as a great place to advance professional skills."

Winnipeg produces and exports high-capacity computer disk systems and printed circuit boards for clients in transportation, financial services, government agencies, health care and telecommunications. Since 1976, the Winnipeg facility has exported over $2 billion of advanced computer storage products globally.

Unisys's technology strategy is to move the Windows NT operating system into the mission-critical enterprise (main frame) market. As this continues to unfold, there will be greater storage requirements to support the demand for information access.

"We see adding NT servers for the open enterprise NT market creating a lot of opportunity," says Hartberger. "We produce state-of-the-art disk enclosures that can be used across multiple hardware platforms and multiple operating systems. In essence, this cutting edge storage technology enables customers to link data storage to a network rather than a server, thus allowing the network to more efficiently process information.

"For example, a county registry of deeds installed a network attached storage subsystem for storing and managing land titles. As a result, the deeds and land record documents are available for viewing on the World Wide Web."

Approximately 50 per cent of Winnipeg's production supports Original Equipment Manufacturer (OEM) business partners. "We perform a number of full-service manufacturing activities for key technology leaders," says Hartberger. "We are experts in the areas of system integration and test, surface mount printed circuit assembly and test and mechanical and electrical design."

State-of-the-art electronic assembly, test equipment, ISO 9000 certified processes, and advance production practices are all housed within the 100,000-square-foot plant located off Lagimodiere Boulevard, just south of the Royal Canadian Mint.

"We have been very successful in deploying the technologies and developing the expertise to support business partners in our expanding contract manufacturing business," says Hartberger. "We also are proud to be the first operation in Canada to achieve ISO 9000 certification, which established, early on, that our processes meet the standard for world-

wide product quality."

The Unisys legacy of technological innovation and quality, instilled within Winnipeg's operating culture, extends for greater than 100 years.

In 1986, two long-established data processing leaders, Burroughs Business Machines and Sperry Univac, merged. The new company was called Unisys, a condensation of "United Information Systems."

Unisys, a $6.7-billion technology solution business in 1997, employs 30,000 people worldwide to deliver enterprise and network solutions serving the leading airlines, telecommunications, banking and financial services, companies and government markets.

Winnipeg employees earn customer confidence by delivering innovative solutions and being dedicated to the customer's success. As one of Winnipeg's

Quality-oriented processes ensure high customer satisfaction.

customers put it, "Thank you! The team overall has been very responsive . . . . Ownership and accountability are constantly in the forefront." ■

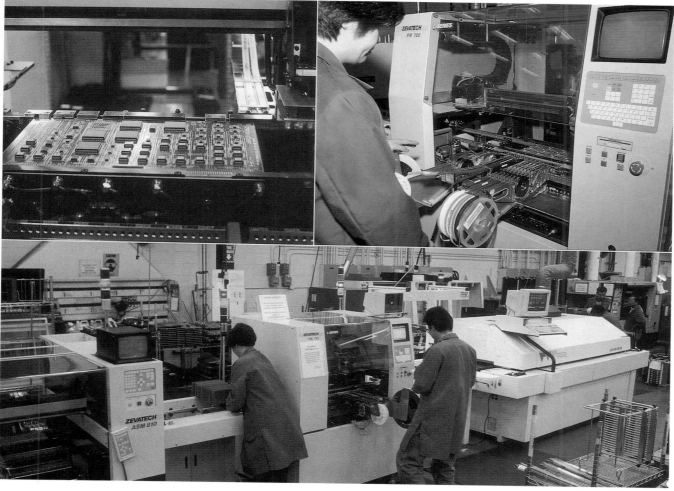

Surface mount automated assembly process for printed circuit assemblies.

Manitoba Hydro

It's a utility that somehow seems at odds with being on the prairies, but Manitoba Hydro is, in fact, one of Canada's largest exporters of hydro-generated electricity.

Water from more than one-million square kilometres, stretching from the Canadian Rockies almost to Lake Superior, eventually empties into Lake Winnipeg, the source of the mighty Nelson River. There, 75 per cent of the province's electrical supply is produced by five hydroelectric generating stations. The remainder is supplied by seven

The Limestone Generating Station on the Nelson River is Manitoba Hydro's largest generating station of 1,294 megawatts.

smaller stations on the Laurie, Saskatchewan and Winnipeg rivers. The corporation also has two thermal generating stations located in Brandon and Selkirk and 12 diesel sites in isolated northern locations.

Manitoba Hydro, a provincial Crown Corporation, generates, on average, 30 billion kilowatt-hours of electricity annually. Just less than one third is sold to the United States, primarily to Minnesota and North Dakota. It is partly due to these export sales that the utility's 391,401 Manitoba customers benefit from one of the lowest rate structures in North America.

The low rate structure coupled with highly reliable service has also provided Manitoba Hydro's industrial and commercial customers with the edge to compete in the global marketplace. Additional benefits of increased customer choice and value-added service is being offered through various energy efficiency programs and innovative rate options.

Manitoba Hydro's customer base covers most of the province, except for the central portion of Winnipeg, which is served by Winnipeg Hydro. It has over 80 years of experience in the development and use of hydroelectric power. And, over the past 25 years, the corporation has established itself as a world leader in high-voltage direct current (HVDC) technology, by operating the world's first major HVDC transmission system. As well, the utility has succeeded in building some of the most technically advanced hydroelectric generating stations in the world in a very challenging northern climate.

While the abundance of low-cost, renewable energy has improved the lives of many Manitobans, Manitoba Hydro's operations have caused some adverse environmental and socio-economic impacts for others. In that regard, settlement agreements with communities impacted by hydro developments continue to be a high priority for the corporation. Successful negotiations have concluded with some of the communities and settlement initiatives are continuing with the remainder.

Manitoba Hydro is also committed to practising sustainable development. The corporation has made progress in integrating economic, technical and environmental

Manitoba Hydro conducts a series of fish monitoring programs that examines fish populations, distribution, habitat and migration, upstream and downstream of generating stations, such as Limestone on the Nelson River.

factors in its decisions. It is working hard to ensure its activities have a minimal impact on fish, birds and wildlife which inhabit the waterways and neighbouring environs, as well as on the quality of the air, land and water. Also, the utility is working towards reducing the peak demand for electricity by 221 megawatts by the fiscal year 2012. This is being achieved through Power Smart programs which identify energy efficient products and provide guidelines on ways to reduce electricity consumption.

Headquartered in Winnipeg, Manitoba Hydro is one of the province's largest employers with 3,926 staff in 77 offices around the province. With assets exceeding $7 billion, it is the fourth largest electrical utility in Canada. ■

CanWest Global Communications Corp.

CanWest Global Communications Corp. has been called the "Cinderella story" of the television industry, having risen from a single station on the Prairies to become Canada's most profitable broadcaster.

The story began when a small border-town TV station in Pembina, North Dakota, which had been purchased by a consortium led by Winnipeg businessman I.H. Asper, was dismantled and trucked lock, stock and barrel to Winnipeg, where on Labour Day 1975, the new station—CKND-TV—broadcast its first show—*The Jerry Lewis Telethon*.

Today, CKND-TV is one of eight TV stations owned and operated by CanWest Global across Canada. Previously known as U.TV in Vancouver, STV-Regina, STV-Saskatoon, The Global Television Network in Ontario, MITV in Atlantic Canada and CKMI in Quebec, the Canadian operations are now collectively known as The Global Television Network.

CanWest Global Executive Chairman I.H. Asper (left) with recently appointed President and CEO, Peter Viner.

such as *Traders, Jake and The Kid, The Outer Limits, NYPD Blue* and *Seinfeld*—to be seen in Alberta on WIC's Calgary and Edmonton stations, allowing the Global Television Network to reach approximately 88 per cent of English-speaking Canada.

It's a success story that's been repeated several times, only farther afield. In 1991, CanWest purchased New Zealand's TV3, which under CanWest management has emerged from receivership to be a dynamic player in the market, reaching 96 per cent of that nation's 3.5 million people. In 1997, TV3 went to air with a second New Zealand network, TV4, which focuses on a youth-oriented audience. Also in 1997, CanWest reached an agreement to acquire MORE FM, New Zealand's top rated commercial radio network.

In 1992, CanWest turned its attention to Australia's Network TEN, acquiring a 57.5 per cent economic interest and a 15 per cent voting interest. Like TV3, TEN had also been in receivership, but today, Network TEN is the second most profitable television network in Australia.

Back home in Canada, CanWest moved into the field of specialty cable television, winning a license for Prime TV, a network geared to an over-50 audience. It launched in October, 1997. And in the Fall of 1998, CanWest will launch TV3 Ireland in Dublin.

To ensure the ongoing financial flexibility to continue such growth, CanWest found it necessary to move into the international capital markets. As such, it completed a public offering of five-million non-voting shares on the New York Stock Exchange in June 1996.

CanWest's touch has literally been golden over the years:
• Combined revenue grew to $835 million in fiscal 1997 from $126 million in 1987, when it broadcast only in Canada.
• Net earnings have skyrocketed to more than $141 million in 1997 from $6.4 million in 1987.
• Shareholders who invested $1,000 in 1991 found their investment worth $22,007 in early 1997.

For Izzy Asper, there's never been any reason why he couldn't succeed in his own hometown, away from Toronto, the industry's perceived centre of power. If Sam Walton could build his Wal-Mart empire from Bentonville, Arkansas, Asper felt he could do the same in Winnipeg. His daughter, Gail, and sons, Leonard and David, all hold senior management positions in the business, although the day-to-day running of the company has expanded beyond the family. In July 1997, Peter D. Viner, former Chief Executive of Network TEN Australia, was named President and CEO of CanWest Global Communications Corp., succeeding Mr. Asper who assumed the new role of Executive Chairman of the Board.

"Peter's magic in transforming Network TEN, in just four short years, from an operation in total disarray to Australia's second most profitable network, is truly remarkable," says Mr. Asper. "His lead-by-example management style has earned him the kudos of our industry worldwide and I have every confidence that he is the right person to successfully lead CanWest into the new millennium." ∎

The new, state-of-the-art headquarters and studio complex of Network TEN in Sydney, Australia.

For company founder I.H. (Izzy) Asper, it's basically the realization of a dream come true to provide a third national voice in Canada. The Global Television Network reaches 78 per cent of the country's English-speaking market, but its influence goes beyond that. An agreement with Western International Communications (WIC) allows CanWest programming—shows

Manitoba Telecom Services

MTS has been a vital part of Manitoba since 1908 when its forerunner, Manitoba Government Telephones, was founded as a provincial Crown Corporation with the mandate to provide universal, affordable telephone service to Manitobans.

MTS has followed that mandate ever since, bringing dial service to all its users in 1926–making Winnipeg the

During 1997's Red River Flood, Manitoba military and emergency organizations relied on MTS Mobility's FleetNet, an enhanced two-way radio system.

MTS's customer care centre showcases the latest advances in call centre technolgy.

first Canadian city to enjoy what was then leading-edge technology. In 1982, MTS was the first telephone company in North America to offer digital voice messaging.

By 1996, switching systems in the entire province were converted to digital technology. MTS had developed one of the most advanced, cost-efficient networks in North America offering the widest cellular coverage in the province and serving two-thirds of the entire cellular market. Now, the company was also well-positioned for the future.

In early 1997, MTS became a publicly-traded company whose initials now stand for Manitoba Telecom Services. The new company remains at the crest of the technological wave, with on-line products, including Sympatico, the largest commercial Internet services provider in Manitoba.

Through its majority share in ViewCall Canada Inc., MTS is developing content for the next generation of Internet direct access tools, like TV set boxes and telephone lines, so users can access the Internet without a computer. Licensed to develop and market the next evolution of cellular technology, the PCS (Personal Communications Services) phone, MTS will be able to provide high-clarity phone communication, enhanced security and mobility and the ability to e-mail, fax and page, in a single package with far more talk and stand-by time than is available with the current generation of cellular phones.

MTS has partnered with the Manitoba government and the city of Winnipeg on the Manitoba Call Centre Team, attracting more than 70 businesses to Manitoba for call centre operations. MTS also joined forces with IBM in 1996, to jointly develop

and market new technologies for the call centre marketplace.

Today, MTS employs more than 3,000 people in cities and towns throughout Manitoba, and is a member of the Stentor alliance of Canada's leading telecommunications providers. In its home province, MTS plays a strong supportive role in sports, community and cultural events, and is the fourth largest contributor (in concert with its employees) to Manitoba's United Way Campaign. The MTS Pioneers are one of the largest and most active volunteer organizations in the province. MTS is proud to be a major corporate sponsor of the 1999 Pan Am Games to be held in Winnipeg.

The company has never lost sight of its original mandate: Manitobans continue to receive top-quality telecommunications service, at costs among the lowest in Canada. ■

Alpha Power Technologies

Alpha Power Technologies, APT (a division of Vansco Electronics Ltd.) provides world leading solutions for Electrical Power Utilities. As Ed Van Humbeck, President of Vansco Electronics Ltd., says, "It made perfect sense for us to create APT. There was already a strong base of electrical power technology in the province. Manitoba Hydro, a major North American utility in generation and export of power, was a pioneer in High Voltage DC transmission. The University of Manitoba had long been recognized for its strong capability in power transmission and distribution

fore created as a division of Vansco Electronics. APT's mission is to design and produce products which integrate and automate the processes of control, data acquisition, information handling and communications for Electrical Power Utilities. Its current products include a series of relays for line and transformer protection, and a flexible multifunctional recording system which monitors power quality and disturbances on transmission and distribution lines. All of these systems are designed to be interconnected. For instance, a power station or a switch yard can be remotely monitored and, if

Sophisticated electromagnetic compatibility test systems ensure that emissions and susceptibility comply with international standards.

Testing the T-Pro Relay on a digital simulator at RTDS Technologies Inc. in Winnipeg.

technology. The HVDC Research Centre was a leading player in digital simulators for power systems. Teshmont Consultants was providing design and consulting to electrical utilities around the world. Pauwels Canada was shipping megawatt transformers internationally. It seemed to be a natural extension to add our exceptional engineering and manufacturing ability to this strong local infrastructure in Power Engineering."

Alpha Power Technologies was there-

necessary, relay settings can be changed without having to go there.

With deregulation and the constant pressure to push systems harder and closer to their design limits, electrical power utilities need increasingly sophisticated protection, control and analysis systems. Growing demand and competitive pressures are driving the need for increased supply of more reliable power at a reduced cost. At the same time, growth in transmission facilities is limited by cost

and environmental constraints. APT is committed to helping its customers meet the challenge of optimizing the delivery of reliable electrical power. To that end, its staff have developed the following simple philosophy:

• We believe our equipment should adapt to (customers') requirements, not the other way around.

• We believe in creating equipment that is easy to use and highly flexible.

• We believe that monitoring, protection and control tools must be able to communicate with each other, no matter what manufacturer has supplied them.

• We believe in bringing information to where it's needed, in the most appropriate form, with a minimum of effort from the user.

APT has enjoyed an ISO 9001 registered quality system since 1995, and its first transmission line monitoring system has been producing reliable data since its installation in 1988. To make sure it fully understands customer needs, APT is supporting an Internet user group. "This way we can learn from customers' questions and suggestions," says Van Humbeck. "It helps us stay in tune with their expanding expectations." ■

Linnet Geomatics International Inc.

Tying together the growing need for integrated resource management with the day-to-day operations of government and business organizations represents a significant challenge as we move into the next millennium. Linnet Geomatics International Inc. is a business solutions developer that is introducing

IDG Stanley Inc. and SNC◆Lavalin Inc.

Today, LGI has restructured its approach to doing business around a packaged product model. By focusing on the natural resource management, agriculture and environment sectors, LGI is able to leverage its experience through the development of a family of products that

integrating on-farm planning with the producer together with precision farming, crop inputs sales, harvested product logistics and commodity risk management through the use of the latest information on local growing areas with historic weather patterns, crop history databases and specific business objectives. As LGI's most mature product environment, *Woodlands-The System*™ provides woodland managers and governments with the capability to plan environmentally friendly harvest plans and link these plans to contract resource allocation, harvested product scaling and performance and regulatory objective tracking.

LGI has also been an innovator in the implementation of development partnerships with key clients that enable them to participate in system design and benefit with downstream royalty payments. Designed from the outset as products, LGI's "The System" family provides optimum business value with minimum risk to the development partner and all future product customers. One example of this approach capitalized on The Nature Conservancy's expertise in the management of rare, threatened and endangered ecosystems to inspire core technologies that form the foundation of several LGI products. These technologies are being rolled out to The Nature Conservancy's 90 offices throughout the Americas during 1998.

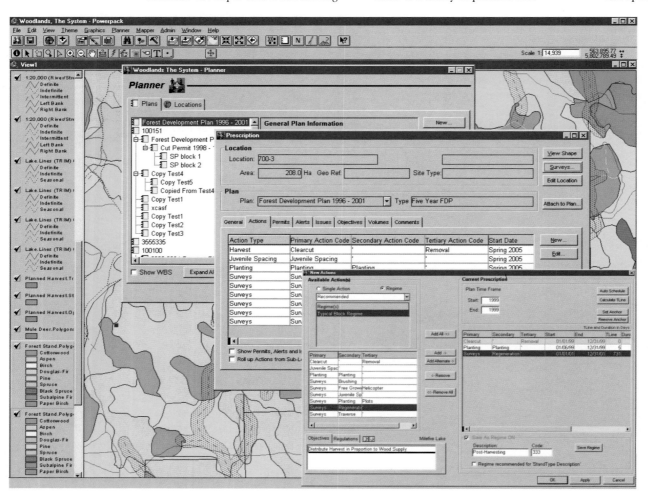

new Geographic Information System-based computer technology to deliver business value for its clients. The company's mission statement embodies its bottom-line focus: "to improve our client's performance by delivering geomatics solutions on time and on budget."

Founded in Winnipeg in 1988, LGI operated throughout its first decade as a custom information systems developer working closely with its clients to develop the applications, programs and GIS databases needed to address their increasingly complex land-based business needs. LGI is a joint venture of senior management,

encompass the best practices in each industry within a highly configurable enterprise system. LGI's three software solutions—*Woodlands - The System*™, *Croplands - The System*™ and *Watershed - The System*™—encompass specific modules that address a hierarchy of business needs.

Local conservation districts can use *Watershed - The System*™ to carry out soil and water conservation planning by developing landscape models to define risk areas, target possible remediation measures and strengthen their project infrastructure management. *Croplands-The System*™ provides an environment for

Bringing international experience from clients as far-flung as the United States, the United Kingdom, Russia, Kenya, Chile, Egypt, Mexico, Venezuela and Argentina, more than 65 highly skilled LGI personnel provide product implementation, support and training on all LGI products. LGI also delivers a number of custom GIS data conversion and integration services on behalf of its clients worldwide. ■

City of Winnipeg

As the waters of the Red River rose and the Flood of the Century hit hard, the eyes of the nation focused on Winnipeg. What they saw was a city that pulled together, a city that by its very nature proved to be resiliant and vibrant. As the call for help went out, volunteers responded—giving 75,000 hours of their time and slinging more than 6.5 million sandbags. The flood of 1997 brought home some important lessons—especially how citizens want access to information about what's happening at City Hall. At a time when the city is embracing a dynamic culture of change, this lesson is one well-learned.

In 1997, the City of Winnipeg underwent a complete restructuring of its civic government, driven by the need to become more affordable and responsive to the community. The board of commissioners was replaced with a chief administrative officer model. An open budget process was introduced in which an ongoing two-year budget forecast now is in place. That, coupled with monthly financial reports, has resulted in enhanced fiscal accountability. Alternative methods of service delivery, such as contracting out and special operating agencies, are also aimed at reducing costs.

As Winnipeg heads into the new millenium, the message Winnipeggers have given is they want a safer city, sound infrastructure, economic opportunities and jobs, responsive and affordable government and Aboriginal communities that are full partners in the city's success. These priorities demand a focused, integrated and targeted approach. The city's role has been and will continue to be to provide the leadership and direction to meet these expectations.

To enhance urban safety, the city has introduced community policing, in which foot patrols now walk the streets of some 20 neighbourhoods. Other programs include late-night bus service in which passengers can get off between regular stops.

Other major initiatives will include the revitalization of Winnipeg's Main Street,

Winnipeg skyline from the Forks.

the heart of downtown and an historical focal point. The renewal strategy focuses on housing, streetscaping, commercial and cultural development, social, health and wellness programs and the Neeginan project. Neeginan, Cree for "Our Place," will be an Aboriginal village, comprising a round house or spiritual and cultural centre, a multi-purpose centre, hall of justice, aboriginal centre, art gallery and centre of excellence for children's well-being. Plans are also underway for a major revitalization of Portage Avenue.

The city's future also depends on economic development. By participating in Team Canada trade missions and in mid-continent trade corridor summits, Winnipeg has strengthened its ties with potential trading partners. It is positioning itself to become a transportation and distribution hub for North America, capitalizing on the 24-hour status of Winnipeg International Airport.

Winnipeg also enjoys the economic spinoffs and the profile of playing host to such events as the Pan American Games, Grey Cup, World Junior Hockey Championship, Labatt Brier and Capital Cities Conference. ■

Portage Avenue looking East.

14

Business & Finance

Photo by Mike Grandmaison.

Winnipeg Chamber of Commerce

The Winnipeg Chamber of Commerce is at the hub of business in Winnipeg, speaking out on policy issues, supporting initiatives that enhance the quality of life in the community and fostering an environment in which businesses, small or large, can prosper.

Incorporated as the Winnipeg Board of Trade by an act of the Provincial Legislature in March 1873, The Chamber is older than the City of Winnipeg by six months. While it has been expressed in many ways over the years, the mission of The Chamber has continuously been to "foster an environment in which

Lake Winnipeg to the City of Winnipeg. Their efforts continue today to reinforce Winnipeg's role as a major transportation and distribution hub. A key to that plan is The Winnipeg International Airport, long recognized as an economic jewel with its central location and 24-hour operation. The Chamber successfully lobbied the Province and the City to ensure that land use surrounding the airport is compatible with its around-the-clock operation. The Chamber also provided the leadership for transfer of the airport from federal hands to community management, a process completed in early 1997. Current

downtown revitalization and transportation planning, all with a view to fostering a positive business climate. On more than one occasion, The Chamber has been instrumental in bringing the community together to discuss what is wanted for the future of the City. A myriad of other issues, from government debt/deficit reduction, workers' compensation rates and labour legislation reform to sustainable development, provincial tax policy and free trade, have also been tackled by The Chamber.

The Chamber is Winnipeg's only business organization open to any and all businesses. Its more than 1,250 member-companies, representing 65,000 employees, reflect a diverse range of businesses from small, home-based enterprises and mom-and-pop operations to Winnipeg's largest employers. However, it mirrors the City's overall business community with two-thirds of its members being small businesses with 10 or fewer employees.

The success of The Chamber largely depends on the involvement of nearly 300 active members who dedicate their time and expertise on more than 20 Chamber committees. In addition to committees dealing with policy issues, there are other committees with a focus on membership activities or business/community development. The Chamber aims to create a competitive advantage for its members through various avenues, and one of those is helping members deal with technology. Each year, a one-day conference is held that looks at how business can use information technology to improve everything from customer service to the bottom line. In a global marketplace, The Chamber plays a key role in encouraging more businesses to become export-ready. It puts local business people in touch with visiting dignitaries from all over Europe, Asia and the Americas. In mid-1997, it signed a Memorandum of Understanding with the Greater Dallas Chamber of Commerce to promote north-south trade.

Business/education partnerships have proven effective in preparing youth for the transition to work. With the support

On location during The Chamber's weekly radio show.

Winnipeg business can prosper." For 125 years, The Winnipeg Chamber of Commerce has served as the voice of business, ensuring that the business perspective is heard on the issues of the day.

Transportation was one of the earliest, and has been one of the most active, long-term interests of The Chamber. Early records document Chamber efforts to influence rail transportation and the building of the St. Andrew's Lock so that the Red River would be navigable from

Chamber initiatives include promoting Winnipeg as the northern terminus of the Mid-Continent Trade Corridor, a trade and transportation corridor stretching from Winnipeg through Kansas City and Dallas in the U.S. to Monterey and Guadalajara, Mexico, in the south.

Civic issues also dominate The Chamber agenda. The Chamber has been a constant and fervent voice on issues like tax and spending reforms, liberalized Sunday shopping, economic development,

1997-98 Chair of the Board, Carol-Ann Borody, meets with Premier Gary Filmon at the Legislature.

guest speakers from across the country. The Chamber also publishes its own full-colour business magazine as a member service, and a biweekly newsletter is faxed out to members telling of Chamber events, lobbying activities and programs. And that's not all. The Chamber hosts The Voice of Winnipeg Business, a one-hour radio show, heard Saturday mornings on AM 1290 Talk Radio.

Membership also has other privileges, including the use of The Chamber Business Centre's private dining facilities and meeting rooms with seating for 2 to 250, located on the sixth floor of downtown's historic Grain Exchange Building. Additional benefits include a group insurance program for companies with fewer than 25 employees, a long-distance telephone savings plan, a credit card merchant-rate discount program and a listing in the annual Membership Directory and Buyer's Guide. The Chamber continually strives to increase the value of membership through enhanced service to its member companies, and as a leader in promoting a prosperous business community within a vibrant city. ■

of Manitoba Education & Training and a local school division, The Chamber has been successful in introducing the use of portfolios, which help students demonstrate marketable skills to potential employers. On the education and training front, The Chamber has also played a role in addressing labour market gaps. Since 1982, The Chamber-sponsored Industrial Training Centre has been training employment disadvantaged individuals in metal trades, and at the same time responding to a demand from the manufacturing industry for qualified entry level workers. The Chamber also reaches out to the Winnipeg community at large, as a founding member of the United Way, and as a sponsor of Crime Stoppers, a cash reward program for anonymous tips leading to arrests in any unsolved crimes.

In today's competitive marketplace, face-to-face, business-to-business communication is essential if one is to keep on top of what's happening and to develop a profile in the business community. The Chamber works hard to provide opportunities for its members to network and

learn through its After Business trade shows, VIP breakfasts and monthly membership luncheons, featuring prominent

An international trade development event in The Chamber's private member dining and meeting room facility.

Manitoba Public Insurance

Manitoba Public Insurance (MPI) is about much more than selling vehicle insurance to all Manitoba motorists. As a public insurance company, it's also about protecting Manitobans from the human and economic costs of vehicle collisions—that includes selling Manitobans on changes in their driving behavior. Ultimately, however, it's about giving Manitobans the best possible protection for the lowest possible cost.

MPI is recognized as an industry leader and innovator. In 1995, it was the first insurance company in Canada to move from using the purchase price for a vehicle in setting its rates to using CLEAR (the Canadian Loss Experience Automobile Rating system).

Autopac premiums now more adequately reflect risk. For each make and model, CLEAR takes into account such factors as repair costs, how often the vehicle is stolen or involved in a collision, personal injury records, and safety and anti-theft features. The goal is to encourage Manitobans to think critically about the vehicles they purchase and to provide

As a public insurance company, MPI's mission is to protect Manitobans from the human and economic costs of vehicle collisions.

manufacturers with an incentive to consider changes which will guarantee both greater safety and reduced insurance costs.

MPI firmly believes drivers with good records, who choose vehicles with less risk and lower repair costs, should pay the lowest possible Autopac premiums, given where and how they use their vehicles. It also believes drivers with poor records, who drive more risky vehicles, should pay more. Therefore, MPI's rates are calculated according to the type of vehicle and the driving record of the owner as well as how and where the vehicle is driven.

The result—according to Runzheimer Canada, an independent management consultant firm—is the most comprehensive vehicle insurance coverage in Canada at some of the lowest rates. That is a tribute to MPI and the corporate values it has stood for, for more than a quarter century. Those values—clearly defined for all Manitobans—are at the centre of everything MPI does.

"Our customers' interests come first.
Our people are encouraged and helped to
*   succeed.*
Our actions are based on trust, respect,
*   appreciation and fairness.*
Excellence and innovation in our work are
*   recognized and rewarded.*
We encourage the involvement of our people
*   and our resources in community affairs.*
We acknowledge our responsibility to exer-
*   cise leadership in our role as a corporate*
*   citizen."*

In keeping with its focus on putting customers' interests first, MPI has introduced a number of major service and product enhancements. In 1994, the corporation

MPI's Personal Injury Protection Plan (PIPP) provides Manitobans injured in vehicle collisions with income protection and unlimited medical and rehabilitation expenses—paid promptly without having to go to court.

introduced its Personal Injury Protection Plan (PIPP) to protect all Manitobans from financial losses caused by automobile injury or death, regardless of who was responsible for the collision and where in Canada or the United States it occurred. PIPP benefits include income protection and unlimited medical and rehabilitation expenses—paid promptly without having to go to court. Without the introduction of PIPP, the average 1997 Autopac policy would have cost an estimated $200 more.

MPI does turn to the courts, however, to protect its customers from the cost of fraud. It actively investigates all suspicious claims. Its Special Investigation Unit, which also helps to detect and recover costs caused by manufacturers' defects, saves Manitobans about $3 million per year. The unit investigates a range of claims, including theft, arson, hit-and-run, as well as comprehensive and bodily injury, and MPI publicizes its success in uncovering fraud to discourage others who might also be tempted to cheat.

A senior Crown attorney has been seconded from the provincial Justice department to ensure MPI-related court cases are prosecuted promptly, and to the full extent of the law. The Crown attorney works with MPI adjusters and investigators to ensure they understand the court process and the rules of evidence. Other insurance companies are looking to MPI as

a leader in this area.

MPI has been first on many fronts, setting standards for others to follow. It's a national leader in the use of recycled parts, not only saving MPI about $7 million per year, but also protecting the environment.

Along with providing the best possible insurance products at the lowest possible cost, MPI is committed to providing the best in customer service.

MPI introduced "plain language" in its customer booklet entitled "Your Guide to Autopac" to make it easier for customers to understand their coverage. It implemented individual renewal dates—four months after customers' birthdates—to spread the renewal process over the entire year and allow its agents to give more personalized service to each customer.

In 1995, MPI introduced Autopac Online, a state-of-the-art computer system, to directly link Manitoba's nearly 400 Autopac brokers with MPI's head office. Autopac Online allows customers to make immediate changes to their policies with no hassle and be issued permanent documents on the spot.

The basic Autopac package—no-fault injury compensation benefits, $200,000 third-part liability coverage, and all-perils coverage—is mandatory for Manitoba-registered vehicles. Many Manitobans supplement their basic policies with optional Autopac coverage. MPI's Special Risk Extension (SRE) division, which operates in the competitive market,

Stressing that 8 out of every 10 collisions are preventable, the province-wide education and enforcement efforts of MPI and its road safety partners encourage drivers to "Be **RoadWise**."

offers more specialized vehicle insurance protection—such as a policy for customers who rent vehicles outside the province.

Since July 1996, MPI's call centre gives Manitobans one centralized telephone number—the Autopac Line—for making claims, arranging appointments, and seeking answers to any questions about their coverage.

But more than just providing the best insurance coverage and service, MPI is striving to prevent the tragedies of traffic collisions before they occur. In 1996, it launched *RoadWise*, a province-wide strategy which unites road safety initiatives in the province under the umbrella of the Manitoba Road Safety Coordinating Committee. Through a combination of education and enforcement, MPI and its *RoadWise* partners stress the role driver attitudes can have in preventing 8 out of every 10 collisions. *RoadWise* uses the principles of social marketing to persuade Manitobans to drive safely.

MPI is also preparing for the future. As part of its preparations for the year 2000, it is looking at how modern technology can increase efficiency, improve customer service, and yet, retain the personal touch. ■

When MPI customers have to make claims, adjusters and estimators in 17 claim centres across the province provide prompt, professional service.

Royal Canadian Mint

Danielle Wetherup, President and Master, The Royal Canadian Mint.

For 90 years, the Royal Canadian Mint has created beautiful, high-quality coins for Canadians and customers around the world. The Mint has two homes, one in Winnipeg and another in Ottawa, where precious metals are refined and collector coins are crafted and their worldwide distribution supported from the imposing, turreted stone building perched on a hill overlooking the Ottawa River. In Winnipeg, a futuristic, glass pyramid rising from its park-like lakeside setting houses the high-speed machinery that produces billions of top quality circulation coins for Canadians and foreign governments every year.

Canada's circulation coins.

The Royal Canadian Mint is an international industry leader in minting. The Mint's reputation for quality, coupled with Canada's international image as an unbiased, fair and democratic nation, are two powerful advantages helping to sustain relationships with established customers and to build relationships with new customers.

This sterling status is built on tradition dating back to 1908, when the Ottawa facility opened as a branch of the British Royal Mint. The new Mint in Ottawa remained a branch of the Royal Mint until 1931, when control passed to Canada and the Mint became an arm of the Department of Finance.

Canada's domestic need for coins grew through the 1960s, and increased demand put a strain on the Ottawa plant. At the same time, opportunities developed to sell Canadian coin-making expertise worldwide, and thereby make a profit for the Canadian government.

In 1969 the government made the Mint a Crown Corporation; the Mint thus gained authority to choose its own business path under an experienced, business-oriented board of directors. The new Crown Corporation wanted to be sure it was never again faced with lack of manufacturing capacity to pursue all the business opportunities available. Planners first considered remodelling the Mint's existing facility in Ottawa, but decided the best solution was a new plant designed specifically for striking coins.

At this time, the government established a policy of decentralizing government departments; Winnipeg began to emerge as a likely candidate for the facility. The Minister of Supply and Services and minister responsible for the Mint during this period was James Richardson, Member of Parliament representing the Winnipeg area. Mr. Richardson was a strong advocate of building the new facility in Winnipeg. One key advantage to the Winnipeg location was its proximity to a supply of nickel from mines in the province of Alberta.

The Winnipeg facility, located on 60.7 hectares (150 acres) of land on Lagimodière Boulevard, is considered one of the world's most modern mints, and can turn out almost three billion coins per year, over 95 coins per second. Over the past 20 years, the Mint has made over 30 billion foreign coins for 60 different countries.

In 1996, the Royal Canadian Mint launched the bimetallic two-dollar coin, the first ever made in Canada, with an inner core and outer ring of different metals. The plant manufactures its own dies, and all auxiliary tooling. Mint engineers in Winnipeg and Ottawa worked together to develop a new locking mechanism linking the two parts. The Mint holds a patent for the mechanism, and, with its production processes modified to produce the two-dollar coin, now offers the technology to worldwide circulation coinage clients.

The foreign circulation coin business brings officials from foreign governments and businesses to Winnipeg, and has helped to give the city an international business profile. Circulation coin launch events are always held here, where the coins are made. Dignitaries including the Minister of Public Works and Government Services, the Minister responsible for the Royal Canadian Mint and the Member of Parliament for the St. Boniface riding,

Winnipeg facility.

where the facility is located, usually attend these events.

The Winnipeg facility of the Royal Canadian Mint has provided approximately 130 permanent, full-time jobs since opening in 1976; among spin-off benefits to the local economy is the employment of shipping and transportation companies with offices in the Winnipeg area to ship Mint products.

The Mint is open to visits from schools and the public and hosts a boutique where Canadian coins may be purchased. The Winnipeg building is designed to offer a unique view of the factory floor and has an elevated tour walkway lined with displays explaining the minting process.

The Royal Canadian Mint believes in giving back to the community, sponsoring cultural organizations such as the Centre Culturel Franco-Manitobain and the Royal Winnipeg Ballet. The Mint entered a team in the 1997 Winnipeg Dragon Boat Race Festival, and supported employees who took time from work to help fight record

flooding in southern Manitoba in the spring of 1997.

The Mint has proven able to adapt quickly to changing circumstances in order to offer clients, both Canadian and foreign, attractive, top-quality products that meet their needs. Throughout the past two decades, metal prices have risen periodically; the Mint has responded by changing the composition of its coins to reduce production costs, quickly identifying and testing new compositions and modifying production to incorporate them.

The Mint in Winnipeg will be expanding by the year 2000, as a coin plating facility will be added to enable the Mint to produce coins using plated metal, instead of more expensive metal alloys.

The change will save the Canadian government millions of dollars each year, and ensure that the Mint remains on the cutting edge of minting technology. The facility will also enable a wider range of products and services to foreign clients, increasing the Mint's ability to compete for international business. With the new facility, the Mint will continue to be a leading world supplier of circulation coins. The Mint will remain an important fixture in Winnipeg's business landscape, as it has been for over 20 years. ∎

Headquarters in Ottawa.

Winnipeg Development Agreement

T he Winnipeg Development
Agreement is a unique program
with a simple goal: to make
Winnipeg an even better place to
live. Civic, provincial and federal governments have joined forces to help
Winnipeggers create more and better job
training, a safe environment in combination with the resurgence of the city's
downtown and the encouragement of
entrepreneurs with dreams who want to
start their own businesses.

Signed in March of 1995, the five-year
Agreement builds on a strong local tradition of cooperation among governments
for responsible management of public
resources. A total of $75 million in fund-
ing, contributed in equal parts by the
three governments, is being put to work
as a catalyst for change. Grass-roots community groups can use this seed funding
to bring their innovative projects and
ideas to life.

*Cutting-edge technology is child's play at Earl Grey
School.*

WDA programs focus on Safety and
Security, Jobs and Developing Strategies
for new resources and investment. Many
of the projects that have come to life
under the Agreement encompass more
than one of these goals. The development
of the Aboriginal Centre renewed an historic building. The project employed a
local workforce of more than 400 workers,
and many of them trained on the job and
learned new skills. At the same time, the
renewed building has become a local

The Honourable Lloyd Axworthy, Mayor Susan Thompson and the Honourable Jack Reimer.

meeting place and centre for some two
dozen service groups.

Education is a key component for successful futures. A pilot program funded by
the WDA has graduated six disabled people from a five-month special training
course in the Canadian Institute for
Barrier-Free Design, enabling them to
become professional disability consultants
advising on building accessibility. At Earl
Grey School, 75 junior high school girls
are working with cutting-edge technology
in a new computer lab, giving them the
opportunity to pursue potential careers in
traditionally male math or science oriented professions.

Through programs like SEED Winnipeg
Inc., people with ideas and energy, but
without financial resources, are able to
start businesses. More than 160 businesses have been helped to start or expand
through SEED Winnipeg Inc. The project's
operating and managing costs are provided by the WDA along with the United
Way, Winnipeg 2000, the Mennonite
Central Committee, charitable foundations
and private donations. The Assiniboine
Credit Union provides loans out of an
allotment set aside just for the program.

Federal Foreign Affairs Minister Lloyd
Axworthy, a Winnipegger, says the WDA
"is really about people. It's about having
three levels of government work together
on issues that affect people's quality of
life, such as getting trained for a good

job or making their neighbourhood a
safer place to live."

Winnipeggers have responded to the
opportunities the WDA Agreement encourages, adds Provincial Urban Affairs
Minister Jack Reimer. "The community
organizations, the volunteers have seen
that if they've got a good project, a viable
alternative for some of the problems fac-
ing the city, they can tap into the
Winnipeg Development Agreement."

The North Main Task Force, in combination with CentrePlan, the City's vision
for the centre of Winnipeg, is using ten
million dollars to revitalize the historic
downtown area, including the world
famous intersection of Portage and Main.
The centre of the city is returning to its
historic roots, sheltering cultural gathering places like Neeginan for aboriginal
people and Oseredok, the Ukrainian
Cultural Centre.

Urban Safety programs are also
designed to attack poverty and lost hopes—
common causes of crime. "Choices", an
award-winning program directed at high
risk teens, shows junior high students
there is an alternative to crime. By com-
bining in-school and extra-curricular activity, students learn about the choices they
have in life, about anger management and
relationship skills. Career Trek gives
youngsters a taste of the sorts of productive careers they can access through higher education, by giving them a chance to

sample programs in post-secondary institutions.

And programs like the Urban Sports Camps give youngsters something safe and fun to do with their time in the evenings—basketball, floor hockey, swimming, karate. The kids spend time just being kids, with caring workers there to act as examples and solid role models.

The Downtown Watch and CounterAction promote a safe, friendly downtown shopping and socializing area. Downtown Watch ambassadors, in their bright red uniforms, walk the city's streets to provide visitors and Winnipeggers alike with the assistance or information they may need. The CounterAction program teaches merchants aspects of crime prevention, and shows businesses how to assess their operations for possible trouble spots, and how to put crime prevention measures in place.

Strategic initiatives encompassing entire industry sectors are also being developed with the support of the WDA. The groundwork has been laid for Winnipeg's resurgence as a ground and air transport hub for North America. As a result, thousands of jobs could open up in and around the Winnipeg International Airport complex and the Winnport cargo-handling, transfer and manufacturing initiative.

A three-year strategy to promote the North American Superhighway Corridor has been funded to share the vision of Winnipeg as the natural northern node in a link from Manitoba through to Mexico for trade, transport and tourism.

Cooperation among all three levels of government has been critical to the

Floor hockey is just one of many activities at the Urban Sports Camp.

Agreement's success. Both Winnipeg Mayor Susan Thompson and Manitoba Urban Affairs Minister Jack Reimer agree. Says Mayor Thompson, "The WDA continues the tradition of tri-level cooperation and has been an effective catalyst in leveraging funds from not only other levels of government, but also from the private and nonprofit sectors."

Many of the programs which have begun through the support of the WDA will continue on their own, fostered and financed in the future by the community groups that founded them. A fresh approach to spur economic development and opportunities for people, the WDA philosophy has been adopted and is being implemented in two more Western Canadian cities, Edmonton and Regina. ■

The Winnport Cargo Complex can fly Winnipeg to the forefront of foreign markets.

The Great-West Life Assurance Company

Winnipeg in the late 1800s was a pioneer town eager to grow and its businesses and farmers were looking for capital to expand and insurance to protect them while they developed the West. Jeffry Hall Brock, a partner in the Carruthers & Brock Insurance Agency, stepped in to lead development of The Great-West Life Assurance Company.

J.H. Brock, developer of The Great-West Life Assurance Company.

Incorporated by an Act of Parliament in 1891, the company began operations in a single room with five staff members. Today, Great-West Life with its subsidiaries, London Life Insurance Company in Canada and Great-West Life & Annuity Insurance Company in the United States, is one of the leading life insurers in North America.

Great-West has become one of the strongest financial institutions in North America. Guided by its Corporate Mission to "achieve excellence in providing financial products and services for people, and to do so in a responsible manner," by the end of 1997 the company had more than $412 billion of life insurance in force. Total assets under administration topped the $75 billion mark; and total premium income surpassed $12.2 billion.

In Canada, Great-West is a leading provider of segregated investment funds, disability insurance and employee benefit plans. The company offers a range of individual life insurance and retirement plans, including an asset allocation system that helps clients choose the right investment blend from among 42 investment funds managed by GWL Investment Management Ltd. with five prominent external fund managers. In the employee benefit market, Great-West helps small and large employers alike manage benefit costs, and offer competitive benefit packages.

One of Great-West's Guiding Principles is to treat staff, clients and the community with integrity and respect. The company's efforts to establish a more diversified work force have been recognized by a certificate of merit award from the Canadian federal government. Community relations programs support a wide range of charitable interests across Canada, and help encourage volunteerism among Great-West's people. Great-West was one of the first to be designated "A Caring Company" by the Canadian Centre for Philanthropy's national IMAGINE program, celebrating corporate financial and volunteer contributions.

With its strong reputation for value, service and integrity, Great-West continues its century-old tradition of helping people achieve financial security. ■

Investors Group

nvestors Group is a national leader in providing financial services to Canadians. The company offers financial planning, a unique family of mutual funds and a comprehensive range of other investment products.

The company's success story began in 1940 when Investors Diversified Services of Minneapolis, Minnesota, established its first Canadian subsidiary in Winnipeg. Since then, the company–renamed The Investors Group in 1964 and Investors Group Inc. in 1986–has developed a strong national presence, while continuing to maintain its Head Office in Winnipeg. Investors Group is a member of the Power Financial Corporation Group of Companies.

Today, the company serves close to one million clients through a dedicated sales-force working from 99 Financial Planning Centres located across Canada.

The focus of the company's efforts is a simple, long-term strategy: a commitment to achieve growth by building enduring client relationships. Investors Group's 3,400 Representatives work closely with clients to understand their current circumstances, long-term goals and investment preferences.

Technology is an important tool in providing superior client service. Every Representative is equipped with a laptop computer or "office in a box," which provides current client data, a reference library and other financial planning tools to provide personalized service to clients at any location.

In addition to financial planning, clients enjoy an extensive range of mutual funds and a complete package of other investment and financial services, including Registered Retirement Savings Plans, Registered Retirement Income Funds, Deferred Profit Sharing Plans, life and disability insurance, Guaranteed Investment Certificates, tax preparation and mortgages.

Today, Investors manages assets of more than $31 billion, administers a mortgage portfolio of more than $4 billion and offers a wide range of insurance products, the face value of which exceeds $11 billion.

In 1996, the company expanded its range of investment opportunities through strategic partnerships with some of the best-known money-management firms in Canada and around the world, including Merrill Lynch Asset Management, Rothschild Asset Management Limited, Sceptre Investment Counsel Limited and Beutel, Goodman & Company Ltd. This move represented the largest single expansion of investment products in its history, making it the largest mutual fund family in Canada, offering 48 mutual funds.

Investors Group is also at work in the community to ensure a better future for all Canadians.

Through donations of more than $1.5 million and sponsorship activities, the company provides leadership and support to a variety of charitable and nonprofit groups and programs in Winnipeg. Investors President and CEO Sandy Riley is Chair of the Pan Am Games Society, which is playing host to nearly 5,000 athletes for the 1999 Pan American Games in Winnipeg. Investors is also a national sponsor of the Games.

Equally important, the company maintains a strong presence in communities across Canada in the areas of education, arts and culture and amateur sport. Investors Group employees and Representatives are also actively supported by the company in their local community involvement. ■

Investors Group, Corporate Head Office, Winnipeg.

Nesbitt Burns

Tom Waitt, Senior Vice-President for Nesbitt Burns, Manitoba-Saskatchewan.

Youth and knowledge–it's a combination that has paid off for the Winnipeg office of Nesbitt Burns. It's what has put the investment brokerage firm out in front with a 38 per cent share of the Manitoba investor market. It's what has led it to have $2 billion of client money under management. And it's what has resulted in its being one of the top three Nesbitt Burns branches in Canada, notwithstanding Winnipeg's ranking as the eighth largest city.

When Tom Waitt, Senior Vice-President for Manitoba-Saskatchewan, moved into management, he was only 24. Now in his early 40s, he has continued to recognize the advantages of a young, aggressive staff. He has built a team that is, on average, 10 years younger than Nesbitt Burns' competitors. Largely because of that, Nesbitt Burns has been keen on embracing change and has concentrated on bringing innovative new products to the attention of its clients before widespread popularity moves the prices up.

Nesbitt Burns has undergone a lot of change itself, having doubled in size in the span of one year. Almost all of Nesbitt Burns' 139 employees now have university degrees, providing a mix of M.A.s, Ph.D.s, M.B.A.s and chartered accountants. They are comfortable with technology and rely on a computer network to help them provide better customer service and information flow. Everyone from the stock boy to the receptionist has a desk with a computer.

Nesbitt Burns, a member of the Bank of Montreal Group of Companies, resulted from the 1994 merger of two of Canada's leading investment firms–82-year-old Nesbitt Thomson Inc. and 69-year-old Burns Fry Limited. The company has had a presence in Manitoba since the early '20s. It continues to be proud of that fact, staffed with Manitobans, taking care of other Manitobans. Nesbitt Burns believes it is making Manitoba a better place to be, whether by ensuring easier access to capital for entrepreneurs and helping create jobs, or advising ordinary Manitobans on how to invest for their future and the future of their children.

Manitobans have a gold mine in their own backyard. There are many Manitoba companies that show better value and investment opportunity than in either Toronto or New York, and Nesbitt Burns is consciously trying to open people's eyes to local opportunities. It has done well listening to itself. When Manitoba Telecom Services Ltd. went public in January 1997, Nesbitt Burns sold the largest volume of shares, more than 20 per cent of the 50.8 million issue. On the first day of trading, the firm handled 67 per cent of the trades on the Winnipeg Stock Exchange.

Since 1988, Nesbitt Burns has increased annual revenues in Manitoba to $30 million from $4 million. ■

Cambrian Credit Union

Cambrian Credit Union is the entrepreneurial credit union focused on customer service through innovation and prudent management. It has served the Manitoba market since 1959 offering professional financial services to its members. Today, Cambrian serves over 34,000 members in 11 locations.

Cambrian has clearly identified its goal–providing top-notch member services. Cambrian has expanded its traditional banking role of gathering deposits and lending money to include the new services its members ask for. Financial planning and wealth management are today's credit union services. Now, members have access to international and domestic equity markets, more than 500 mutual funds, government and corporate bonds, treasury bills and other investment instruments through its full-service brokerage, Credential Securities.

And all Cambrian members are also shareholders and owners. As an owner of the business, each member shares in the profits of the company through dividends and shares. The management team treats its responsibility to shareholders with care, knowing that strong management and solid financial position generate profits and other benefits for the member-owner. Over the last three years, Cambrian members have enjoyed refunds and dividends of over $3 million. Not to mention over $300,000 in refunded service fees in 1997 alone! This credit union fully rewards its members for putting their banking trust in Cambrian.

In addition, Cambrian has the vision to identify the benefits technology can offer its members. Eight years before the major banks offered telebanking, Cambrian members were using their phones to check their account balances and pay their bills. In 1997, its members said they wanted another way to access their accounts. Cambrian became the first credit union in Manitoba to "get wired." Cambrian members go on-line to do their banking–from their PCs at home over the Internet to make the Cambrian connection! Cambrian information systems are constantly being improved to provide the best in technological innovation in the branch and on-line.

As well as serving its members,

Cambrian delivers traditional member service using today's leading technology.

Cambrian believes in its corporate responsibility to contribute to quality of life in the community. As an employer, Cambrian provides a learning environment for its staff and supports them with generous education subsidies. Over 40 per cent of its employees are enrolled in advanced professional training in the fields of management, securities and chartered financial planning. In keeping with its focus on education, Cambrian supports young people through contributions to such programs as Rossbrook House, Aboriginal Youth Achievement and Manitoba Winter/Summer Games. Cambrian views its contribution in the framework of people helping people supporting organizations such as Habitat for Humanity, Winnipeg Harvest and the Salvation Army.

Cambrian continues to build a strong organization dedicated to identifying and serving the ever-changing needs of its community, its employees and its members. ■

Cambrian Credit Union celebrates Winnipeg winter at the Festival du Voyageur.

Health Care, Education & Quality of Life

The University of Manitoba. Photo by Mike Grandmaison.

St. Boniface General Hospital

In an era of technological advances that have created a society grown almost inured to startling change, St. Boniface General Hospital maintains its original values while contributing to significant changes in health care services and delivery. By holding firm to the mission of its founders, the Sisters of Charity of Montreal "Grey Nuns," the hospital endeavours to keep the human element in the science of health services.

The Grey Nuns' mission is to promote excellence in patient care. That mission began over 125 years ago when they founded the first hospital in Western Canada on the banks of the Red River. From a simple beginning, St. Boniface General Hospital has kept pace with, and often led the way in advances in health care. While the kinds of services and their delivery may have evolved dramatically since 1871, what has never changed is the hospital's mission to "serve all those who call or need our services."

Thanks to their dedication to the real focus of health services—the patient—members of St. Boniface General Hospital's staff and volunteers have rallied to meet the challenges of health reform and looked for the opportunities it presents. Photo by Bill Peters.

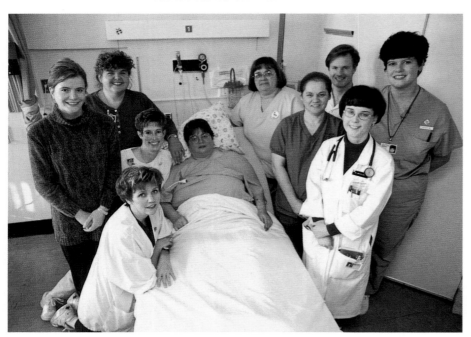

Multidisciplinary care teams include the patient and family along with physicians, nurses, physiotherapists, social workers, pastoral care associates and nursing assistants in the delivery of care. This initiative has been implemented with success in many areas of the hospital and creates more opportunities for better patient care. Photo by Mike Deal.

The hospital's mission is to provide excellence in patient care and to provide leadership in research and education which reflects compassionate care of the persons served. These latter two fields of endeavour ultimately bring the focus back to quality patient care. For without health research there would be no advances in the prevention and treatment of disease. Without education, there would not be the qualified health professionals to care for the people served by the hospital.

In the past few years, the external environment in which the hospital functions has altered in significant ways. Health care reform is changing how provinces fund and manage health services. These changes have affected fiscal policies and service delivery. The creation of the Winnipeg Hospital Authority adds to the external pressures to which the hospital must adapt while maintaining its autonomy and unique mission.

There is no doubt that health reform has generated some anxiety and uncertainty among health professionals and others in the hospital. Thanks to their dedication to the real focus of health services—the patient—members of St. Boniface General Hospital's staff and volunteers have rallied to meet this challenge and looked for the opportunities it presents. In exploring the hospital's many activities, and how it accomplishes them, it becomes apparent that the hospital on the Red will find new ways to meet the needs of the population it serves.

PATIENT CARE

St. Boniface General Hospital has long valued collaboration and teamwork, emphasizing the opportunities they create for better patient care. This has translated into partnerships with other agencies in the community and internally into the implementation of a patient focused care team.

Although surrounded by modern technology, hospital staff endeavour to keep the human element present in the care provided to patients. Photo by Paul Martens.

The multidisciplinary care team includes physicians, nurses and physiotherapists, as well as social workers, pastoral care associates and nursing assistants. More importantly, the team includes the patient and his/her family in the delivery of care. This approach has been implemented with growing success on the Medicine, Neurosciences, Geriatric Medicine and Post Anaesthesia Recovery Room units. Plans are to expand the initiative to other units in the hospital. Internal Medicine has opened a Family-Centred Care area to facilitate family involvement in caring for terminal patients.

As the 21st century dawns, the hospital is seeking new partners in the community to provide care to those in need. This is particularly important in discharge planning. Including community-based organizations and/or services in this process helps the team ensure individuals return to their home environment as soon as safely possible with the resources at hand to assist them once they leave the hospital.

Recently, St. Boniface entered into a three-year agreement with the Manitoba Cardiac Service Program and the Kinsmen Reh-Fit Centre, establishing a community-based program to provide rehabilitation services to people who have undergone heart surgery. The goal of this venture is to promote and encourage a long-term approach to supporting lifestyle changes for improved health. The initial six-month project was so successful that the hospital has signed a three-year agreement to continue the project. Cost savings have also allowed the hospital to extend the service to patients from the Health Sciences Centre. This type of project provides for an integrated continuum of care from the point the cardiac patient undergoes a heart operation to the point where he or she is fully recovered and prospering in the community.

St. Boniface General Hospital, in collaboration with other city hospitals, has also expanded its Community IV program which allows patients to return to their homes and often to their work environments, while continuing a treatment of intravenous antibiotic therapy. Initially involving only patients at St. Boniface, the Community IV program is now based out of St. Boniface to provide care to patients throughout the city.

These and other community-based programs are expected to reduce hospital admissions, length of stay and ambulatory visits to hospital. More importantly, for individuals admitted to the community-based programs, it means going home sooner or being able to stay home.

In the coming months and years, the hospital's five program areas—Medicine, Surgery, Woman and Child, Mental Health and Emergency Services—will continue to seek new ways of caring for patients both in hospital and through partnerships with community-based agencies as part of the hospital's commitment to quality patient care and to the community it serves.

The hospital provides rehabilitation services to people who have undergone various types of surgery. The goal of community-based programs is to promote and encourage a long-term approach to supporting lifestyle changes for improved health. Photo by Mike Deal.

RESEARCH—CREATING HEALTH AND ECONOMIC BENEFITS

Although patient care may be the link that most Manitobans have with St. Boniface General Hospital, its research and education activities ultimately benefit them as well. Through research and education, health care itself is moved forward, allowing care providers to offer patients the best available services.

In 1971, St. Boniface General Hospital and the Grey Nuns rededicated their focus on education and research, establishing them as pivotal to the hospital's activities. At that time, they established the St. Boniface General Hospital Research Foundation, which since has raised more than $42 million for research. It's been a tremendous catalyst for world-class

The mystery of many diseses such as those afflicting the aging population are being unraveled at the Research Centre. Scientists such as Dr. Francis Amara are seeking answers into Alzheimer's, stroke and viral dementia. Photo by Mike Deal.

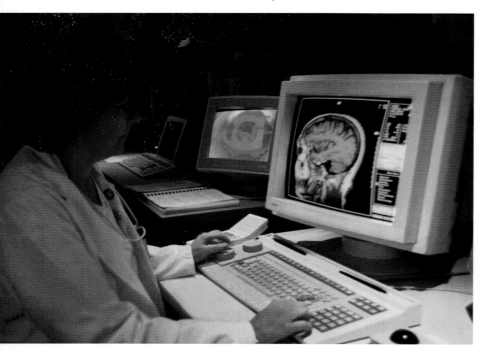

The magnetic imaging scanner at St. Boniface is a major focus of research and patient care, helping to diagnose thousands of patients each year. Soon a new interventional MRI will be located in the Centre to further research in deep-seated tumours and diseases associated with aging. Photo by Mike Deal.

research taking place at the St. Boniface General Hospital Research Centre. Opened in 1987, this free-standing research facility is home to more than 190 researchers and support staff who currently are involved in projects in three primary areas: cardiovascular sciences, magnetic resonance imagery and spectroscopy and degenerative disorders associated with aging.

Some of the most advanced health research in the world, primarily in the field of basic heart research and diagnostic technology, is conducted at the Research Centre. The Division of Cardiovascular Sciences, now the Institute of Cardiovascular Sciences, one of the first areas of research to be established when the Centre opened, is involved in groundbreaking research. Investigators are looking at areas such as the possible repair of injured heart muscle and of arteries that may be scarred when blockages must be surgically removed. Researchers also are looking at genetic questions that may lead to the prevention or correction of heart disease.

Health research not only leads to health benefits, but to economic spin-offs as well. Some of the Centre's activities have rewarded Manitoba economically by creating employment opportunities and demand for products and services from Manitoba suppliers. From the hospital's perspective, having a world-class facility allows it to attract and retain top-notch scientists whose research and academic activities ultimately benefit the patients whom it serves.

EDUCATION—A COOPERATIVE VENTURE

From an early stage in the hospital's development, the Grey Nuns recognized that teaching future health care professionals was an integral responsibility of a quality health care institution. A partnership with the University of Manitoba was natural. Since the late 19th century, the hospital has worked with the university to provide health sciences education that combines the academic strengths of the university with the health care services and unique philosophy of the hospital.

A recent agreement between St. Boniface General Hospital, the Health Sciences Centre and the University of Manitoba will enhance medical education. This agreement emphasizes St. Boniface's role as an academic health centre. It also demonstrates its importance to the university in health science education and research.

Last fall, after the closure of its School of Nursing, St. Boniface began a new relationship with the university through the establishment of several Faculty of Nursing Practice Units on site at St. Boniface. This change mirrors a national trend which has seen a gradual shift from diploma to degree education for registered nurses.

The relationship between the hospital and the university goes beyond the strictly medical component of patient care, teaching and research. Eventually, other disciplines will likely fall under the new affiliation agreement. Already the hospital, with the university, offers clinical programs in physiotherapy, occupational therapy, registered dietetics, pharmacy and social work.

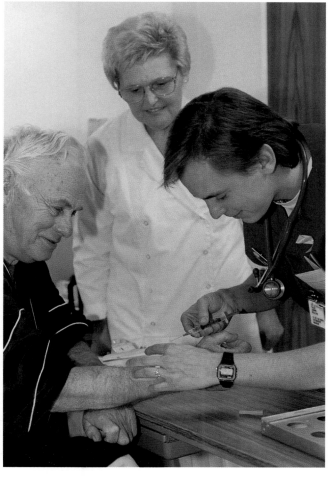

The Grey Nuns recognized early that teaching future professionals was an important responsibility. A recent agreement with the University of Manitoba has resulted in the establishment of several Faculty of Nursing Practice Units on site at St. Boniface General Hospital. Photo by Paul Martens.

A BRIGHT FUTURE
BUILT ON A SOLID FOUNDATION

In the coming years and decades, St. Boniface General Hospital will continue its mission to serve those in need. The pioneering legacy of the earliest Grey Nuns lives on in the hospital as it seeks to build on its past while striking out into new ground. Whatever technologies develop, whatever partnerships it forms, as it looks ahead to the new century, St. Boniface General Hospital will continue to provide compassionate, quality care to the community it proudly serves.

L'HÔPITAL GÉNÉRAL SAINT-BONIFACE

Situé aux confluents des rivières Rouge et Assiniboine, l'Hôpital général Saint-Boniface a été établi par les Soeurs de la Charité de Montréal «Soeurs Grises» en 1871. En tant que premier hôpital dans l'Ouest canadien, l'Hôpital général Saint-Boniface a aidé à jeter les bases du système de santé au Manitoba.

Malgré les nouvelles technologies et les nombreux changements au système de santé au cours des dernières années, l'Hôpital demeure fidèle à la mission de ses fondatrices et réussi à joindre l'élément humain à la science des soins de santé.

Le patient et sa famille sont une partie intégrante de l'équipe soignante et les équipes multidisciplinaires établies dans les divers unités connaissent un grand succès auprès des professionnels de la santé aussi bien qu'auprès des patients.

L'Hôpital a toujours travaillé en collaboration avec la communauté et à l'aube du 21e siècle, il continue à forger de nouveaux liens avec la communauté afin d'assurer des soins continus à ses patients.

Par exemple, l'Hôpital vient de signer une entente avec le Service manitobain de cardiologie et le Kinsmen Reh-Fit Centre pour offrir des services de réadaptation à partir de la communauté. Ce service, destiné aux personnes qui ont subi une intervention cardiaque, encourage et appui des changements dans le mode de vie pour une meilleure santé.

Ce projet, comme bien d'autres, vise à réduire les admissions, la durée de séjour et les visites aux cliniques externes de l'Hôpital. Ce qui est plus important encore pour les personnes touchées par la maladie, ces programmes communautaires leur permettent de rentrer plus rapidement à la maison et même de demeurer chez eux.

Quoique sa mission principale soit d'assurer des soins de qualité à ses patients, l'Hôpital croit également à l'importance de l'éducation et de la recherche.

En 1971, l'Hôpital a établi la Fondation de recherche dans le but de financer la recherche, les soins aux patients et l'éducation. Depuis, la Fondation a recueilli plus de 42 millions de dollars dont une partie a servi à la construction du Centre de recherche en 1987.

Les chercheurs qui y travaillent s'intéressent principalement aux domaines de la cardiologie et de la technologie diagnostique, particulièrement celle de l'imagerie par résonance magnétique. Les maladies liées au vieillissement font également l'objet de recherches intéressantes alors que les chercheurs tentent de percer les mystères de la maladie d'Alzheimer, des démences et des accidents cérébrovasculaires.

Ces projets de recherche contribuent également à l'essor de l'économie manitobaine, car ils créent de l'emploi et nécessitent des produits et des services de fournisseurs de la province.

Avec ses partenaires, l'Hôpital continue de jouer un rôle de chef de file en contribuant à la prestation des soins de grande qualité, à la mise en oeuvre de programmes d'éducation et à la réalisation de travaux de recherche. Au cours des années à venir, l'Hôpital général Saint-Boniface continuera à chercher de nouvelles façons de mieux servir les patients qui font appel à ses services. ■

The University of Winnipeg

I ts roots set deep in Manitoba's history, The University of Winnipeg began as Manitoba College in 1871, just months after this province joined Confederation. Since its birth, the university has worked to nurture the development and growth of the community it serves, and has fostered a similar sense of responsibility among its graduates.

In the finest, most traditional sense of a college, The University of Winnipeg retains smaller classes than many other similar undergraduate Canadian institutions, and encourages its nearly 7,000 students to work closely with highly qualified academic staff, acclaimed in their fields, in studies and research. With an annual budget of just under $50 million, the university relies on government for little over half its funding; the remainder derives from tuitions, gifts, bequests, investments or other revenues.

Applications from The University of Winnipeg for funding from the Natural Sciences and Engineering Research Council, for example, have an impressive success rate well above the national average.

Yet this academic community of interests has also embraced newer philosophies, helping to define the value and role of higher education within society by fostering strong, active partnerships with others: universities, businesses, government and research groups, and by recognizing practical applications of post-secondary education and research.

The University's Business Computing Program steadily turns out graduates to fill the significant gap identified by business between industry needs for suitable employees and existing skills of software workers. The program equips students with the vital combination of technical knowledge, business acumen and people skills needed by today's employers, and has attracted students from as far away as Sedaya College in Malaysia, where

Although the University of Winnipeg has grown beyond its century-old flagship building, Wesley Hall, it has retained the tradition of small classes and faculty/student interaction.

an arrangement between institutions allows them to complete the business computing program in Winnipeg. They come because this university offers what few other programs in Canada provide— a practical balance of skills.

That balance is further reflected by the Division of Continuing Education, which offers programs, designed in consultation with industry, to provide employees with new skills relevant to current business needs.

In partnership with the Women's Health Clinic in Winnipeg, and together with other Prairie universities and 31 more cooperating organizations, the university was able to establish a Centre of Excellence for Women's Health in Manitoba and Saskatchewan. With a mandate from Health Canada and a $2 million budget, the Centre defines the health status of Canadian women, identifies key issues requiring investigation and action and informs policy.

The Prairie Centre of Excellence for Research on Immigration and Integration

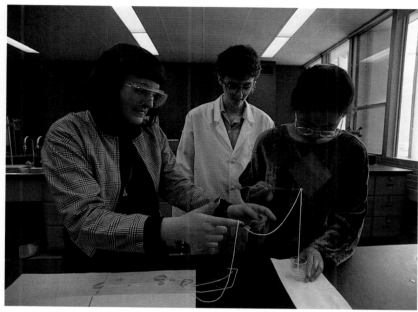

is one of four established by the Canadian government, and involves The University of Winnipeg and five others across the Prairies in a $2.4 million, six-year-long study to better understand the impact of immigration and contributions made to Canadian society by immigrants. These centres, coordinating the research efforts of some of the finest social scientists in Canada, are major components of an international project to gather information through which government, community and business leaders can base policies and services.

Academic and research partnerships have been formed close to home and around the world. Several joint programs are offered with Winnipeg's Red River Community College, including degrees in Applied Chemistry, Developmental Studies and Applied Environmental Studies. Through an agreement with Ain Shams University in Cairo, Egypt, researchers from both centres work together examining environmental applications of photoenergy. Closer to home, the College and University Bound Project (CUB) is a unique collaboration with Seven Oaks School Division, Red River Community College and the private sector. With funding from the Royal Bank, it encourages those faced with cultural, economic, racial or physical barriers to obtain post-secondary education.

The university partnered in the Manitoba Model Forest, part of a federal program to introduce the concept of sustainable development into forest communities. The Manitoba forest was one of the top-rated examples in Canada of diverse stakeholders working together to accommodate the needs of logging companies, aboriginal people, recreational users and governments, while protecting the future of this valuable natural resource.

Collaborative research between the university and the National Research Council Institute of Biodiagnostics in Winnipeg uses magnetic resonance imaging to study brain function—and has begun to pave the way for dramatic developments in medical science, such as ways to help protect the brain during traumatic events like neurosurgery. These techniques could also lead to advances in the treatment of attention deficit disorder in children, and better ways to relieve pain.

The University of Winnipeg's Institute of Urban Studies serves as a community-based resource centre. Funding for IUS projects is largely derived from contracts with external organizations and industry, and the institute has a solid reputation for bridging the gap between pure research and commercial potential. The institute, and the university's Division of Continuing Education, are located in a downtown Portage Avenue building, an

excellent example of downtown revitalization and a demonstration that old buildings can be recycled and renovated effectively.

And Canada's first undergraduate program in Environmental Studies, saluted by the United Nations as a model for such programs, has a history of breaking new ground in environmental sustainability and urban environmental policy.

This stimulating blend of academics, in an atmosphere conducive to personal growth, cutting-edge research and practical, collaborative partnerships, have produced a proud roster of notable graduates like CEOs Ray McFeetors of Great-West Life Assurance and Michael Phelps of WestCoast Energy Resources; nationally-popular children's entertainer Fred Penner; acclaimed writer Margaret Laurence; Joanne DiCosimo, President and CEO of the Canadian Museum of Nature and Canadian external affairs minister Lloyd Axworthy. Dedicated teachers, talented scientists, innovative researchers, successful business people and others have moved on from this undergraduate university to make significant contributions to society. ◾

The University of Manitoba

Firm commitment to quality in teaching, research and community service has resulted in a roster of top-notch professors and researchers at the University of Manitoba. The University of Manitoba's staff, students and graduates routinely collect prestigious awards and accolades for major contributions in their chosen fields of endeavour, whether scientific, artistic, business-

Fort Garry Campus. Photo by Robert Tinker.

oriented or devoted to studies in the humanities and social sciences.

Founded in 1877, the University of Manitoba began in downtown Winnipeg with the merger of St. Boniface College, St. John's College and Manitoba College. But the young university quickly outgrew its original location, as it expanded to include the sciences, medicine, architecture, the Manitoba Agricultural College and fine arts faculties. Today, with the main campus at the south end of the city on its 274-hectare Fort Garry location,

University of Manitoba sites include faculties of medicine and dentistry and major research facilities adjacent to Manitoba's major medical facility and Winnipeg's largest teaching hospital, the Health Sciences Centre; far-flung agricultural research stations, biology field stations and nursing education sites; more than 20 teleconference sites and the Winnipeg Education Centre with innovative teacher-training and social work programs in the core area of the city.

Through more than a century of dedication to the development of excellence in post-secondary and post-graduate education, this university, Western Canada's oldest, has become the largest in the province, with a current annual total enrollment of more than 44,000 students, more than half of whom study in regular session degree programs. Well over 5,000 students in 20 countries enrol in distance education courses, delivered in five different formats. From architecture to zoology, this university offers 78 degree, diploma and certificate programs. All of the province's professional programs are delivered here, as is the only Faculty of Graduate Studies for masters' and doctoral programs.

Continuing education courses, off-campus programs and special access programs are offered through this university, with its $240 million annual operating budget. The university's library boasts more than 2 million volumes. The University of Manitoba is also recognized as one of

The University of Manitoba's Fort Garry Campus in South Winnipeg. Photo by Robert Tinker.

Canada's major research universities. Roughly $70 million in research funding—two-thirds of which is received from organizations outside the province which seek the specific talents and expertise of University of Manitoba faculty—is received annually by the university in the form of grants and contracts, and those studies have contributed results on a regional, national and international scale.

Hundreds of research projects are tackled every year here, in a remarkable cross-section of disciplines including the processing of materials in outer space, quality assurance in commercial baking, effects of annual flooding in Bangladesh, spinal cord injuries and other medical disorders. Plant scientists here have developed improved grains, and are investigating the greenhouse effect on prairie agriculture and industry. One of the world's leading AIDS researchers, Francis Plummer, is studying the biology of

sexually-transmitted infections. Cancer research is being tackled on fronts ranging from ways to block cancer cells through gene modification, to work by foods and nutrition professor, Ranjana Bird, on the role of fat in the development of colon cancer, which earned a Canadian Society of Nutritional Sciences Borden Award for outstanding contributions to nutrition research.

Awards and accolades garnered by staff, students and graduates at this prestigious university range from an Academy Award Oscar for Technical Achievement (Nestor Burtnyk, for National Research Council work developing ground-breaking software techniques in computer-assisted animation) to the highest number of students in any Canadian university to receive the Special Corporate Awards for Canada Scholarships, a program by the Association of Universities and Colleges of Canada which recognizes Canada's brightest students. In 1996, eighteen University of Manitoba students received such awards, more than twice the number given to runner-up universities of Toronto and Alberta. Professor of geology, Vacliv Smil earned the Joseph Levenson Book Award which named one of his books as the best in the world on China.

The wide-ranging list of faculty, student and graduate achievements includes Prime Minister's Awards for Teaching Excellence, Canada Council's Killam Fellowships, the Three M Teaching Fellowship, a *Reader's Digest* Leadership in Education Award, the Royal Institute of British Architects Gold Medal award to internationally-recognized outstanding architects, the Prix St-Exupéry award (author, children's book category) from France's national library, numerous inductions into the Canadian Business Hall of Fame and the Order of Canada for meritorious public service, Queen's Fellowships, Rhodes scholarships and prestigious Interior Design scholarships.

Brodie Centre, on the University of Manitoba's medical and dental campus in downtown Winnipeg. Photo by Tony Nardella.

But there's more at work here than fine minds, top-quality academics and internationally recognised research in both the sciences and humanities. The university's sports facilities are the most extensive in the province, taking in racquet sports, an ice arena, indoor and outdoor tracks, gymnasia, stadium and pool. These facilities play host not only to the university's athletic teams, but to national and international competitions, including many of the events of the 1999 Pan Am Games. University of Manitoba Bison teams in volleyball, basketball, track and field and wrestling, have been national champions. And this is a university dedicated to its students; the annual *Macleans Magazine* ranking of Canadian universities, based on student surveys, gave the University of Manitoba its top mark for going the distance with its students.

In its first century of teaching, this prestigious Canadian institution has graduated more than 130,000 students. The University of Manitoba looks forward to the next century, in which faculty and staff will continue to rise to the challenge of providing outstanding teaching, research and community involvement of internationally impressive calibre. ■

Fort Garry Campus. Photo by Robert Tinker.

Health Sciences Centre

The largest health care referral, teaching and research centre in Manitoba, Winnipeg's Health Sciences Centre serves patients from areas as distant as the Northwest Territories and Northwestern Ontario. In addition to providing a full range of hospital services from surgical inpatient care to outpatient day facilities and services, the Health Sciences Cente is the designated trauma centre for this entire area. When Canada's Armed Forces needed to ensure complete medical resources and the capacity for rapid trauma treatment, in case of emergencies during Manitoba's worst flood of the century in 1997, they turned to the Health Sciences Centre as the designated facility.

More than 20,000 patients are admitted each year to this health care complex, founded in 1972 with the amalgamation of the Winnipeg General Hospital, The Children's Hospital of Winnipeg and The Manitoba Rehabilitation Hospital.

Today, 6,000 staff members in the combined hospitals operate a total of roughly 800 beds, almost half of those in the General Hospital and Respiratory Unit.

Because the Centre is located in an area of Winnipeg where many aboriginal people live, and because many patients from more distant areas are aboriginal, the hospital has become the single largest health care provider for aboriginal people in Manitoba. The Health Sciences Centre, through its Aboriginal Services Department, provides language translators for half-a-dozen aboriginal languages, and patient intermediaries to handle questions or concerns and to ensure patients are comfortable, and are treated

FROM CHILDHOOD . . .

with the respect appropriate to their own cultural traditions.

Emphasis on the human being is not confined to this department; it is the ubiquitous philosophy at Health Sciences Centre. Roughly 14,000 outpatient procedures and more than 10,000 inpatient surgeries are performed here each year, including the most complex surgery done in the city. The Adult Surgery program utilizes a same-day admission policy; ninety per cent of surgery patients here are admitted on the day of their operations, and are able to spend the night prior in the comfort of their own homes.

The Facilitated Recovery Program speeds the recovery process for cardiac patients here—the length of some patients' stays has been reduced by half as a result of the use of sophisticated anesthesia techniques which enable prompt transfer from the step-down unit to inpatient beds. And the Health Sciences Centre has begun a trial phase of bloodless surgery.

The Women's Health Program includes gynaecology and gyne-oncology programs, as well as full birthing facilities where post-natal care is emphasized through outpatient services to improve parent-child development at home, drop-in centres for parents and children, the Ante-Natal

A CITY WITHIN A CITY—Beyond the doors of Health Sciences Centre lies a community as complex as any city, a community made up of people dedicated to using the very best in medical practice to bring hope to those in need.

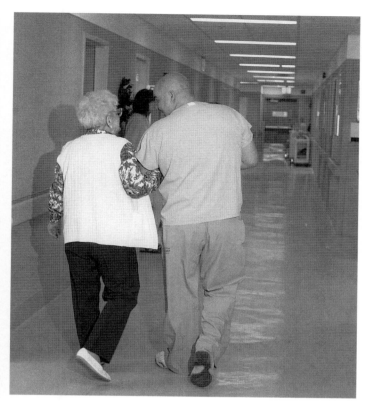

...THROUGH ALL THE ADULT YEARS...

Home Care Program, a breastfeeding clinic and hotline and a Family Planning Service and Pregnancy Counselling. The evolving nature of North America's adult population is recognized through the establishment of Manitoba's first Mature Women's Health Clinic.

At Children's Hospital, the Child Health Program, the sole in-hospital pediatric program in the catchment area of Manitoba, Northwest Ontario and the Northwest Territories, is dedicated to giving children the best care possible. Active in community outreach and education, the hospital maintains a "Family Information Library" on a vast range of topics from childhood diseases, to developmental disorders, to safety in the home.

The Children's annual Teddy Bears' Picnic in Assiniboine Park has become a Winnipeg tradition with its BASH (Bears' Ambulatory Surgical Hospital) Tent, where children bring "injured" bears to be cured, and volunteer staff bandaging furry toy limbs use the opportunity to teach children about safety and hygiene. Children's Hospital works closely with the Winnipeg Fire Department and others to encourage the installation and use of smoke detectors in homes with children, and to educate parents and children about fire safety.

The Medicine Program at the Health Sciences Centre includes the Rehabilitation Hospital and the Infectious Diseases Unit, and functions as Manitoba's hub hospital for treatment of renal disease and kidney dialysis. The Medicine Program also maintains a Diabetes Education Centre, providing written materials to patients and their families and operating group and individual education sessions for patients and families, as well as daily outpatient clinics for diabetics.

An annual public symposium on aspects of diabetes is designed to inform the general public of the warning signs and dangers of diabetes. With a statistically high prevalence of diabetes among aboriginal people, the Health Sciences Centre provides a regular fly-in service to Thompson, Manitoba, by a physician with a special interest in the disease's treatment. Actively involved with pharmaceutical companies handling advanced clinical trials of leading edge medications for diabetes treatment, the Health Sciences Centre provides a strong educational component for from 50 to 100 patients in those trials.

The Mental Health Program at the Health Sciences Centre serves as the forensic psychiatry centre for the province, and operates a full-service mental health program, including inpatient treatment with more than 90 beds, general psychiatry and day hospital facilities, as well as outpatient services. Specialized programs that tackle specific disorders include a unit for treatment of adolescent eating disorders like anorexia nervosa and the treatment of SAD (Seasonal Affective Disorder), a form of depression linked with seasonal fluctuations in natural light levels.

As well, the Schizophrenia Treatment and Education Program offers a full spectrum of treatment for patients suffering from this devastating disease, and support and advocacy for both patients and families.

In the ever-changing world of health care, and with increasing regionalization of health care delivery systems, Winnipeg's Health Sciences Centre looks forward to continuing to play a key role in Manitoba's health care services system, through its medical resources, research and treatment facilities and with its dedicated staff and health outreach, education and support programs. ■

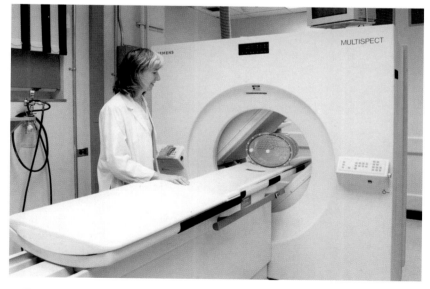

...THE HEALTH SCIENCES CENTRE brings together the best people and the best in technology to promise Manitobans a secure present and promising future in health care.

NRC Institute for Biodiagnostics

I f science sufficiently advanced is indistinguishable from magic to the layman's eye, then magic is being done at the National Research Council's Institute for Biodiagnostics in Winnipeg. A biomedical research lab specializing in medium- to long-term research, the Institute was founded here in April 1992 by the National Research Council of Canada, Canada's foremost federal government research organization.

The NRC wanted to decentralize its laboratory operations across Canada, and Winnipeg was in many ways the ideal place for a biomedical research facility.

The NRC Institute for Biodiagnostics is located on Ellice Avenue in downtown Winnipeg.

The Institute for Biodiagnostics is conducting research on new diagnostic methods such as infrared spectroscopy for potentially non-invasive disease diagnosis.

The Manitoba government's Health Industry Development Initiative had spurred a rapid increase in the number of local health industries. A strong "critical mass" was forming in the area of health and biomedical research, and of the health industry itself, in Winnipeg–a critical mass that sparked a synergy of talent, education, knowledge and creative thought, which in turn has begun to result in remarkable scientific breakthroughs.

By 1997, the health industry in Manitoba would number over 100 companies and agencies, multiplying from less than ten just a decade earlier. Strong professional collaborations had been forged between health research facilities like the St. Boniface General Hospital Research Centre, the Health Sciences Centre and the Universities of Winnipeg and Manitoba.

In addition, an excellent, relatively new NRC-owned facility was available in central Winnipeg. Four diverse biomedical research groups distributed among the Ottawa NRC Institutes had the potential for strong synergies, if grouped together in a single facility.

Director General Dr. Ian C. P. Smith, originally from Winnipeg, came back to the city to head the Institute, bringing a combination of strong civic pride and a desire to be a part of regional economic development through leading-edge research. The establishment of the Institute in Winnipeg resulted in positions for 90 people with another 20 to 30 staff as visiting researchers, industrial collaborators and grant-funded researchers. In summer months, the total number of people in the building balloons to over 150, as the organization takes on outstanding science and engineering students. The Institute also participates in programs for master's and doctoral level students.

Many of the senior scientists and research group leaders here are Adjunct Professors at the Universities of Manitoba and Winnipeg; Dr. Smith holds an executive position on the U of M's Alumni Association; the Research Group Leaders serve on granting committees of the Natural Sciences and Engineering Research Council (NSERC) and the Medical Research Council of Canada (MRC). The Institute and Red River Community College operate a unique training program for technicians who will operate magnetic resonance imaging (MRI) instruments in Canadian hospitals.

Twenty-five different languages can be heard in the IBD building; that's how far-flung its reputation has spread, attracting researchers from around the world who are eager to work in the Institute's four disciplines: magnetic resonance technology, bioinformatics, physiology and infrared spectroscopy. Simply put, all four combine to enable medical practitioners to examine the insides of patients in three-dimensional microscopic detail, without having to cut them open. The

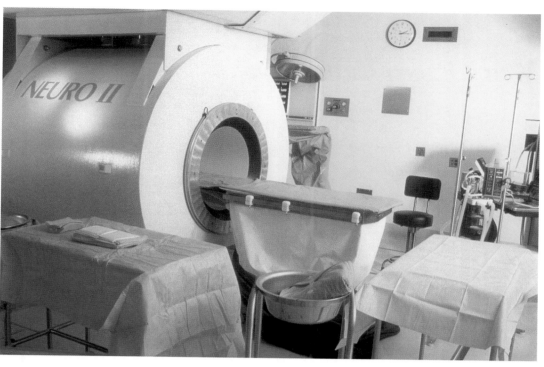

Institute specializes in the invention of Star Trek-style diagnostic tools that need not poke, prod or otherwise invade a patient's body to determine what's wrong.

While it may seem unimaginably far-fetched or based strictly on science fiction concepts of medicine, this progress is real. It is an outgrowth of the National Research Council's vision and commitment to utilize leading-edge research and development to generate economic benefit for Canadians—medical research that's oriented toward building industries and making jobs, both directly and by forging partnerships with private industry.

The Institute is working on early warnings for osteoporosis, studying how the brain recovers from strokes and how to sideline the effects of strokes. They are examining the impact of strokes on the one to three per cent of newborn babies who suffer a form of stroke that can lead

The Institute for Biodiagnostics is a key collaborator in the intraoperative MRI project. A spin-off company called IMRIS Inc. has been formed to commercialize the technology resulting from this project.

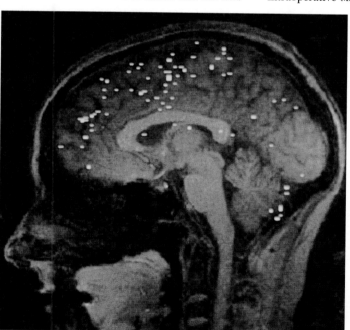

Functional magnetic resonance imaging (fMRI) is a powerful research tool which could provide clues toward the treatment of stroke, dementias and other neurological diseases.

at the forefront of exciting new developments on technological fronts, including the establishment of the world's first Intraoperative Magnetic Resonance Imaging system, EvIdent, a paradigm-free image analysis software used to study functional magnetic resonance images of the brain, and the use of infrared spectroscopy as a biomedical diagnostic tool.

The Institute for Biodiagnostics receives about $6 million a year from the federal government, but spends about $10 million, with the difference sourced from business partners, grants, other organizations and pharmaceutical companies (some of them based offshore) willing to invest in projects here because the research at the Institute possesses genuinely incredible potential.

The results of the remarkable research being conducted at the Institute for Biodiagnostics are now appearing in the form of products, as the Institute forges

partnerships with pharmaceutical companies, diagnostic instrument manufacturers and others to introduce new Canadian products and innovations with applications for the international marketplace, as well as to give existing products a competitive advantage.

A wide variety of additional products, in the form of non-invasive medical diagnostic systems, are expected to appear over the next few years. The Institute's links to medical, research and university communities have spread to include collaborations at many different levels, and with organizations as close as hospitals a few blocks away from the Institute, to companies in countries as distant as Australia, Brazil, Poland and the Czech Republic.

The Institute for Biodiagnostics will continue to press forward, along the leading edges of biomedical technological research, creating even more magic for the future. ■

to epilepsy, cerebral palsy or learning disabilities. They're finding non-invasive ways to diagnose early, and to monitor, diseases like cervical cancer, multiple sclerosis, Alzheimer's disease and arthritis.

What's more, IBD scientists have been

Merck Frosst Canada Inc.

The prevention and treatment of disease . . . that is the mission, the heritage and the business of Merck Frosst Canada Inc., Canada's leading research-based pharmaceutical company.

In pursuit of its mission, Merck Frosst excels in breaking new ground through Therapeutic Research, and in collaboration with many scientists from universities and hospitals across the country, Merck Frosst is on the leading edge in many of today's most important areas of health care research, such as respiratory, inflammatory and neurodegenerative diseases.

where Charles E. Frosst founded the company at the turn of the century. The company, however, has a strong presence in Canada through nine regional offices, one of which is in Winnipeg.

Merck Frosst also understands it has a much broader role to play, one of which involves working with various players in health care to find solutions which will enable them to better prevent and treat health problems.

The creation of a Patient Health Management (PHM) division is a direct result of this understanding. This initiative represents our commitment to advancing health and health care.

Patient Health provides the leadership necessary to mobilize stakeholders from a cross-section of areas, including government, academia, community medicine, pharmacy and industry, and works on several fronts to improve the effectiveness and efficiency of Canada's health care delivery system. Patient Health initiatives focus on the following areas:

Mobilizing stakeholders to establish a system of integrated, seamless health care delivery; this provides the ability to track patients across the continuum of care and addresses the costs and inefficiencies associated with the current, fragmented delivery system.

Measuring "usual care" across the continuum of health care delivery in order to uncover important care gaps that deliver sub-optimal outcomes; with this information providers become better equipped to develop targeted interventions that move usual care more in line with best practices.

Finally, with the application of an evidence-based approach to health evaluation and intervention, patient health initiatives help to assure appropriate care is available to all Canadians.

In the field of asthma, Merck Frosst works in collaboration with a research team involved in allergy and clinical immunology at Winnipeg's Health Sciences Centre. These scientists play a major role in a Canadian-wide, multi-centre study of young sufferers of chronic asthma.

In addition, Merck Frosst is involved in a large number of clinical trials to develop

Merck Frosst Canada Inc., Canada's leading research-based pharmaceutical company.

the talents of approximately 300 world-class scientists and researchers, who are part of the broader Canadian team of over 1,300 employees engaged in the discovery, manufacturing, marketing and distribution of medicines and vaccines for human health.

The company markets an extensive line of cardiovascular products for high blood pressure, heart failure, elevated cholesterol, as well as a broad range of vaccines. Merck Frosst is also a recognized leader in the treatment of osteoporosis, HIV/AIDS, glaucoma, prostate disease and other diseases.

With the Merck Frosst Centre for

These advances are not chance occurrences. In the last decade alone, Merck Frosst has invested more than $450 million in pharmaceutical research and development. Canadian researchers from Winnipeg's Health Sciences Centre, St. Boniface General Hospital, Children's Hospital and the University of Manitoba also benefit from the strong dedication of Merck Frosst to research and development. The company's commitment to pharmaceutical innovations places it among the top five research and development corporations in the nation.

Merck Frosst has its head office facility in Kirkland, Quebec just outside Montreal,

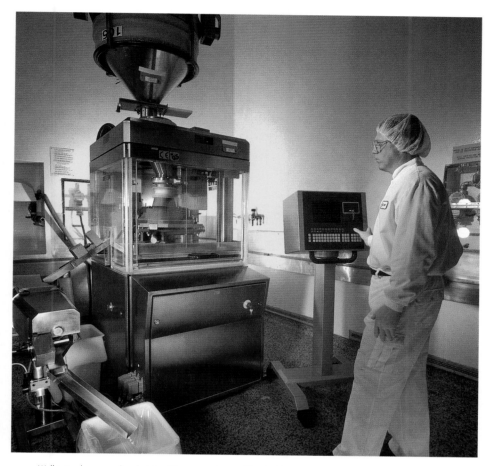

Well-trained personnel and state-of-the- art equipment like the Fette P1200 ensure that the Merck Manufacturing Division maintains the highest quality standards for its customers.

long-term partnerships aimed at enhancing the delivery of care for the population.

In addition, Merck Frosst supports organizations that focus on patient education, including the Lung Association of Manitoba and the Heart and Stroke Foundation of Manitoba. Merck Frosst was a major sponsor of "A Breath of Fresh Air" campaign, aimed at educating young children and adolescents on how they can live with asthma and still fully enjoy participation in sports activities.

Its corporate philosophy is very much to be involved in its communities. During Manitoba's worst flood of the century, Merck Frosst recognized the needs of those who were forced to leave their homes, and contributed to a flood relief fund. The company also contributed to the Christmas Cheer Board, which ensures that some of Winnipeg's less fortunate families have food on the table and a few gifts to open during the holiday season.

Merck Frosst is proud of being a part of the community and of its commitment to advancing health and health care for all Canadians. ■

and evaluate new therapies to treat heart failure, coronary artery disease and acute coronary syndromes, utilizing the expertise of primary investigators from the University of Manitoba's Department of Medicine, Cardiology division. It is also supporting the educational initiatives of the University of Manitoba's Lipid, Lipoprotein and Atherosclerosis Research Group, which is doing research into cholesterol and cardiovascular disease, and the work of the Health Sciences Centre Lipid Clinic, to which it provides an annual grant. In cooperation with the St. Boniface General Hospital Research Centre, Merck Frosst established and financially supports the Merck Frosst Distinguished Lecturer Series in cardiovascular research and medicine. Along similar lines, it provides funds for the University of Manitoba Research Faculty's Research Day, which focuses on a central topic with world renowned speakers and also features the research projects of local graduate students.

As a company, Merck Frosst has experienced growth in Manitoba in the past couple of years as a result of an expanding product line for the prevention and treatment of important diseases. Staffing also

reflects a changing health-care environment and the need to work with health-care decision makers and to develop

The researchers in this laboratory are involved in process development to support the various medicinal chemistry programs. The ultimate aim is to identify and develop new medicines for various treatments.

Manitoba Blue Cross

Since its formation in 1938 as the Manitoba Hospital Service Association, the corporation that ultimately emerged as Manitoba Blue Cross has become one of the 50 largest employers in the province. Although much has changed over the years, one thing hasn't. Formed to fill a need for health care costs not borne by government, Blue Cross remains committed to that purpose, both for individuals and for companies seeking administered benefits packages for their employees.

Today, the not-for-profit Blue Cross annual income is divided between a variety of individual subscriber plans addressing the needs of Manitobans of all ages, and leading-edge group health care programs handled for a range of companies. Group plans are custom tailored for a

Manitoba Blue Cross Senior Management Team (left to right): John Henson, Vice-President, Finance and Operations; Aidan O'Brien, Vice-President, Sales and Marketing; Leon Ganas, Vice-President, Management Information Systems; (seated) Kerry Bittner, President, Manitoba Blue Cross.

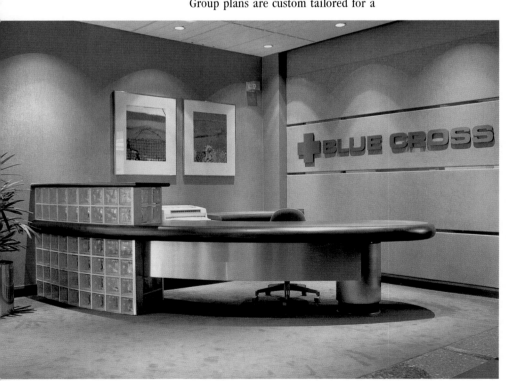

Manitoba Blue Cross, Main Reception.

company's specific needs, and individual subscriber plans offer a full range of health and travel benefits.

A member of the Canadian Association of Blue Cross Plans and an associate member of the Blue Cross and Blue Shield Association in the United States, Manitoba

Blue Cross has pioneered initiatives in the suplementary health benefits field, and has worked to remain at the forefront of innovation in individual and group plan services. The first travel health plan of its kind for Blue Cross in Canada was pioneered here in 1975, and is the "flagship" by which most Canadian Blue Cross plans are known. In 1982, another Canadian first, the "Plus Plan," included dental and vision coverage for subscribers, and in 1986 Manitoba Blue Cross was the first Canadian Blue Cross organization to introduce an Employee Assistance Plan.

Blue Cross believes in proactive health care; the ounce of prevention theory is evident in its community involvement, which includes grants to the Manitoba Medical Service Foundation Inc. and Foundations for Health, as well as sponsorship of the Blue Cross 10K Walk in the annual Manitoba Marathon and the yearly Age and Opportunity Lifestyles Conference for Manitobans over 50.

Now, in the 1990s, as baby boomers age and begin to face increased health costs in tandem with strained pension plans, Blue Cross is working with other agencies to ensure continued quality care will be available to older people. With cuts to the health care system combined with public demand for various forms of elder care, supplementary benefits are undergoing major revamping. At the same time, a "Gen X" Plan has been designed for those under 30, and travel coverage adjusted to respond to changing travel patterns.

In addition, Manitoba Blue Cross has prepared for another evolution in its customer base. As shifting economic patterns cause more people to become self-employed, work out of their homes or for smaller businesses, they seek different health benefit packages. In response, Blue Cross has developed plans suited to these new economic realities. Now all individuals, and groups both large and small, can select packages specifically designed to meet today's changing needs. ■

St. John's-Ravenscourt School

SJR students are well-rounded, motivated individuals, who lead active lives and have many outside interests.

SJR enrols boys from Grade One through Six, and becomes coed with the introduction of girls into Middle School at Grade Seven and beyond.

In many ways, it's like a small town. There's a real sense of community at St. John's-Ravenscourt, where teachers and students not only get to know each other in the classroom, but also over lunch, at the hockey rink, the fundraisers or at drama practice. Long after the final bell goes for the day, and even on weekends, the school remains open and filled with students. It's the type of atmosphere that fosters mutual respect, self-confidence and a willingness by students to risk failure in order to succeed. It's no accident that SJR has taken top honours in the world public speaking and debating championships for 8 of the past 10 years. SJR teachers never say, "Don't argue with me," but on the contrary, they encourage thoughtful argument in the classroom, letting students know their ideas matter.

Founded in 1820 by the Rev. John West, St. John's-Ravenscourt was originally established as a mission school for the children of the Selkirk settlers. Today, it's an independent day and boarding school devoted to helping young men and women prepare for university through the pursuit of academic excellence. SJR graduates are sought after by universities across the country, with 40 to 45 per cent of graduates winning university entrance scholarships.

The school has a selective entry policy, accepting only students with average to above average abilities. SJR students are well-rounded, motivated individuals, who lead active lives and have many outside interests. The school enrols boys from Grade One through Six, and becomes coed with the introduction of girls into Middle School at Grade Seven and beyond. The students come from close to home and from around the globe—the Pacific Rim, Saudi Arabia, Germany, Ukraine, Colombia and the U.S. Sixty enrol as boarding students, making one of the school's three residences their home away from home. Canada is recognized as a safe country for children, and that, together with the school's reputation for being strong in math and science, has attracted many international students. The school has established a yearly $400,000 financial aid program, which includes scholarships and bursaries, to assist families with financing their child's SJR education.

In 1997-98, over $6 million was spent on renovations and additions to the school, providing larger classrooms, new science labs, a second electronically equipped library and a brand new music centre. However, what makes a great school great is its teachers, and SJR is proud to say its teachers are outstanding. For them, teaching goes beyond a career—it's a lifestyle. They enjoy the subjects they teach from a personal perspective. Many are published authors of textbooks, periodicals, curriculum and other works. They believe in the school's philosophy of fostering a sound mind and body, and, like the students, participate in the many extracurricular activities at the school, ranging from soccer, wrestling, judo, hockey and golf, to chess, ham radio, debating and public speaking, band, photography and choir.

St. John's-Ravenscourt has its roots in the past, but it is investing in the future—developing a generation of confident, resourceful and contributing members of society. ■

Collège universitaire de Saint-Boniface

Located in the largest francophone community west of Ontario, the Collège universitaire de Saint-Boniface (CUSB) is Western Canada's oldest post-secondary educational institution and also its only French-language university. Founded by Bishop Provencher, who arrived at the Red River Colony in 1818, the CUSB has been a leader in French-language education and training for almost 180 years.

Affiliated with the University of Manitoba, the CUSB offers bachelor's programs in arts, science, education and translation, as well as a master's degree program in education. The CUSB's Faculty of Education is Manitoba's only recognized faculty for persons wanting to teach in the Français and French Immersion schools of the province.

Au niveau académique, le CUSB offre tous les avantages des grands campus universitaires sans leurs inconvénients. Les installations sont modernes; les services axés sur les besoins des étudiantes et étudiants. Le rapport étudiant/professeur est l'un des points

Collège universitaire de Saint-Boniface. Photo ©Henry Kalen.

forts du CUSB: les membres du personnel enseignant connaissent leurs étudiantes et étudiants et ils leur sont accessibles.

The CUSB will soon be offering a four-year business administration degree which will require a working knowledge of a third and even a fourth international language (Spanish and German). In antici-

pation of the future needs in the international marketplace, the CUSB has signed cooperation agreements with universities in France, Germany and Chile.

The CUSB is a recognized leader in training Winnipeg's bilingual workforce. The CUSB's École technique et professionnelle (ETP) is a technical college offering one- and two-year diplomas in business administration, office management, early childhood education and computer analyst-programmer. The ETP also offers certificates in the growing field of health-care aide and call-centre client services.

The CUSB's Continuing Education Division offers conversational French and Spanish courses to anglophones and francophones wanting to learn another language. It also provides language skills upgrading courses tailored to the needs of government departments and agencies, as well as private corporations.

St. Boniface, Winnipeg's francophone community, is the centre of francophone artistic and cultural life in Manitoba. St. Boniface is the home of all of Manitoba's francophone provincial institutions and associations. The Franco-Manitoban Cultural Centre, the Cercle Molière (Canada's oldest theatre company), two French-language radio stations, two French bookstores and the St. Boniface Municipal Library are but a few of the Franco-Manitoban institutions found within minutes of the CUSB.

Une rivière seulement, la Rouge, sépare Saint-Boniface du centre-ville de Winnipeg. C'est à dire que la vie sociale, sportive, commerciale et culturelle de Winnipeg est facilement accessible aux étudiantes et étudiants du CUSB. Parmi les joyaux de Winnipeg, signalons le Ballet Royal, l'Orchestre symphonique, le Musée des beaux-arts, le Musée de l'homme et de la nature et le Parc national et le marché de La Fourche.

The CUSB genuinely offers the best of both worlds, in a city unique in Canada that embraces both English and French culture. ■

The Misericordia Hospital

Misericordia has served the City of Winnipeg and Manitoba since 1898 as a Catholic health care provider. It has become known as the "hospital without walls"—a hub of health care delivery, focusing on providing inpatient, ambulatory care and community outreach services, and on building partnerships with patients and the community.

The Eye Care Centre of Excellence is one of Misericordia's cornerstone programs and offers a comprehensive service. Consolidation of eye care has resulted in an increase in the number of eye surgical procedures and improved efficiencies. Each year over 6,000 cataract surgical procedures are completed at Misericordia, improving and restoring eyesight to Manitobans.

This comprehensive approach includes a partnership with the Manitoba Cancer Treatment and Research Foundation (MCTRF) to provide a site for the Provincial Breast Screening Program and the HOPE Breast Cancer Information and Resource Centre.

To meet the needs of an ever changing society, the Misericordia has pioneered many new health care delivery programs.

Health Links phone line, available 24 hours a day, everyday, makes it possible for people to call a professionally trained nurse to ask health questions, receive information and referrals. Follow-up is an important part of this program.

The hospital's unique Care-A-Van takes to the streets with health care professionals who offer mobile blood pressure

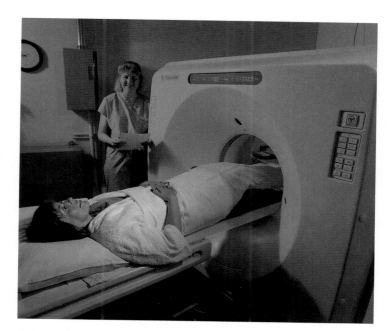

At Misericordia, caring is their tradition.

Compassion of the heart to those in need.

Misericordia has played a leading role in women's health.

The Breast Care Centre is a one-stop location for assessment, diagnosis, treatment and support. The Centre provides a holistic approach to care, including teaching breast self-examination, breast health clinics and wellness seminars.

clinics, breast health clinics, Peripheral Vascular Disease (PVD) screening, nutrition and eye safety clinics.

"Easy Street" is a re-creation of a city street set inside the safety of the hospital and includes a bank, a supermarket, restaurant, department store, a car, a bus and curbs, doorways and steps. This

rehabilitation environment prepares people in a positive way to manage some of the real obstacles of everyday life.

Wolseley Family Place is a community resource centre with a nurturing environment for young parents, especially single moms, and their children. Parents learn about nutrition and how to stretch precious dollars when shopping. Pre- and post-natal child care classes enhance parenting skills. Young fathers and mothers participate in employment readiness programs. While parents are learning, children are nearby in a safe fully equipped daycare environment filled with love, laughter and activity.

MGH (Maximizing Good Health) for lungs is a program designed to teach people with lung disease how to deal with their breathing difficulties.

Misericordia means "Compassion of the Heart to Those in Need." At the beginning of another century of service to the community, the Misericordia embraces its Core Values of Caring, Respect and Trust and prepares for the next 100 years based on a proud tradition of caring. ■

16

The Marketplace

Photo by Mike Grandmaison.

Place Louis Riel All-Suite Hotel

Place Louis Riel All-Suite Hotel is located in the heart of downtown Winnipeg, close to attractions and business centres.

One of the largest private collections of original aboriginal art in Manitoba does not hang on an art gallery wall. Each year, thousands of visitors to Winnipeg take in the works of art in the warm, welcoming atmosphere of the Place Louis Riel, a 280 room all-suite hotel in the heart of downtown. The artwork is a visible commitment to Canada's First Nations people and to the hotel's returning guests, drawn back by its friendly, first-name hospitality.

The collection, from some of Canada's most prominent native painters, began in much the same way as did another collection, in another hotel half-way around the world. The Colombe D'Or, an elegant hotel in France's upscale Côte D'Azur, acquired art from the likes of Picasso and Matisse, who in their struggling years paid their tabs with paintings. Similarly, prominent Canadian aboriginal art is on display in many of the suites of the Place Louis Riel All-Suite Hotel—from its well-appointed studio suites to its exclusive premier suites. Some of the earlier works were traded for a place to stay, but today the hotel's owner, Martin Tallman, actively purchases the art.

Place Louis Riel's commitment to First Nations people stems from a decades-long loyalty on their part in choosing the hotel as a home away from home. Callers to the hotel switchboard may request reservation service in Cree, Ojibway or OjiCree, in addition to Canada's official languages. That's just one example of the people-first philosophy Place Louis Riel has put in place. The hotel and its staff are truly committed to ensuring all its guests—whether performing artists, film crews, athletes, corporate executives, tour groups or out-of-town families whose children are sick and in the hospital—have a sense of belonging. Many keep coming back—60 per cent of Place Louis Riel's business is repeat—drawn by that personal touch.

Guests are especially made to feel welcome, whether it's by being greeted on a first-name basis or being surprised with an anniversary card signed by the staff. Professional service is combined with a lot of caring. Special bonds are formed. When a family with a young baby in the hospital went home after staying at the Place Louis Riel, the family kept in close touch with staff to let them know how the baby was doing. When Manitobans were faced with the worst flood of the century, an elderly woman called the hotel for a friendly voice at the other end of the phone to reassure her that everything would be OK if she had to evacuate her home.

Place Louis Riel All-Suite Hotel would be nothing without its staff—people like executive housekeeper Barbara Scerbo, who started with the hotel more than 15 years ago, or Marcel, the bell captain, who knows everything that's going on and frequently has guests send parcels to his attention prior to their arrival, knowing the parcels will be there waiting for them.

Many of the staff at Place Louis Riel have gone through a six-month certification program by the Manitoba Tourism Education Council, which has a strong focus on recognizing professional industry standards.

Place Louis Riel offers a choice of studio or one or two-bedroom suites, as well as superior executive suites, all equipped with data ports, voice mail, cable television and pay movie channels.

There is truly a sense of family among the staff, and that is because many staffers are, in fact, related to each other—cousins, aunts and uncles. Many, like Barbara and Marcel, have been with the hotel a long time and have been given the opportunity for career advancement. Most have been there more than five years, a rarity in the hospitality industry. It's the result of a basic operating philosophy that a caring attitude to the staff will project itself onto the clients.

Many of the staff have gone through a six-month certification program by the Manitoba Tourism Education Council, which has a strong focus on recognizing professional industry standards. Also more than fifty per cent of the staff have been through "The Manitoba Best" customer service workshop. The staff has achieved such high service standards that Place Louis Riel has become popular as a centre of training excellence. Many trainees come from First Nations communities to learn the ropes of the hotel industry and to take those skills back home. Two northern Manitoba hotels, operated by First Nations communities in The Pas and Garden Hill, are staffed by graduates trained at the Place Louis Riel All-Suite Hotel.

Place Louis Riel was originally a luxury apartment block when it opened its doors in 1970, Winnipeg's centennial year. The building's name was chosen to reflect the combined heritage of the province's pioneers. Louis Riel, the founder of Manitoba and a historic Metis figure, championed the rights of his people, but was hanged for treason in the late 1800s, after a failed rebellion against the ruling government.

In the mid-1980s, the Place Louis Riel All-Suite Hotel made the transition from an apartment hotel with limited service to a full-service all-suite hotel. Twenty-two residential apartments are still intermixed held under long-term lease by permanent residents, who have been told by the present owners they can stay as long as they wish. Hotel guests have all the benefits of a traditional hotel, plus more—24-hour guest service, room service, kitchen facilities (full-size stove, refrigerator, microwave, coffeemaker and cooking and eating utensils), valet service or laundromat, grocery store and restaurant. The hotel offers a choice of studio, one or two-bedroom suites, as well as superior executive suites, all equipped with data ports, voice mail, cable television and pay movie channels.

Place Louis Riel All-Suite Hotel is more than a perfect place to stay. It's also the ideal place to hold a business meeting, wedding reception or banquet. The hotel has 16 meeting rooms for groups as small as five or as large as 125. A business service centre in the hotel's lobby is capable of handling the routine needs of the business traveller, from photocopying to receiving e-mail.

Place Louis Riel is part of the community. It is involved with the Winnipeg Chamber of Commerce, Downtown Biz, and Winnipeg 2000, the city's economic development agency, working to keep Winnipeg a strong, safe city. The hotel is involved in promoting Winnipeg as a tourism destination, not just a stopover, and is working hand-in-hand with Tourism Winnipeg and Travel Manitoba. It's also involved in cultural and sporting events, whether through fundraising, helping to create community awareness or reducing accommodation costs so organizers can continue to put on these types of unique events that attract visitors to Winnipeg. ■

For business or pleasure, Place Louis Riel is an ideal choice.

The Lombard

Queen Elizabeth II, Mick Jagger, Bobby Hull, Celine Dion, Pierre Elliot Trudeau—they all have one thing in common. They have all stayed at The Lombard, located on the most famous intersection in Winnipeg—Portage and Main.

The 21-storey hotel, owned by Winnipeg's Richardson family, not only sets the standard for elegance in Winnipeg, but for comfort and personalized service. No touch is too small, whether it's sending dog treats up to the room for pets travelling with their families, welcoming joggers back from a run with a cold drink and towel at the front door or greeting a returning guest by name. It's about putting people first.

Officially opened in 1970, the hotel was known as The Winnipeg Inn. It became the Westin Hotel in 1980 and enjoyed a further renaissance, when in September 1996 Canadian Pacific Hotels assumed the management contract and its name was once again changed. For Canadian Pacific Hotels, The Lombard

marks the return to Winnipeg 25 years after closing its doors to the historic Royal Alexandra Hotel. The Lombard was a perfect fit with the company's collection of 26 heritage and distinctive properties across Canada, including Chateau Whistler Resort in British Columbia, the Banff Springs Hotel in Alberta and Le Chateau Frontenac in Quebec.

With 350 guest rooms, 16 suites and two superior suites, The Lombard is a "home away from home" for many business travellers. Roughly 20 per cent of the hotel's guests represent firms with which The Lombard has established long-standing relationships. To make it easier for business travellers to conduct business while away from the office, they can stay in rooms fully equipped with the appropriate amenities—a large working desk with computer hook-up, a halogen desk lamp, desk drawer organizer and supplies, two telephones (including a portable speaker phone), in-room coffee-maker with complimentary coffee and tea, hairdryer, terry bathrobe and iron and ironing board. Hotel staff will assist with business needs, making restaurant reservations and arranging tickets for local theatre productions and entertainment events.

All Canadian Pacific Hotels offer an innovative guest recognition program for frequent travellers. By tracking the stays of Canadian Pacific Club members and

creating personal profiles, guests are ensured their preferences will be met as far as room requirements—smoking or non-smoking, floor level, bed type and even the type of pillow. Members also enjoy special benefits such as a reservation number for members only, instant check-in/check-out, priority room access, complimentary luggage storage, late check-out privileges and cheque-cashing privileges.

All guests of The Lombard are offered the use of the hotel swimming pool, sauna, whirlpool, exercise room, services of a massage therapist and unlimited free local calls.

Nearly 350 people are employed by The Lombard to ensure that service and hospitality consistently exceed guest expectations. However, one can't forget that the hotel not only caters to out-of-town visitors, but to Winnipeggers themselves. Many citizens of Winnipeg have grown up with the hotel. They've celebrated key events in their lives there—from high school graduations to engagements, weddings and 25th anniversaries. The hotel's four-diamond award-winning restaurant, The Velvet Glove, has been where many a suitor has popped the question, having conspired with the waiter to add a diamond sparkle to the champagne or to put a little surprise in the chocolate mousse. In recognizing that memories such as those are special, the hotel often sends guests home with complimentary photographs, taken at the table.

In its first 25 years, The Lombard saw more than 2,000 couples hold their wedding receptions there. That translates to more than 503,750 meals being served, along with 16 tons of wedding cake. It's that attention to detail that's kept people coming back. So what did it take to run The Lombard in its first quarter century? That's simple:

- 720,000 rolls of toilet paper
- 432,000 boxes of facial tissue
- one-million notepads for the rooms
- 31-million pounds of laundry (guest room and table linen)
- 20.4-million feet of saran wrap
- 300,000 pounds of coffee
- 792,000 cases of beer
- three-million room guests
- 17-million restaurant and banquet facility guests

Over the years, The Lombard has changed with the times. What was once The Stage Door night club is today the Wellington Ballroom, having been a dinner theatre and three-meal-a-day restaurant in between. The Top of the Inn Bar, once a trendy after-five meeting spot, is now replaced by a health club and

meeting room with wall-to-wall windows, giving a bird's eye view of the city.

As The Lombard looks to the future, it also looks to play an important role in the community. In 1997, during Manitoba's flood of the century, it provided free babysitting for Winnipeggers who wanted to help sandbag. It sent out a van-load of food for people assisting in the flood effort daily. And it provided stress counselling for those families forced to relocate, whether they were guests of the hotel or not.

Every Christmas, all Canadian Pacific hotels open their doors to make "Room at the Inn" for needy out-of-town families visiting relatives in hospitals. The hotels work with local partners—hospitals, cancer clinics and AIDS hospices—to refer families to the program, which provides free accommodations for each family for

up to seven days.

As part of a first-of-its-kind national program, each Canadian Pacific hotel across Canada has "adopted" a local battered women's shelter. Through the program, furniture, bedding and other household items belonging to the hotel are donated to the shelters on an ongoing basis.

The Lombard, a Canadian Pacific hotel is as committed to taking an active role in the community as it is to providing excellent customer service. In fact, The Lombard is the only hotel in Winnipeg to receive the CAA/AAA Four Diamond award for 15 consecutive years. Through its service both to the community and to its guests, The Lombard has shown itself again and again to be the choice for excellent hotel accommodations. ■

Murray Chevrolet Oldsmobile

From early roots in the picturesque Manitoba town of Souris, to the office towers and the broad streets of Winnipeg, Murray Chevrolet Oldsmobile has been matching Manitobans to GM cars for more than 70 years—and the company continues to grow and expand across the Canadian Prairies.

It's a long way from where it all began for the Murray family, back when cars were a novelty. It was the spring of 1926, when Andrew A. Murray first opened his business in the small town of Souris. He began raising a family, and he sold Star cars—later, Essex and Hudson vehicles. In 1934, Murray's Garage began handling General Motors cars and trucks.

By 1945, sons Ewart, Del and Clair had joined the business and soon were employing two dozen people in Souris. The family expansion gathered steam, expanding to Brandon, Manitoba, in the '60s and early '70s, and by the late 1990s shows no sign of slowing down. Clair, with more than 50 years as a GM dealer, remains actively involved in all the dealerships now run by his four sons. The eldest, Doug, is in Brandon; Dan operates the Winnipeg location, opened in 1994 and Chris is in Oak Bluff, Manitoba. Brother Paul has moved on to Alberta with a dealership in Medicine Hat and a satellite location in nearby Bow Island. The Murray dealership family also has a location in Moose Jaw, Saskatchewan. The Manitoba dealerships employ well over 200 people.

The Murray philosophy revolves around the slogan "Our Reputation is Your Guarantee," and company employees live that slogan as a genuine mission statement. The close-knit group of Murray staff approach their jobs with dedication to quality service, and commitment to ensuring customer satisfaction. In an industry where personnel change employers frequently, it's an unusual characteristic of the Murray dealerships that staff turnover is low; the professional relationships that are forged tend to last over the long-term, fostering growth and development opportunities for staff.

Several of the Murray team members have gone on to acquire their own successful GM dealerships, building on the experience gained as Murray employees. This has been the case in Dauphin and Portage la Prairie. The success of these former employees indicates both the high quality and professional approach of the staff who work at Murray Chevrolet Oldsmobile, and the opportunities that exist within the Murray family chain of dealerships.

The future is bright. As the millennium approaches, it is time for the Murray dealership family to expand again. The dealership purchased in Winnipeg in 1994 has outgrown its leased location in downtown Winnipeg. That location will be replaced by one in the undeveloped south end of the city which will allow for acres of

New Image 2000 Winnipeg Dealership opening Fall 1998. Bishop Grandin & Waverley.

Paul Murray, Chris Murray, Doug Murray and Dan Murray at the 9th hole, Clear Lake Golf Course.

storage as well as far more display space for vehicles.

The new location for the Winnipeg dealership will be an Image 2000 General Motors dealership, and will incorporate the full range of GM sales and service facilities. These will reflect new, improved methods and approaches to customer service, developed through GM's research and marketing arm. In addition, Murray Chevrolet Oldsmobile has expanded into cyberspace, moving onto the Internet with a fully interactive website.

But while the trappings may change, one thing remains constant through the continuing growth and expansion: the guarantee to customers that is based on the Murray reputation, and the dedication of all Murray Chevrolet Oldsmobile staff to ensuring that pledge is kept. ■

Clair & Mildred Murray celebrating Clair's 51st year as a General Motors dealer.

Manitoba Lotteries Corporation

Modern lotteries were introduced in Manitoba in 1970 as part of this province's 100th anniversary celebrations, and evolved over the years in response to consumer demand. Today, the Manitoba Lotteries Corporation operates or facilitates a wide range of entertainment possibilities in this province, from break-open tickets to free-standing casinos.

A provincial Crown Corporation, Manitoba Lotteries is responsible for lottery and gaming operations in the province, enabling some 800 retail outlets throughout Manitoba to provide a full range of lottery services and products, including lotto and add-on spiel games, instant tickets and sports wagering, through lotteries operated by the Western Canada Lottery Corporation and the Interprovincial Lottery Corporation.

The MLC also manages and operates the jewels of the gaming industry in Manitoba, three casinos in Winnipeg: Club Regent with its tropical theme, the nostalgia-oriented McPhillips Street Station and the Crystal Casino's Monte Carlo-style environment emphasizing classic table games. Manitoba was the first province to develop year-round casino gaming in Canada. The Crystal Casino in downtown Winnipeg, opened in 1989, was the first Continental-style facility in North America.

Club Regent and McPhillips Street Station both opened in 1993. Each offers a full 50,000-square-foot facility, where ample parking is easy to find and road access is fast and convenient. The two provide the latest in gaming entertainment.

Club Regent and McPhillips Street Station remain open seven days a week, and form the number one attraction for hundreds of bus tours and thousands of convention delegates that visit Winnipeg every year. The two full-service casinos are significant economic contributors to the province's tourism economy; since their opening in 1993, they have grown annually, and by 1997 were attracting 300 tours a year.

With this steadily increasing demand by consumers for the leisure entertainment options provided by a range of

There is always a warm "tropical" Manitoba welcome at Club Regent for the more than 300 inbound tour groups that visit the casinos of Winnipeg annually.

gaming, the MLC embarked on an exciting redevelopment phase for the popular casinos. Construction for this redevelopment began in the fall of 1997 and was targeted for completion to coincide with the 1999 Pan Am Games being held in Winnipeg.

Traditional table games with proven popularity will be added to the variety of gaming options already provided at these two casinos, and an expanded full range of live entertainment, food and beverage services, including licensed lounge facilities, will be developed in answer to recent, greatly increased competition in the gaming industry in the Midwestern U.S. and Canada, and to attract additional

tourism to Manitoba. These expansions will add another 325 new jobs to the gaming industry in this province; the growth in capacity will fill anticipated rising demand from tourism over the coming decade.

By 1999, the Crystal Casino will have been phased out in favour of expanded, full-service operations at the McPhillips Street Station and Club Regent sites. Coupled with the expansions of these two gaming facilities, the compelling use of theme architectural styling ensures the casinos are "must see" attractions in Winnipeg, creating a marketing catalyst that will drive the doubling of tour volumes by the year 2000.

Gaming has been one of the fastest growing industries in North America for the past quarter-century, increasingly popular everywhere as a full-service form of consumer recreation, and an important factor in the expansion of tourism. At least five Canadian provinces now offer casino facilities, and 90 per cent of Canadians find gaming an acceptable form of entertainment.

Gaming activities administered by the MLC, which employs 1,200 people directly, sustain almost 10,000 additional jobs in the economy. And entertainment events that are an integral part of the gaming experience also support Manitoba's well-known entertainment industry. Local entertainers with national reputations have appeared at MLC entertainment venues.

Tourism is a major industry in Manitoba, a source of revenue that helps diversify the province's economic base. Overall, Manitoba's tourism industry generates over $1 billion in expenditures

McPhillips Street Station's unique themed architectural styling ensures that it is one of Winnipeg's "must see" attractions and sets a distinctive mood for the entertainment experience awaiting within.

annually, roughly 3.5 per cent of the $30 billion total for Canada. Gaming draws thousands of visitors here from outside our province each year. During their visits, they discover the multitude of cultural, recreational and historic attractions Winnipeg offers, as well as the genuine

hospitality and warmth of the city's residents. Once visitors have experienced the rich mosaic of entertainment and cultural and natural attractions Winnipeg offers, they put this vibrant Prairie city on their list for return individual visits, group tours and conferences. ■

A solid focus on customer service coupled with an exciting entertainment experience attracts thousands of visitors from outside Manitoba to the casinos of Winnipeg, the most popular group tour attraction in the province.

Keystone Ford

R.M. (Bob) Kozminski, Corporate Headquarters.

Most Winnipeggers know Keystone Ford as the car dealership whose name reflects the Manitoba nickname of the Keystone province. But this Ford dealership is actually the largest member of the stable that makes up the RMK Automotive Group, including Jaguar and Hyundai dealerships, and the local Budget Rent-A-Car franchise. All of them reflect the distinctive personal style fostered by dealer principal and RMK corporate head Bob Kozminski: a firm belief in the provision of quality and insistence on customer satisfaction as a solid basis for success.

This principle has been operative since the beginnings of RMK Automotive Group in 1973, the year Mr. Kozminski bought a small car rental franchise operation, Arro Rent A Car, in downtown Winnipeg. His brother-in-law Glenn Cross, who has partnered with him ever since, took on the job of General Manager for the small company.

Bob Kozminski grew up with cars; his father was in the business. The younger Kozminski learned early the principle of good customer relations, as he ran errands and helped out at his father's various business locations. The rental agency reminded him that his first passion was cars; he had purchased himself a 1974 Jaguar E type as a special treat on graduating from law school. Though a successful lawyer, he began looking for new challenges, and the idea of the car business intrigued him.

In 1975, he and Glenn Cross bought the franchise and assets (two city locations and approximately 150 cars and trucks) of the existing Budget Rent-A-Car operation in Winnipeg. By 1986 he had taken over as Dealer Principal of Keystone Ford Sales Ltd. after acquiring the controlling shareholder's interest in the local Ford franchise. This was the original Dominion Motors that was operated at the corner of Fort and Graham in Winnipeg for many years and the dealership assets had been sold to Keystone Ford Sales Limited.

With his law practice left behind, Mr. Kozminski took on the dual positions of President and Chief Executive Officer of Keystone Ford. The dealership had just been moved in August of 1986 from the corner of Fort and Graham into a brand new facility on Regent Avenue in Transcona, spreading over roughly five acres of land, with a building that provides more than 30,000 square feet of office, showroom and service space. Keystone Ford is known for competitive advertising, progressive sales and marketing techniques and solid customer service based on

R.M. (Bob) Kozminski and Glenn Cross in the showroom at Keystone Ford Sales Ltd. on Regent Avenue in Winnipeg.

integrity and respect for the customer.

Bob Kozminski's strong convictions revolving around customer satisfaction, hard work and service haven't been restricted to the successful development of RMK Automotive Group. Employees are encouraged to follow their CEO's lead to take leadership roles in improving their community; the list of donations Mr. Kozminski routinely makes on behalf of RMK includes dozens of organizations ranging from the University of Manitoba to Manitoba Riding for the Disabled, Canadian Cancer Society, Winnipeg Habitat for Humanity, Manitoba Theatre Centre and the Prairie Theatre Exchange.

for the Progressive Conservative Party of Manitoba.

Budget has grown to four locations including the Winnipeg International Airport, and its summer fleet numbers peak at over 450 rental cars and trucks. Starting with 26 per cent of the local market share when Mr. Kozminski and Mr. Cross took over, the car rental franchise in just over a decade captured almost half the market at the Winnipeg Airport location and continues to be the market leader.

By April 1990, the group of companies and the Executive Management team were brought together at the corporate head-

Glenn Cross and R.M. (Bob) Kozminski at main office Budget location at Ellice and Sherbrook in Winnipeg.

Corporate Headquarters and Jaguar/Hyundai dealership, as well as Budget truck rental location at Sargent and King Edward in Winnipeg.

Kozminski has worked tirelessly with the United Way to help establish a 25th Anniversary Foundation and with the Variety Club of Manitoba to help organize their fundraising mechanism. He also supports the Winnipeg Symphony Orchestra's annual fundraising raffle of a new Jaguar. He was heavily involved in the late '90s local citizens' campaign to save the Winnipeg Jets hockey team, and has worked actively for years as a fundraiser

quarters at the Budget Administration building on Sargent Avenue at King Edward, in the St. James area of Winnipeg. RMK Automotive Group now has 150 full-time and 30 part-time employees.

In November 1990, the local Jaguar franchise became available, and Bob Kozminski, with fond recollections of his 1974 Jag, bought it—though not before studying the market and realizing the

high-end dealership would require balance with quality product for mid- and lower price range customers. So he married the Jaguar franchise with a Hyundai dealership, putting them together on Sargent Avenue along with the Budget administration building, to offer customers a broader range of choice and price. The dealership has become the top-rated Hyundai dealership in Canada for customer satisfaction, and Jaguar on Sargent remains Manitoba's only Jaguar sales, service and parts facility.

While Budget makes up about 22 per cent of total annual sales now for the Group today, and the Jaguar/Hyundai combination accounts for approximately 8 per cent, Winnipeg's Keystone Ford accounts for about two thirds of the RMK Group's total annual sales of $70 million on its asset base of $29 million. The dealership ranks 13th in Ford customer satisfaction ratings across Canada, and is among the largest car and truck dealerships in Manitoba, thanks to the company's continued commitment to its founding philosophy of customer satisfaction. ■

Lakeview Management Inc./Country Inn & Suites By Carlson

L ook around Winnipeg, and the Lakeview stamp is clearly visible on the city's distinctive Prairie skyline. In the suburbs, apartments and condominiums dot the landscape: the Courts of St. James, or the country-style Kenaston Village. The downtown hub of the city includes Lakeview's home offices, located in the company's substantial hotel-office-apartment-restaurant complex

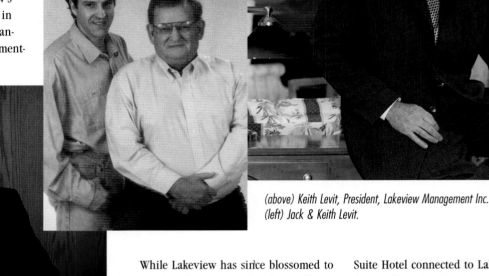

(above) Keith Levit, President, Lakeview Management Inc.
(left) Jack & Keith Levit.

Jack Levit, CEO, Lakeview Management Inc.

development adjacent to the Winnipeg Convention Centre and originally known as Lakeview Square.

Connecting the hotel/office complex with the convention centre are the first Winnipeg skywalks built, to enable guests at the then-Holiday Inn to reach meetings at what was a brand-new convention centre, without having to go outside during the winter. The idea for the walkways came from Lakeview founder and current Chief Executive Officer Jack Levit; it was quickly borrowed by civic developers to become a honeycomb of sheltering walkways over much of the downtown landscape.

While Lakeview has since blossomed to international status as a developer of top-quality hotel properties with luxurious amenities at affordable guest rates, the Lakeview head office remains here, faithful to its Prairie roots.

Lakeview's origins are in Winnipeg. In 1964, founder Jack Levit began the firm to design and build multi-tenant warehouse and showroom facilities for the city's distribution industries. From the beginning, Mr. Levit believed in growth and evolution. Lakeview would move quickly into the development of multi-family residential/commercial complexes like the Courts of St. James and Lakeview Square.

Lakeview soon established its innovative style: acting as the catalyst for investment, the company would provide design, financial and project construction management expertise for major developments, and would manage the properties into highly profitable, successful ventures. By the 1980s, these operating principles would draw Lakeview into the hotel development field, and the construction of showplace hotels in cities across Canada— the Sheraton in Winnipeg, Hamilton and Edmonton, and the 160-room Radisson

Suite Hotel connected to Lakeview's Airport Executive Centre near the Winnipeg International Airport.

Lakeview had the distinction of being the only developer which opened three major Sheraton Hotels in one year. The year was 1985.

The Radisson Suite Hotel fast became one of the most successful in the Radisson chain worldwide, and was the only hotel in the entire chain to receive 100 per cent guest satisfaction ratings twice in one year.

In the early '80s, Jack's son Keith Levit joined his father at the helm. Keith directed his own creative bent to the company his father had founded; the younger Levit brought to Lakeview a strongly innovative approach and the solid academic credentials of a Bachelor of Commerce (Honours) degree at the University of Manitoba, in addition to his Masters' degree of Real Estate and Regional Sciences obtained from the prestigious Southern Methodist University in Dallas, Texas. Keith's keen creative eye also lent itself to supporting Jack's energetic vision of growth for Lakeview. Recently, Jack moved to the CEO position, and Keith

Country Inn & Suites By Carlson Exterior.

took on the responsibility of President.

Then Carlson came along. The Levits saw an intriguing concept in the Carlson Corporation's limited-service luxury hotel, and negotiated an exclusive Canadian franchise pact with the American firm to develop Country Inns & Suites across Canada. Construction began in 1988, during a major Canada-wide recession, at a time when others were nervous about the economic future.

Keith Levit successfully took on the massive responsibility of bringing together an international pool of a thousand investors from around the world, and Lakeview forged ahead, building 12 Country Inns & Suites across Canada and one hotel in Grand Forks, North Dakota. The concept behind the hotels, all with fewer than a hundred rooms, was to provide luxury-style accommodation at affordable rates, "A Cozy Stay at a Comfortable Price," with the emphasis on room quality and amenities like free local calls, extensive complimentary Continental-plus breakfasts and 24-hour free coffee for guests.

The Inns also provide a Moviebar "Free to Guest" concept, with video cassette players in each room and a fully stocked computerized video vending machine located in hotel lobbies. The movies are offered free to hotel guests. Lakeview expanded the country-style, warm, inviting atmosphere concept by ensuring half

the rooms at the Inns were two-room suites, enabling a more diverse range of accommodation choice. Carlson, the original franchisor, liked the idea and picked it up for its own future developments.

Within months of their openings, the Lakeview-run Canadian hotels were drawing room occupancy rates so high the hotels began receiving awards for both occupancy rates and top-notch management: the Carlson Presidential Award for excellence and the Gold Award for occupancy rates over 90 per cent. Twelve of the properties in 1996 joined the 98 per cent Club—an award for hotels achieving repeat business of more than 98 per cent, as evidenced by returned survey cards. Eleven properties repeated their performance again in 1997.

The Winnipeg property opened its doors to receive the New Property of the Year award, then won the highest occupancy

award for seven consecutive years. The Gimli, Manitoba, Country Resort and the New Glasgow, Nova Scotia, properties received awards for increase in sales growth in lodging. The Regina, Saskatchewan, property took the 1995 Presidential Award for the highest standards of excellence in marketing, sales, guest service and profitability. Outstanding housekeeping awards, employee of the year, standards of excellence awards, general manager of the year—the list of kudos spreads across all the Inns in the Canadian system, all managed by Lakeview.

Lakeview continues to believe in growth; President Keith Levit envisions the company's next major project as utilizing a very aggressive development approach developing Country Inns & Suites in the provinces of Ontario, British Columbia and Alberta. In addition, the younger Levit foresees other branded lodgings with Lakeview's commensurate quality in management and service will be developed in cities across Canada; and envisions a new chain of hotels which will include the stamp of thick-towel luxury combined with enhanced business class services—affordable luxury for both business and pleasure discerning travellers. ■

Country Inn & Suites By Carlson Lobby.

Tourism Winnipeg/Travel Manitoba

Imagine one destination where you can explore a landscape from arctic tundra and lush forests to pristine lakes, desert and multicultural cities. Diverse and vast, Manitoba offers these experiences and many others. It is this wealth of wonders that draws visitors from around the world year round.

The gateway to Manitoba is Winnipeg—a capital city that brims with the vibrant culture of a large metropolis—ballet, theatre, symphony and opera for a start. Its attractions let you star gaze, sail the seas, hit the jackpot and sneak a peek at exotic wildlife and birds. Restaurants with cuisine from around the globe, colourful festivals, professional sports and a mecca of shopping bargains abound.

It is a city of sunshine and endless blue skies. However, it is the warmth of the city's more than 675,000 residents that ensures each stay is a memorable one and contributes to Winnipeg's success in winning bids to host major events such as the 1999 Pan American Games.

For Winnipeg and Manitoba, tourism

The gateway to Manitoba is Winnipeg—a capital city that brims with the vibrant culture of a large metropolis. Photo by Dave Reede. Courtesy of Tourism Winnipeg.

means big business. Nearly $341.5 million per year is spent on accommodations, meals, entertainment, retail purchases and transportation in Winnipeg. Add to that

what is spent outside Winnipeg and the total is more than $1.1 billion—making tourism the third largest industry in the province.

Tourism is also the fastest creator of new jobs. In Manitoba, that translates into approximately 29,000 full-time jobs and more than 50,000 part-time and seasonal positions.

It is meetings and conventions that offer the most lucrative opportunities for Manitoba. Each year, Winnipeg hosts more than 200 major conventions, attracting upward of 55,000 delegates. These delegates contribute more than $45 million to the city's economy.

Tourism Winnipeg, the city's marketing agency and Travel Manitoba, a department of the provincial government, work together with industry partners to bring the economic benefits of tourism to the province. Their role is to market the city and province as a travel destination for consumers, group tours and as a business destination—a preferred place to host conventions, trade shows, corporate getaways, board meetings and special events.

Tourism Winnipeg and Travel Manitoba target their meeting and convention promotional efforts in the Ottawa-Toronto-Montreal triangle, where a majority of

The Forks in Winnipeg. Photo by Henry Kalen. Courtesy of Tourism Winnipeg.

Canadian associations are headquartered, and in the United States where the focus is directed to Minneapolis, Chicago and the Midwest region.

Advantages to meeting in Winnipeg and Manitoba are clear. Winnipeg is centrally located, just 100 kilometres from the Canada/U.S. border and easily accessible by land, air and rail. Its 24-hour airport is served by several major airlines. Accommodations, facilities and meeting services are the most affordable of any comparable Canadian city. Half of the city's 6,000 first-class hotel rooms are

Inuit art at the Winnipeg Art Gallery. Theatre, symphony, opera, wildlife and waterfowl, the heritage of the fur-trade and more round out the diverse entertainment options.

In striking contrast to the capital city's sophistication is the natural beauty at its doorstep. With adventure travel, eco-tourism and agri-tourism growing in popularity, particularly in international markets, Winnipeg stands to benefit from its position as a gateway to the north. Manitoba's holiday and convention resorts provide year-round luxury, set amidst

Manitoba is not only home to great culture and heritage, but also to striking examples of nature's beauty. Photo courtesy of Travel Manitoba.

world's finest freshwater fishing. The many lodges welcome anglers looking to land one of the 28 species of trophy fish found in Manitoba waters, as well as those looking to take a quiet canoe trip across a pine-ringed lake or a photo safari through the forest, checking out the flora and fauna or perhaps prehistoric rock paintings.

Brandon, Manitoba's second largest city with a population of 40,000, can also serve as a hub for day trips to see the desert-like sand dunes of the Carberry Sand Hills and the International Peace Garden on the Manitoba/United States border. ■

Whiteshell Provincial Park. Photo courtesy of Travel Manitoba.

located downtown, within walking distance of the Winnipeg Convention Centre, a three-level, multi-purpose facility designed to host groups of all sizes—from a meeting for 50 people to a crowd of 15,000.

The cosmopolitan culture of Winnipeg is apparent in its range of attractions and events. The city is home to the Royal Winnipeg Ballet; casinos; top-rated Manitoba Museum of Man & Nature; Folklorama, the world's largest multicultural festival and the finest collection of

nature's beauty—from grassy meadows to rich forests and shimmering lakes. Within a three-hour drive of Winnipeg, it's possible to catch a glimpse of black bear, elk, moose, whitetail deer and beaver, and to still enjoy the amenities of fine dining, an indoor pool or playing a round of golf on an 18-hole course. Equipped with meeting, banquet and seminar rooms, these resorts offer an idyllic option for a working holiday.

The province's remote fly-in fishing lodges in the north promise some of the

Bailey's Restaurant & Bar

Winnipeg is blessed with one of the finest collections of turn-of-the-century architecture on the continent, and when one walks through the doors of Bailey's Restaurant and Bar in the city's Exchange District, one is indeed walking back into history. Less than a block from the famous corner of Portage and Main, Bailey's quiet charm remains true to the building's origin in 1900. Architect F.W. Griffiths is noted not only for his work on this building, but Winnipeg's first all-stone office tower, which was equipped with an electric passenger elevator. Apparently fascinated by modern inventions, Griffiths was reportedly the first Winnipegger to drive an automobile through the city's streets. He was a forward thinker and built a strong foundation for the future in the heart of Winnipeg's downtown.

Today, it's easy to forget the hustle and bustle of modern city when one steps into Bailey's—with its vestibule lined with

Enjoy the pleasures of fine continental cuisine at Bailey's intimate surroundings, where uncompromising quality and service awaits you.

Located on Lombard Avenue, in the heart of the Theatre and Business Districts, Bailey's is one of the city's most popular destinations.

dark-stained oak panels and authentic leaded-glass. A sweeping grand staircase leads to the main dining room where imported wrought-iron grillwork, carved wooden pillars and ornate sideboards which once graced the halls of old English castles provide an elegant backdrop for diners to enjoy the fine continental cuisine. From Bailey's signature rack of lamb to its Shrimp Provençale or stuffed Chicken Chartreuse, the quality is uncompromising. Its selection of wines, fine Cognac and Scotch is practically unparalleled. Regardless of whether patrons drop by for food or libations, Bailey's courteous, friendly staff is committed to making the experience a memorable one, no matter what the occasion.

Just minutes from nearby office towers, Bailey's is a place to meet and do business. Located within a stone's throw of the concert hall and live theatre, Bailey's is the ideal prelude to an evening on the town. Its four dining rooms provide an intimate atmosphere, whether for individual dining, weddings, banquets or seminars. "The Library," with its sconce-lighting, rustic brick walls and bookshelves lined with more than 1,200 worn volumes, is well-suited to small groups of between 10 and 20. "The Boardroom," with its rich mahogany panelling brought from Europe, sparkling chandeliers and doors inlaid with stained glass, accommodate somewhat larger groups of up to 45. Nestled next to the main dining room (which has a seating capacity of close to 120 people) is "The English Garden," a cheery, bright room—reminiscent of the 1920s—that looks out on the avenue. This room can accommodate up to 70 people. Located on ground level, Bailey's lounge features the sound of live jazz on Sunday nights. For those individuals interested in gambling entertainment, nestled in the Hunts Room of the lounge is the gaming room which houses video lottery terminals. ■

Hotel Fort Garry

Winnipeg's unique Fort Garry Hotel has played host in its time to prime ministers, members of British royalty, entertainers like Benny Goodman, Harry Belafonte, Charles Laughton and Sir Laurence Olivier—and to generations of graduating classes, brides and couples celebrating silver anniversaries or marking special occasions with celebrations that demanded the finest in both form and content.

The Fort Garry is one of few Canadian structures with the distinction of holding Historic Site designations from three levels of government: civic, provincial and federal.

This chateau-style, 11-storey, great old railway hotel and its 243 rooms, has since it first opened in 1914 represented classic affluence, rising out of the historic centre of Winnipeg like a castle transported in time and place from 19th-century Europe's Loire Valley. The Fort Garry is one of few Canadian structures with the distinction of holding Historic Site designations from three levels of government: civic, provincial and federal.

Like many of the grand old distinctively Canadian chateau-style railway hotels, this one had its share of hard times through the '60s and '70s, passing through a short series of owners to close, reopen and close again, until finding its current saviours in an improbable partnership: two successful local restauranteurs and the Quebec-based Laberge hardware store family—accidental owners of the Fort Garry after taking it over due to a defaulted debt.

Under the onsite stewardship of husband-and-wife team Ida Albo and Rick Bel, the Fort Garry has risen again. The couple had a local reputation for flair and panache as a result of two nearby restaurants they had founded, the Sandpiper and the Prairie Oyster. They've brought the same energy to the restoration of the Fort Garry.

By 1997, almost five million dollars had been spent of what may ultimately total almost ten million dollars in work. The building's exterior was repaired, while its magnificent interiors were slowly, carefully returned to their early lustre. Ceramic tiles overlaying original marble floors were chipped away by hand, to avoid marring the polished stone beneath. New design features were carefully incorporated into the classic details, creating an eclectic blend of gleaming brass, glowing granite and ornate vaulted ceilings.

At the same time, the hotel has evolved as a haven for business people and tourists seeking top-quality accomodations close to the cultural attractions of the city's vibrant historic centre. Rates substantially reduced from historic highs include a full breakfast with room, in the dining room open for breakfast and dinner. Lunches are served in the airy lounge, once called the Palm Room, off the main lobby.

The hotel is a haven for business people and tourists seeking top-quality accomodations close to the cultural attractions of the city's vibrant historic centre. Rates include a full breakfast with room, in the dining room open for breakfast and dinner. Lunches are served in this airy lounge, the Palm Room, off the main lobby.

For business travellers or companies seeking meeting venues with a full range of facilities, the Fort Garry provides meeting, banquet or reception space for as few as a dozen or as many as 500 people, with support services including full fitness centre, business services, valet parking, room service and in-room coffeemakers. The Fort Garry now blends chateau-style grace and elegance with the conveniences modern travellers expect in their accommodations. ■

Hospitality Corporation of Manitoba Inc.

Hospitality Corporation of Manitoba Inc. has been chosen as one of Canada's 50 Best Managed Private Companies in a national competition undertaken by the *Financial Post* and Arthur Andersen & Co. Hospitality stands out for having taken a unique approach to the hotel and entertainment industry. All of its properties are in essence huge "amusement shopping centres," boasting food and beverage services, entertainment and accommodation. Each of these elements compliments the other, resulting in high volume turnover and occupancy rates that are outstanding in the industry.

Hospitality Corporation, the largest chain of its kind on the provincial landscape, attracts more than three-million customers a year. It employs a dedicated team of more than 700.

Originally established in 1965 as Ledohowski Hotels Limited, Hospitality Corporation has always been solely owned by the Ledohowski family. However, it was long before that, that Walter Ledohowski, a farmer and truck driver, bought his first hotel. He, together with his wife, Anne, got into the business

in 1948. Twelve years later, hotels had become the family passion exclusively.

When the company changed its name in June 1984 to Hospitality Corporation of Manitoba Inc., the senior Ledohowski indicated it was about time he stepped aside, leaving his sons Leon, Christopher and Ronald to take over the operation. His eldest son Ben, who was also involved in the business, chose to leave about the same time to pursue a separate success in Alberta.

Hospitality Corporation has taken a different approach to its organizational structure at the home office level. Each facet of the operation is overseen by departmental directors. The directors, specialists in their fields, act in an advisory role and provide a managerial service to each property. This "horizontal/vertical structure" and approach, integrated with the on-site operations, has resulted in a diverse, yet uniquely strong, organization.

Hospitality Corporation has consistently shown itself to be committed to the community, donating more than $100,000 to the Variety Club over a two-year period.

Having a firm belief in the need to be socially responsible, Hospitality

Corporation designed a comprehensive, media-driven Designated Driver Program and presented it to the appropriate government agencies and the industry. This program has now been adopted province-wide and is the industry standard.

Leading into the next millennium, Hospitality Corporation has shown that it is a company with deep roots in Manitoba and that it will continue to thrive despite years of industry uncertainty and evidence of shaky economic times. It is a company that seems limited only by the reach of its people–their ideas, dedication and willingness to succeed. What started as a small family business has grown to include a solid, professional team of employees and management, whose creativity and uniqueness have driven its success. Yet, it has not lost the true family cohesiveness that was one of its original strengths. ■

Leon N. Ledohowski, B.A., B.COMM., M.B.A., C.M.A., C.H.A., President and CEO of Hospitality Corporation of Manitoba Inc.

Christopher W. Ledohowski, Vice-President; General Manager, Transcona Inn.

Ronald S. Ledohowski, Secretary-Treasurer; Director of Marketing & Entertainment.

Winnipeg Convention Centre

Located in the heart of downtown, the Winnipeg Convention Centre was Canada's first convention centre.

Winnipeg Convention Centre's exhibition areas offer the ultimate in flexibility.

The Winnipeg Convention Centre is a place for people to come together to exchange ideas, see new things and celebrate life. Every year, 1.5-million visitors from far away and close to home pass through its doors to shop, dine and attend any number of special events, conferences, meetings and trade shows. The Winnipeg Convention Centre, though it might be small compared to other centres in the U.S., prides itself in being the ninth busiest convention centre in North America with no less than three events per day on average.

The mandate of the city-owned facility is to bring people to Winnipeg, to fill the city's hotels and restaurants and to promote the city's economic well-being. Since 1975, it has done just that—generating $408 million in spending by convention delegates and exhibitors and contributing $130 million in federal, provincial and civic taxes. It creates employment for 1,100 Manitobans, resulting in an annual payroll of upward of $4 million. It is virtually a city within a city—providing jobs for everyone from plumbers to dishwashers, receptionists to parking attendants, ticket sellers to payroll clerks, housekeepers to stage handlers and chefs to security guards.

Located in the heart of downtown, 10 minutes by car from Winnipeg International Airport, the Winnipeg Convention Centre is a three-storey, 150,000-square-foot building that, when built 20 years ago, was Canada's first convention centre. At the time, it was state-of-the-art, and even today visitors look at it and take away ideas. Its third-floor exhibition hall offers the ultimate in flexibility—whether it's accommodating seven semi-trailers at a time in a heated, indoor loading dock or providing 78,000 square feet of pillarless display space that can be divided into two rooms of 50,000 square feet and 28,000 square feet. Its high ceilings—30 feet from floor to open grid and then 20 feet from grid to roof—have enabled everything from sailboats to cement trucks to be displayed.

On the floor below, retail shops and eateries intermingle with a variety of meeting space—a 600-seat lecture theatre,

two 1,000-square-foot boardrooms, an upscale ballroom for small weddings and receptions and three meeting rooms, which combined can handle a banquet for 600 or theatre-style seating for 1,300.

The convention centre's more than 21,000-square-foot main floor offers 20 meeting rooms, which together or individually can meet the needs of any size of gathering. An executive conference centre provides video and teleconferencing capabilities, together with surround sound, a

14-person boardroom table, bar and reception area with comfortable wingback chairs. A separate VIP salon is also ideal for receptions, as is a carpeted and draped concourse leading off the larger meeting rooms.

The convention centre caters to all events in the building, having its own kitchen and award-winning chefs. ■

Bibliography

Photo by George Siamandas.

Artibise, Alan F.J. *Winnipeg: A Social History of Urban Growth 1874-1914*. Montreal and London: McGill-Queen's University Press, 1974.

Artibise, Alan F.J. (ed). *Gateway City: Documents on the City of Winnipeg 1873-1913*. Winnipeg: the Manitoba Record Society in association with the University of Manitoba Press, 1979.

Arbitise, Alan F.J. *Winnipeg: An Illustrated History*. Toronto: James Lorimer & Company and National Museum of Man, National Museums of Canada, 1976.

Bellan, Ruben C. *Winnipeg, First Century: An Economic History*. Winnipeg: Queenston House Publishing Co., 1978.

Bumstead, J.M. "1919: The Winnipeg General Strike Reconsidered." *The Beaver*, (June-July 1994): 27-44.

Into the 21st Century: Arts and Culture in Winnipeg. Report of the City of Winnipeg Cultural Review Panel. Winnipeg, 1997.

Jackson, James A. *The Centennial History of Manitoba*. Toronto: McClelland and Stewart, 1970.

Kurnarsky, Larry and Smith, Murray. *Famous and Fascinating Manitobans*. Winnipeg: Face Publications, 1982.

Kuz, Tony J. (ed). *Winnipeg 1874-1974: Progress and Prospects*. Winnipeg: commissioned by the Manitoba Department of Industry and Commerce, 1974.

Levine, Allan. *The Exchange: 100 Years of Trading Grain in Winnipeg*. Winnipeg: Peguis Publishers Limited, 1987.

Manitoba Travel Guide. Winnipeg: Manipeg Publications Inc., 1995.

Morton, W.L. *Manitoba: A History*. Toronto: University of Toronto Press, 1957.

Winnipeg Facts. Winnipeg 2000 Economic Development Corp., Winnipeg, 1997.

Extensive use of material from the *Winnipeg Free Press* and the *Glove and Mail* newspaper was indispensable in writing this book.

Photos by Mike Grandmaison.

Enterprise Index

PATRON

The North West Company

Photo by Mike Grandmaison.

Index

Photos by Mike Grandmaison.

Index

Photo by Mike Grandmaison.

Index

Photo by Mike Grandmaison.

Index

Photo by Mike Grandmaison.

253

Photos by Mike Grandmaison.

Index

Photo by George Siamandas.